IMAGES
of America

ARTESIA

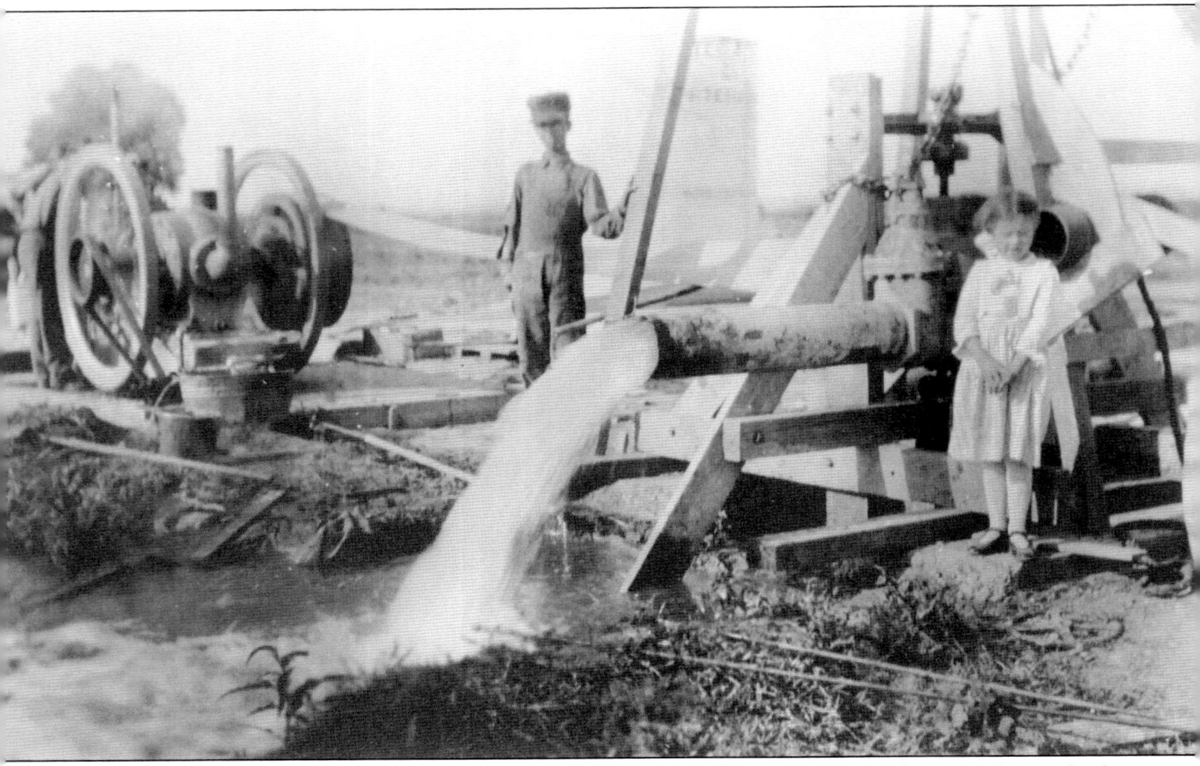

Paul and Beth Rogers pose by their family farm's artesian well. The Rogers farm was located a few miles southeast of Artesia. The area's early farmers all relied on artesian wells to water their crops and livestock. The stock ponds also served as swimming holes in the hot summers. (Courtesy of Artesia Historical Museum and Art Center.)

On the Cover: The Artesia Machine Shop-Auto Hospital was owned and operated by Joseph Schenck. Built in 1909, the business was located on the corner of Fifth and Main Streets. It offered supplies and repairs for automobiles. (Courtesy of Artesia Historical Museum and Art Center.)

IMAGES
of America

ARTESIA

Nancy Dunn, Naomi Florez
Artesia Historical Museum & Art Center

ARCADIA
PUBLISHING

ISBN 978-0-7385-7628-2

Published by Arcadia Publishing
Charleston, South Carolina

Printed in the United States of America

Library of Congress Control Number: 2011936442

For all general information, please contact Arcadia Publishing:
Telephone 843-853-2070
Fax 843-853-0044
E-mail sales@arcadiapublishing.com
For customer service and orders:
Toll-Free 1-888-313-2665

Visit us on the Internet at www.arcadiapublishing.com

Dedicated to the memory of Lela and Rufus Waltrip,
authors of Artesia: Heart of the Pecos

Contents

Acknowledgments		6
Introduction		7
1.	The City through the Years	9
2.	Farming and Ranching	35
3.	Schools and Churches	45
4.	Clubs and Organizations	55
5.	The Oil and Gas Industry	63
6.	Artesia's Contributions to the Military	73
7.	Going the Distance	83
8.	Enjoying Life	95
9.	Sports—The Tradition Continues	105
10.	Celebrations of Yesterday and Today	117

ACKNOWLEDGMENTS

The Artesia Historical Museum and Art Center opened its doors in 1970. Since then, the collection has grown through the generosity of our donors and their many contributions. Without their support, this book could not have been written, and we are grateful to everyone who has contributed to the museum's collection over the years.

We want to acknowledge former museum director Terry Koenig; we made use of a lot of his research and newspaper columns for historical information. We also want to acknowledge former museum registrar Sarah Quiroga; we relied on her research and exhibit materials for chapter six. The Artesia Chamber of Commerce was very supportive of our efforts, and we want to thank everyone on its staff. Administrative assistant Lisa Johnson at the Artesia City Hall helped in a pinch, and we appreciate it. Gayla Ivy of the B&B Newsstand also helped with historical perspectives; thanks for all your support! Former Arcadia Publishing acquisitions editor Jared Jackson was very helpful in getting this book started, and we appreciate his efforts.

We appreciate all of the support from Mayor Phillip Burch and the Artesia City Council. We would especially like to thank city clerk–treasurer (and museum department head) Aubrey Hobson and the Artesia Historical Museum and Art Center board members.

All images appearing in this book are from the collection of the Artesia Historical Museum and Art Center.

Introduction

The earliest inhabitants of the Artesia area appear to have arrived around 7,000 years ago. They were hunter-gatherers and settled along established area waterways. Changes in the environment caused these early inhabitants to move on, but the climate in the Lower Pecos Valley has been relatively stable for the past 5,000 years. Later inhabitants migrated into the region and produced the first pottery around 1,000 years ago. Ancestors of the Apaches moved into this area soon afterwards and were established by the 1400s.

The first Europeans to visit southeastern New Mexico were a group of four men who were shipwrecked along the Texas-Louisiana coast in 1528, including the first person of African heritage known to set foot in North America. Alvar Nuñez Cabeza de Vaca, Esteban (also Estevan or Estevanico) the Moor (as African people were often referred to at the time), and two others spent several years wandering through parts of New Mexico, Texas, and Mexico before finally reaching Mexico City in 1536. Antonio de Espejo led a group along the Pecos River in 1582–1583, and colonizer Gaspar Castaño de Sosa took a caravan of settlers up the Pecos in 1590. De Sosa became lost near Artesia and was guided back to his camp by *muchas luminarias* (many signals or bonfires)—possibly the first use of luminarias in New Mexico.

The Mescalero Apaches and their main enemies, the Comanches, roamed throughout southeastern New Mexico and parts of southwestern Texas. They were so fierce that pioneers were largely deterred from establishing homes in this area, but a few brave Hispanic settlers established homes in the Seven Rivers area, 20 miles south of Artesia, by the early 1860s. Cattlemen Charles Goodnight and Oliver Loving drove the first large group of cattle through the Pecos Valley in 1866. The Anglo settlement of Seven Rivers was established by 1867, and cattle king John Chisum's vast ranch reached south to the Seven Rivers area as well.

A railroad was built through the Lower Pecos Valley in 1894, and the small settlement of Miller was later established along one of its sidings. As more people settled in Miller, it was granted a post office and was briefly known as Stegman after its first postmistress, Sallie Chisum Robert Stegman. Stegman continued to grow, and with the discovery of the settlement's abundant artesian water wells, the town was named Artesia in 1903 and formally incorporated in January 1905.

Artesia has seen many changes through the years; it has gone from water wells to oil wells, weathered the Depression, and survived two World Wars. In this book, we have tried to bring Artesia's history to life through photographs, and we hope that you all enjoy it.

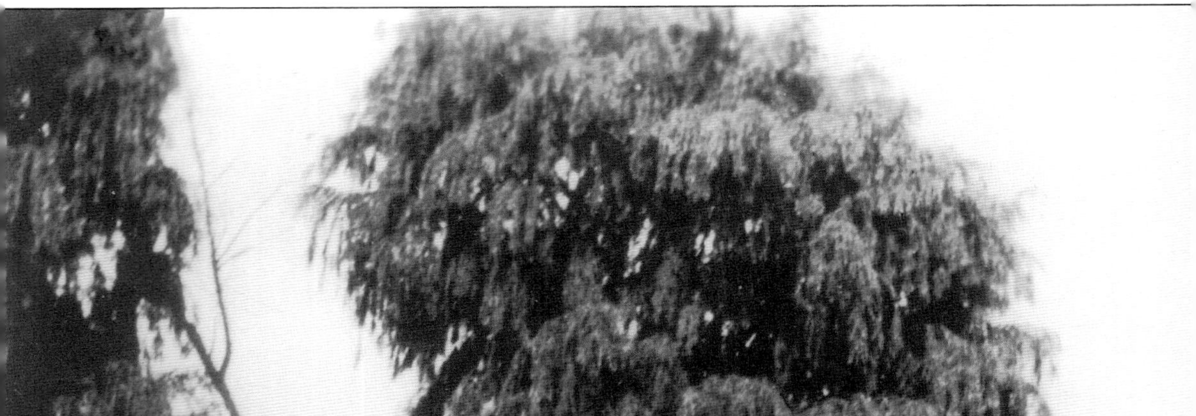

At the beginning of settlement in the area, there was a spring at what is now Eagle Draw and Roselawn Avenue. Early Native American and Hispanic inhabitants relied on many of the local natural springs. When John Chisum drove his first cattle herds up the Pecos Valley in the 1860s, his cowboys became accustomed to stopping and watering the herd at this spring, which became known as Chisum Spring Camp. Later, a stagecoach line ran through the Lower Pecos Valley (1874–1894), and the spring became known as Blake Spring. John Chisum's niece Sallie Chisum Robert built her first Pecos Valley home nearby around 1890, but because it was constructed from adobe bricks, it was easily swept away in an early flood. A few years after that, the small settlement of Miller was established near the spring around 1899, and as it grew into today's Artesia, the spring dried up. Today, there is nothing left on Eagle Draw and Roselawn Avenue to show that a spring was ever there.

One

The City through the Years

An early real estate booklet for Artesia mentions the town as "born of water." While this may have been true for early area promoters, the story is not that simple. In 1894, the railroad came through the Lower Pecos Valley to link Roswell to Eddy, today's Carlsbad. The siding halfway between the two towns was named Miller after a brakeman who worked for the railroad (other sources cite G.E. "Jeff" Miller, a construction engineer). The town's second name, Stegman, came about because Sallie Chisum was the first postmistress, from 1899 to 1903, and was married to a man named Stegman at the time. Artesia is actually the town's third name, adopted in 1903.

Merchant Bill Whitaker opened a store at the Miller siding in 1898, and other buildings soon joined the business. More settlers moved into the community, and as they drilled for water, the area's artesian wells were discovered. By that time, Miller had a post office, but the community's name was officially changed to Stegman in 1899.

By 1903, the Artesia Townsite Company and the Artesia Improvement Company had been formed by businessmen to promote settlement in the town. Their first project was to change Stegman's name to Artesia to capitalize on the abundant water available. Artesia was officially incorporated in 1905.

The artesian wells were a visual and agricultural attraction to early settlers until the early 1920s, when the wells began to dwindle because of 20 years of unchecked flow. Not only did the artesian wells draw in settlers, but the discovery of oil also became a top-seller to prospective investors and settlers several years later. Today, the oil and gas industry continues to flourish in the Artesia area, along with farming and ranching.

Over the years, Artesia has gone from a dusty settlement to a well-established city. Changes in the community coincided with fluctuations in the economy, technological advancements, and the need for new, improved ways of working and living. Many changes have taken place throughout Artesia over the years, and not everything is the same as it once was.

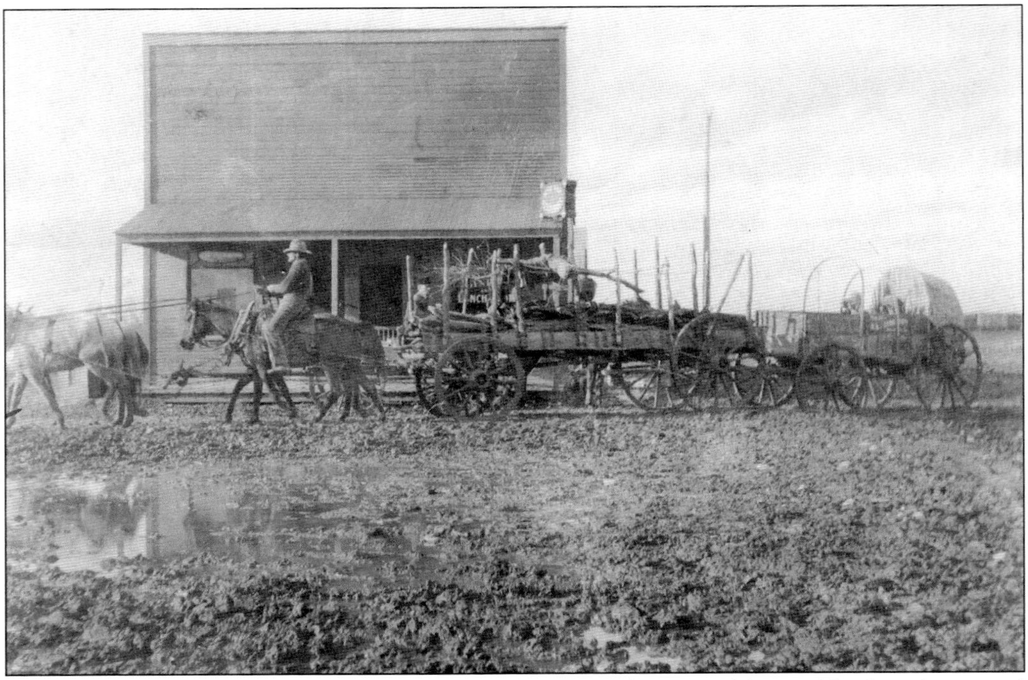

In 1898, Bill Whitaker, of Hope, New Mexico, (about 20 miles west of Artesia) built and operated a store at the Miller railroad siding along with his nephew Hugh Gage. The store stocked basic items and also housed the Ocean Wave Restaurant. A few buildings soon joined the store, and as a more settlers entered the small community, they began drilling for water and discovered the area's artesian wells. The very first artesian well in the area was the Bruce Well, drilled by L.R. Sperry in 1902. In the photograph below of the Bruce Well are, from left to right, ? Hoagland (Lydia Bruce's mother), Lydia (Mrs. John) Bruce, John Bruce, and well-driller L.R. Sperry.

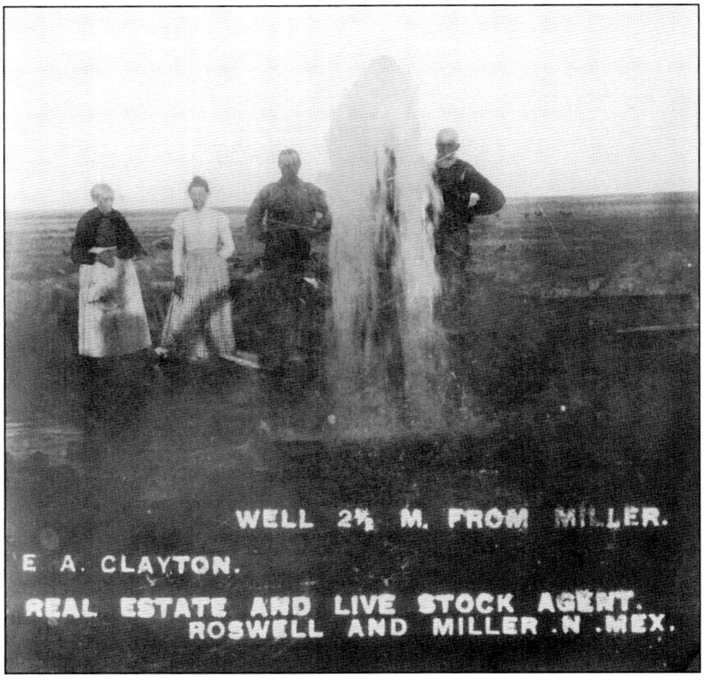

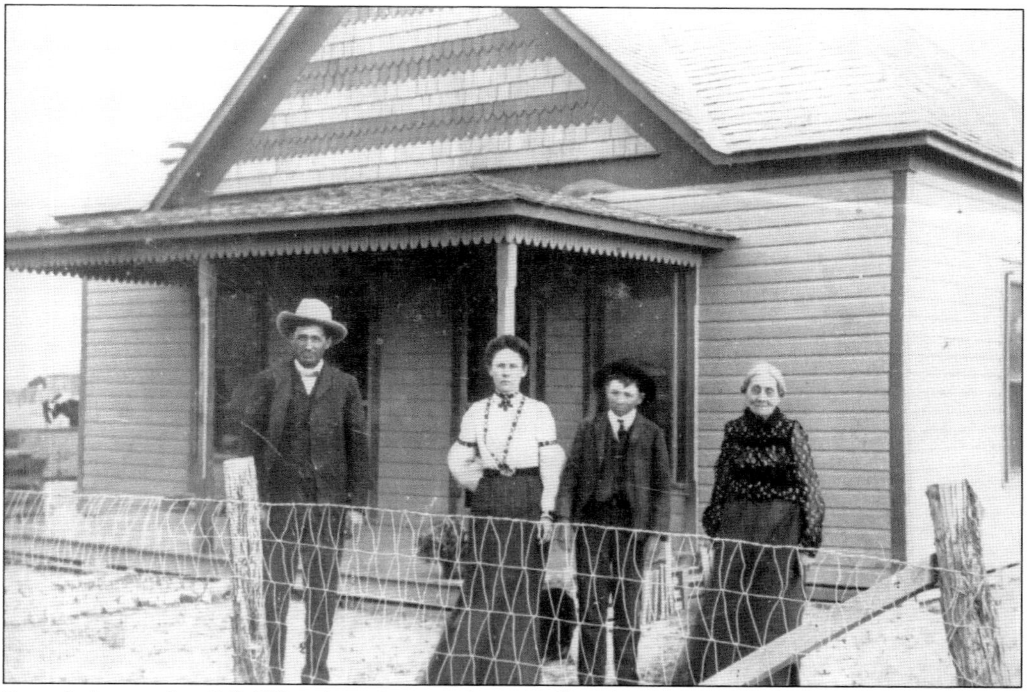

From left to right, Bill Whitaker, Georgia (Mrs. Bill) Whitaker, Earl Whitaker, and Madeline Johnson (Georgia's mother) pose in front of their home in Hope, New Mexico. Bill owned the first store at the Miller railroad siding. The Miller store never did much business; there just were not enough people in the area. In 1902, he sold the mercantile to another Hope resident, M.H. Beckett, who kept it open for another year.

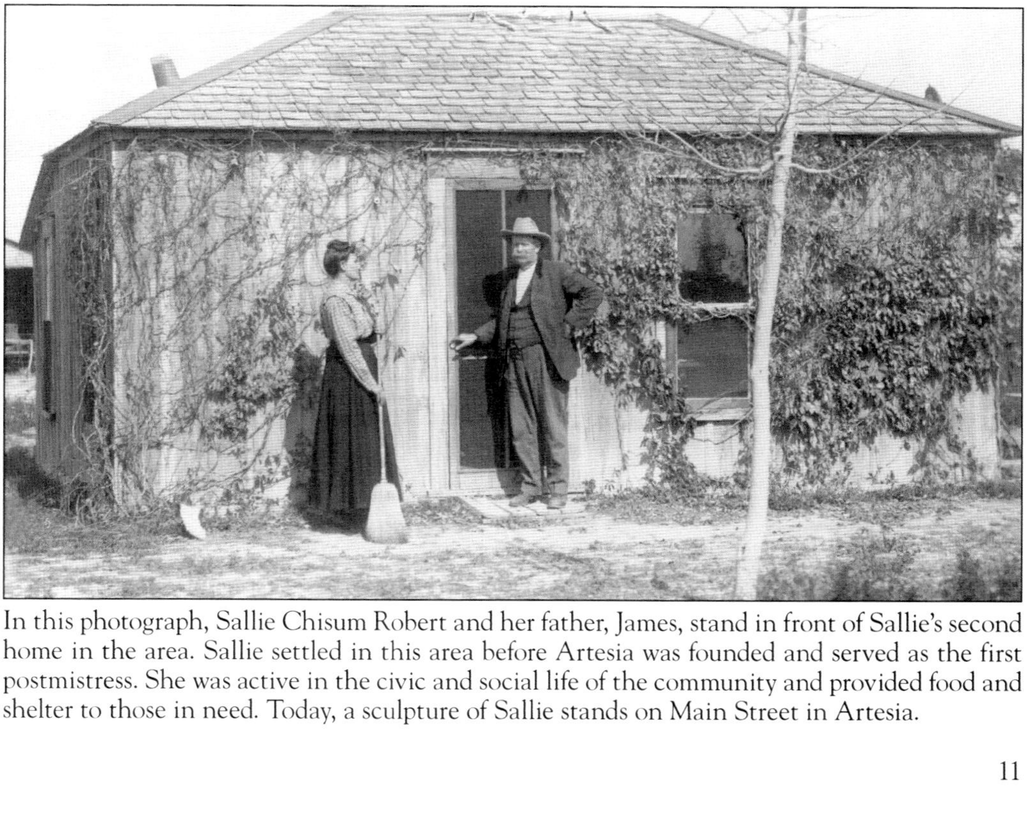

In this photograph, Sallie Chisum Robert and her father, James, stand in front of Sallie's second home in the area. Sallie settled in this area before Artesia was founded and served as the first postmistress. She was active in the civic and social life of the community and provided food and shelter to those in need. Today, a sculpture of Sallie stands on Main Street in Artesia.

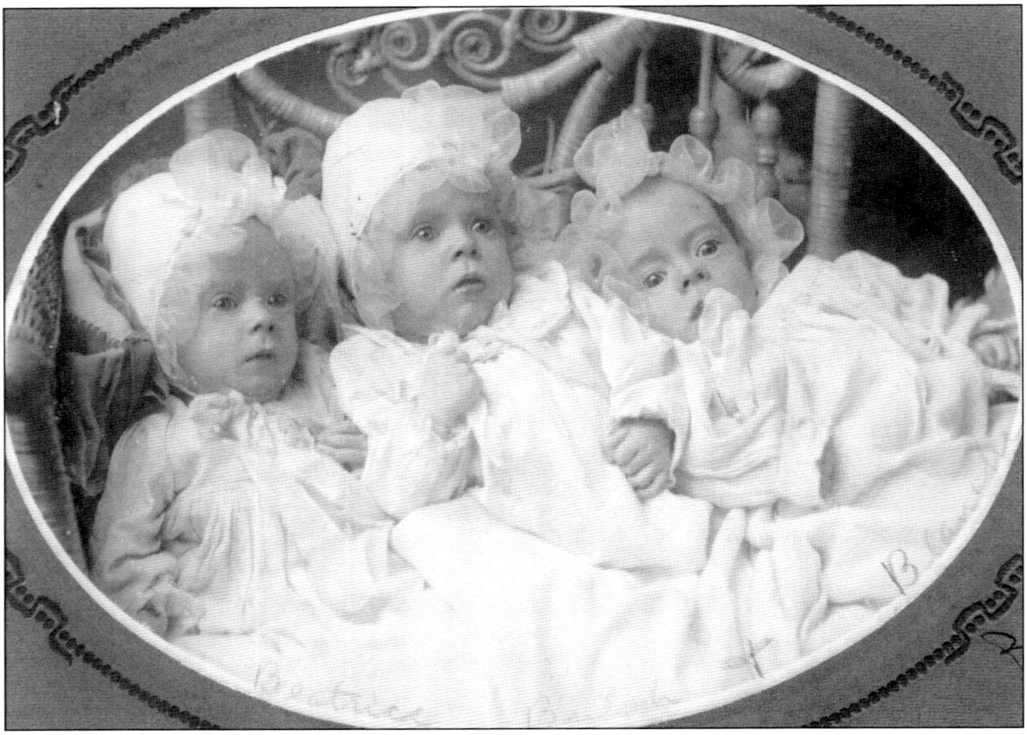

Mr. and Mrs. Will Greene arrived in Artesia on December 24, 1904. Mrs. Greene was feeling unwell, so Will rented a small shack for them to stay in. Feeling unwell soon became labor pains, and on Christmas Day, triplets Beatrice, Blanche, and Beulah were delivered by a midwife. All three babies thrived and are believed to be the first babies born in Artesia.

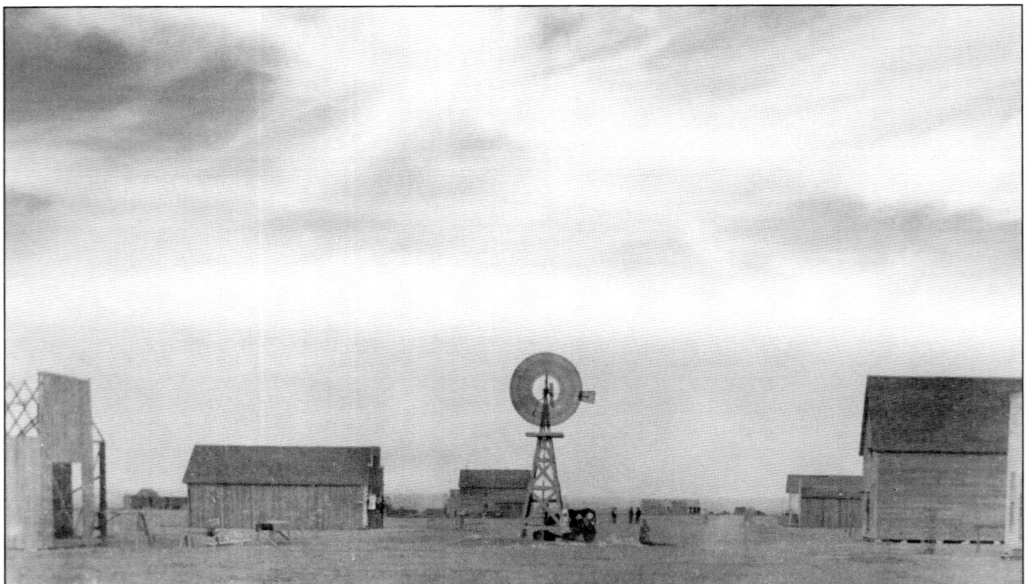

This is an eastward view of Artesia's Main Street around 1901. These earliest buildings in Artesia are simple, frame structures. At least one is a saloon, and the others be boardinghouses, stables, and/or dry goods stores. The town quickly began to grow and take shape within a few years.

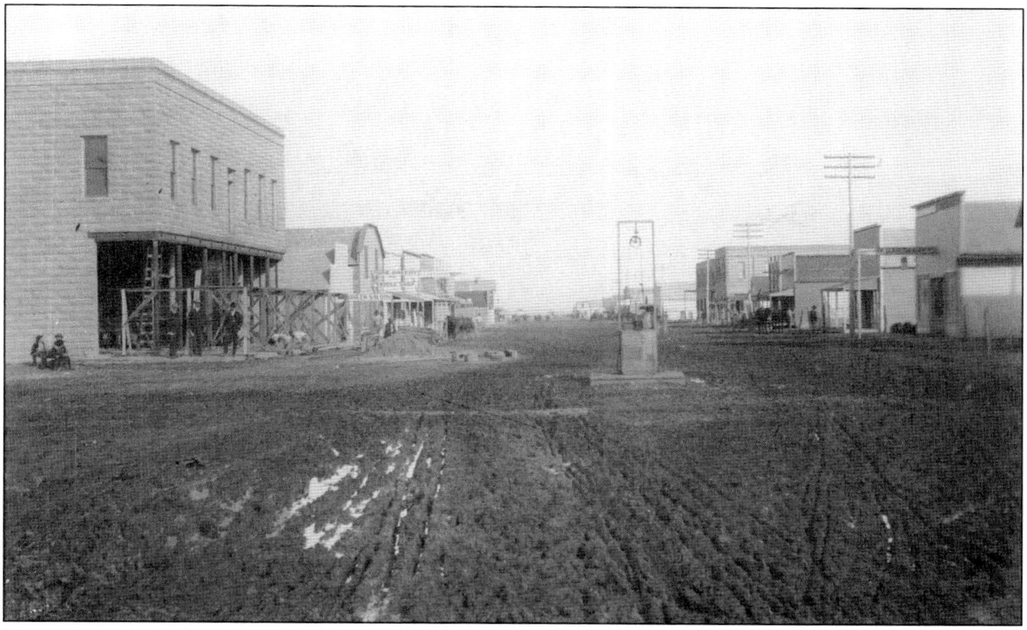

By 1904, Artesia had grown significantly, as this east-facing photograph taken at the intersection of Fourth and Main Streets shows. More substantial brick and stone structures were being built, but high railroad freight charges for construction materials forced local builders to make their own artificial-stone blocks from concrete, as seen in the first building on the left. Businesses included a home bakery, a saddle shop, a hardware store, and several saloons, restaurants, and banks.

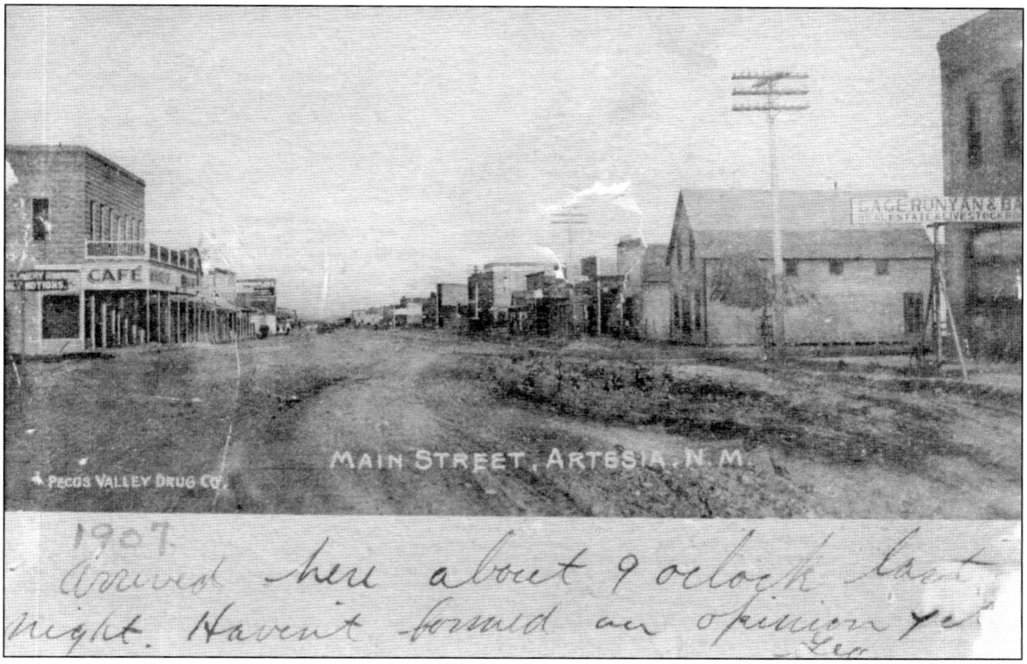

"Arrived here about 9 o'clock last night. Haven't formed an opinion yet—Geo," reads this early postcard sent by George Ferriman to his family in Medina, Ohio, when he arrived in Artesia in November 1907. The Ferrimans must have liked what they saw because the family later relocated to Artesia, and George's father, Myron, served a term as mayor from 1922 to 1926.

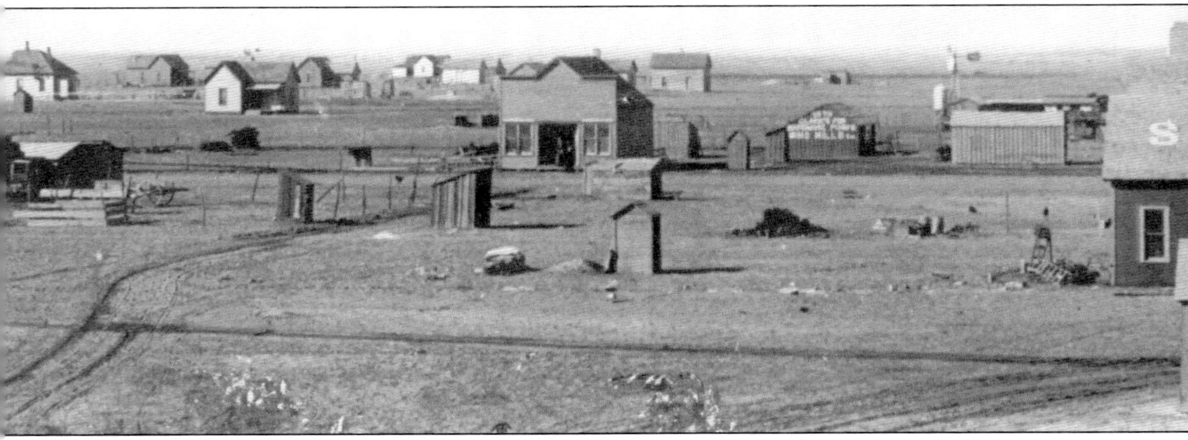

Artesia is pictured in 1902. The saloon sits on Main Street, which is heading west in this photograph. The dirt track across the bottom of the image is today's First Street. The barn located to the back left of the saloon has an early advertising sign painted on it that reads, "Go to Clark's for

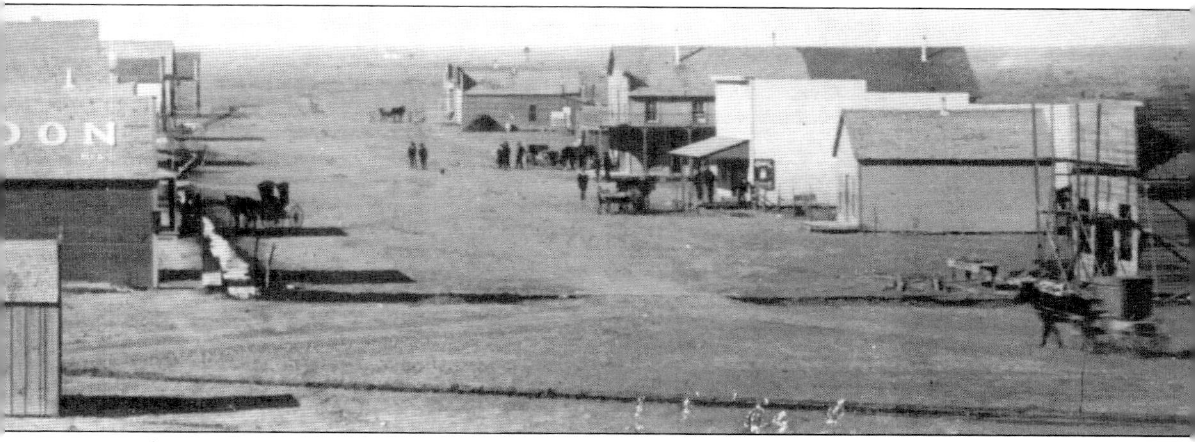

National Pumps Windmills Etc." A comparison to the scene in the earlier photograph on page 12 shows that a lot of building progress has been made in just one year.

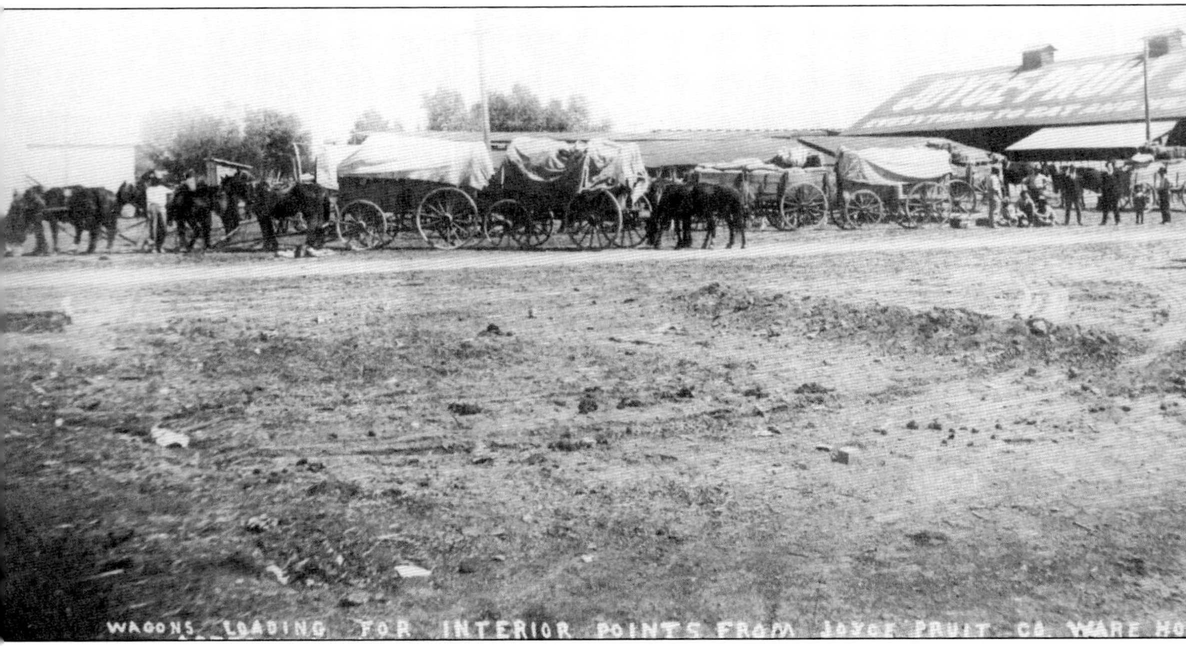

The text on this image reads, "Wagons loading for interior points from Joyce Pruit Co. Ware House, Artesia N.M." The Joyce Pruit Company was formed in 1888 by John R. Joyce and his business partner, Aurelius Pruit. After the original partners passed away, descendants J. Frank Joyce and Albert Pruit took over the business. The company had several stores in Texas and had newly opened stores in Carlsbad and Roswell when it opened the Artesia site in 1905. The Artesia Joyce Pruit store was *the* place to shop for anything and everything; as its sign proclaims, it had everything to eat and wear. A second story was added to the building in 1912. The Joyce Pruit Company had a separate warehouse to receive and store merchandise to supply inventory to its area stores. The Artesia location was the only one to survive the 1929 stock market crash.

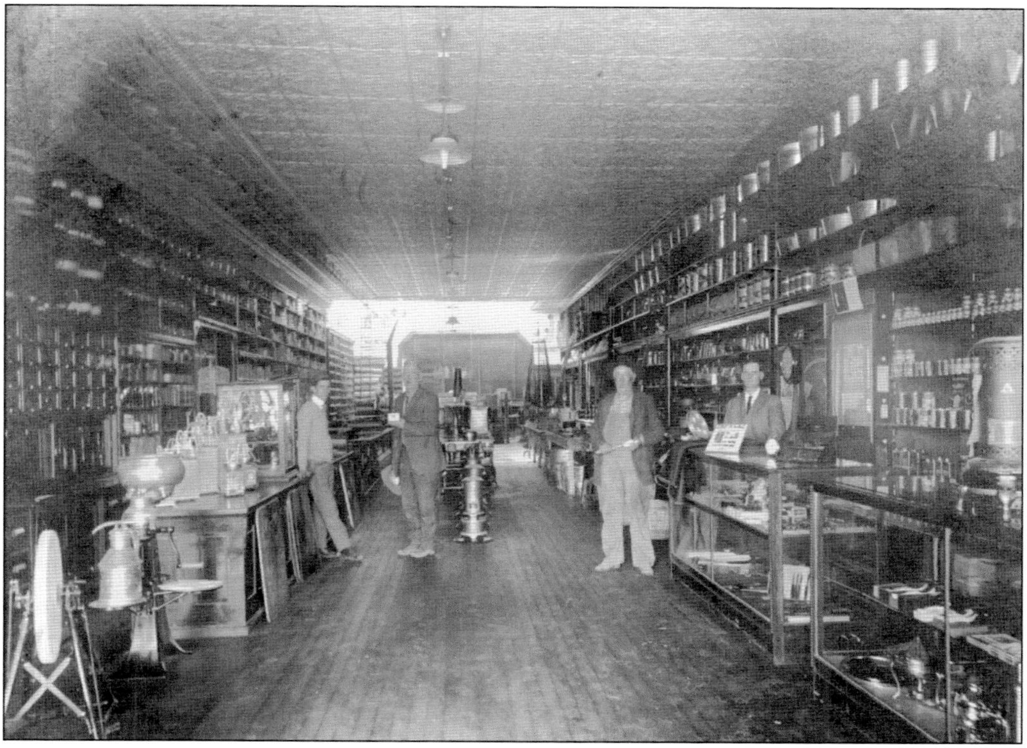

In the photograph above, the Joyce Pruit Company store's hardware department is shown in 1910. Shown from left to right are unidentified, dairyman J.M. Jackson, justice of the peace Tom Stagner, and store manager V.H. Doubek. In the photograph below, a china display is featured in the hardware department in the mid-1920s. Shown from left to right are Clint Cole, unidentified, C.A. Sipple, and hardware department manager R.G. Knoedler. The store employed 31 people at a time. A fire partially destroyed the business in 1934, but it managed to survive until 1940. The Joyce Pruit Company store led the way for many other early mercantiles.

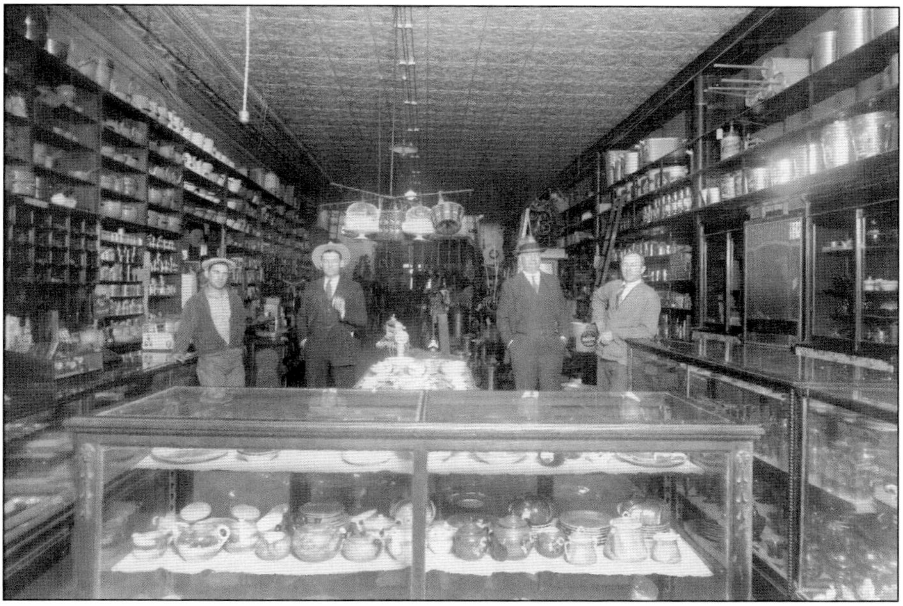

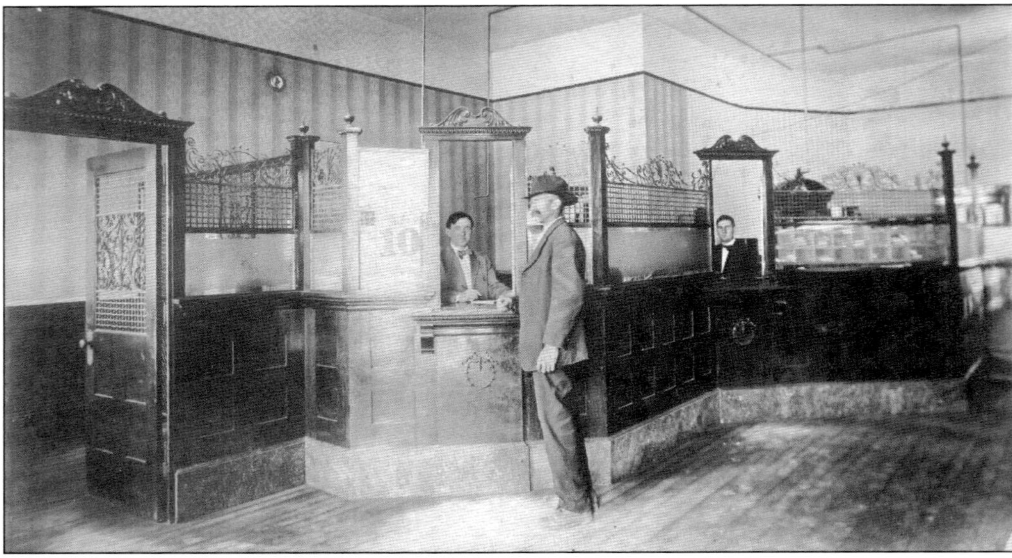

Artesia's First National Bank opened in 1903 and over the years merged with several other early financial institutions. First National Bank was one of few area banks to survive the 1929 stock market crash. It was also one of the very few allowed to open immediately after the mandatory four-day bank holiday in March 1933. Local rancher Tim Flint bought up 51 percent of the bank's stock and sponsored a return to full services in July 1933. During this period, currency issued by the bank (below) briefly bore his signature and that of bank cashier Landis Feather. The lobby of First National Bank in 1910 or 1911 is shown above. From left to right are J.E. Robertson, J.S. Worley, and John McIlhaney.

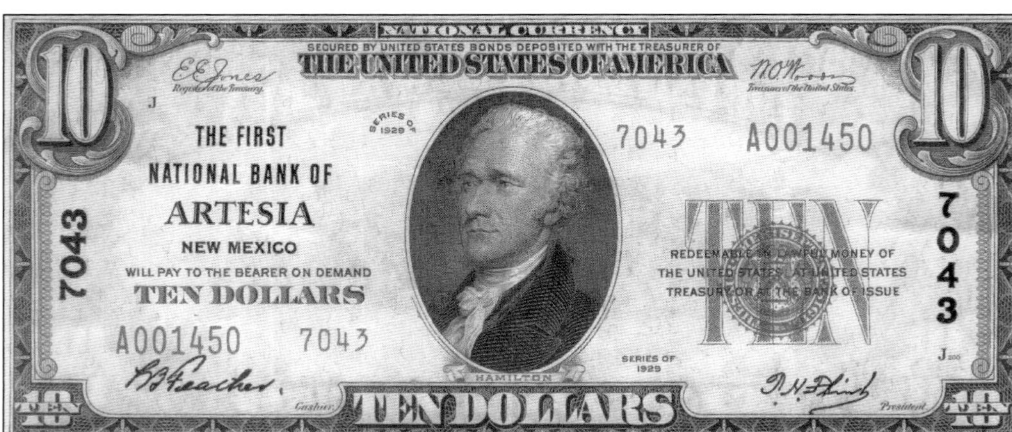

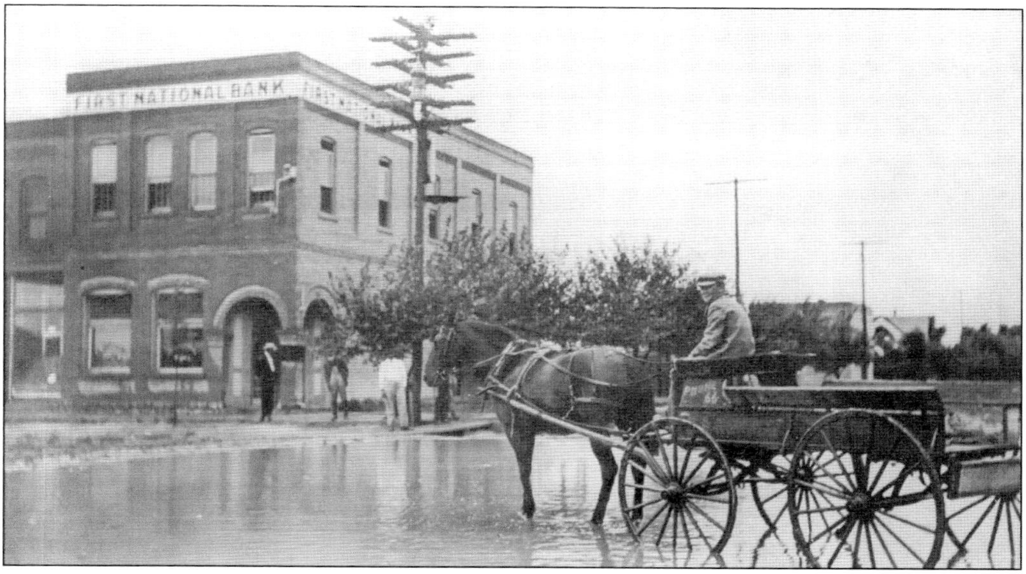

Above, the exterior of First National Bank is shown after a summer storm in 1912. Below, the lobby of the First State Bank of Artesia is pictured around 1916. From left to right are unidentified, teller Kenneth Rowan, and Beecher Rowan. The First State Bank of Artesia was previously the Bank of Dayton; its name was changed after it relocated to Artesia in 1914. The bank was rechartered as the Citizens' State Bank in 1919, and it merged with First National Bank in 1931. Another early bank with a similar name, the State National Bank of Artesia, had merged with First National Bank in 1914.

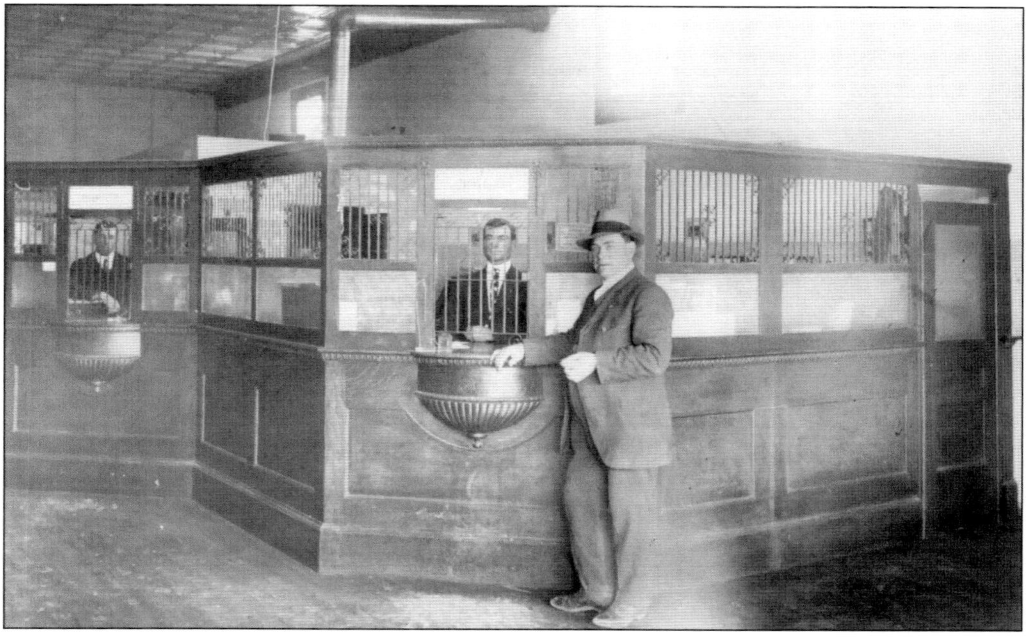

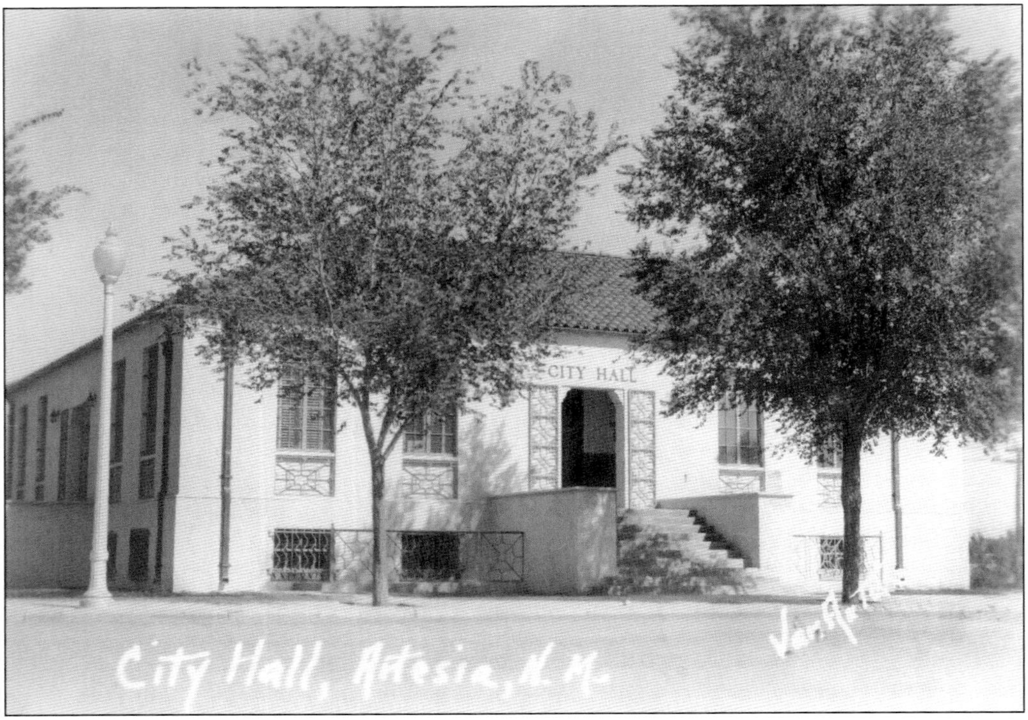

Pres. Franklin Roosevelt's Depression-era projects were active in Artesia. The city received several Works Progress Administration (WPA) public projects: in the photograph above, Artesia's new city hall is shown soon after its construction in the late 1930s. The Artesia Public Library was also located inside the structure. In the photograph below, the Artesia Municipal Hospital is shown after its official opening in August 1939. The hospital was equipped with 28 beds: 10 private rooms, 3 two-bed rooms, and 3 four-bed rooms. There were an operating room, an obstetrics room and nursery, and offices as well as an emergency room, a kitchen, a laboratory, and a surgery room.

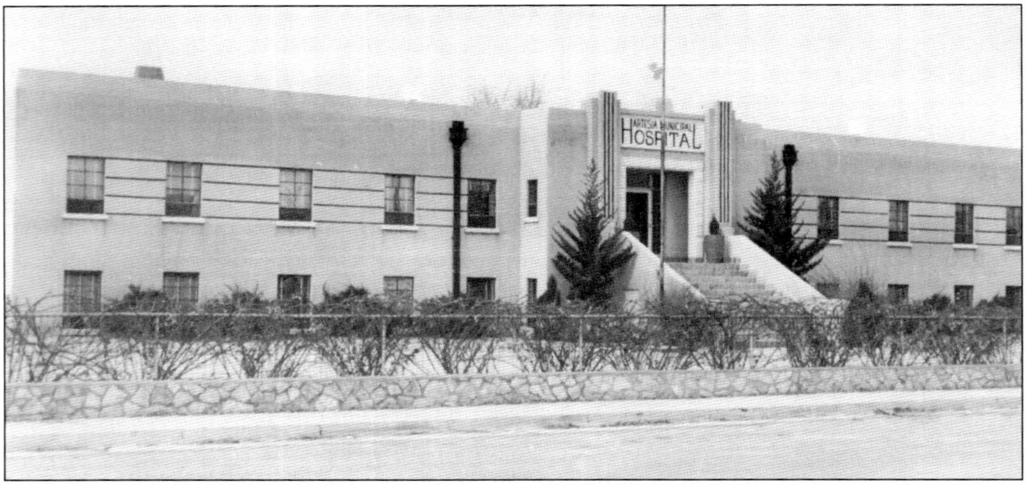

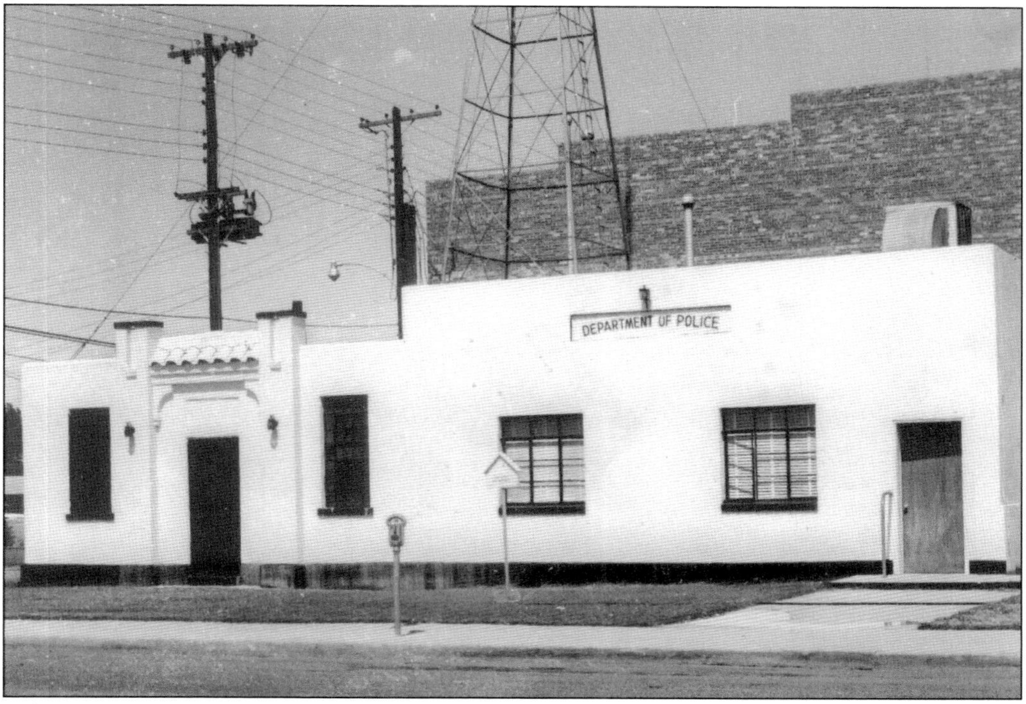

Other WPA projects in Artesia included new homes for the police and fire departments. The police department had an adjoining jail, and the fire department had bays for three response vehicles. All of the WPA building projects provided much-needed jobs to local residents during the dark days of the Depression and gave Artesia several modern, up-to-date buildings and facilities to be proud of. Both departments moved in 1976 to new, improved facilities. In the spring of 2011, the City of Artesia's new Public Safety Complex opened and allowed both departments to greatly expand their services to the public.

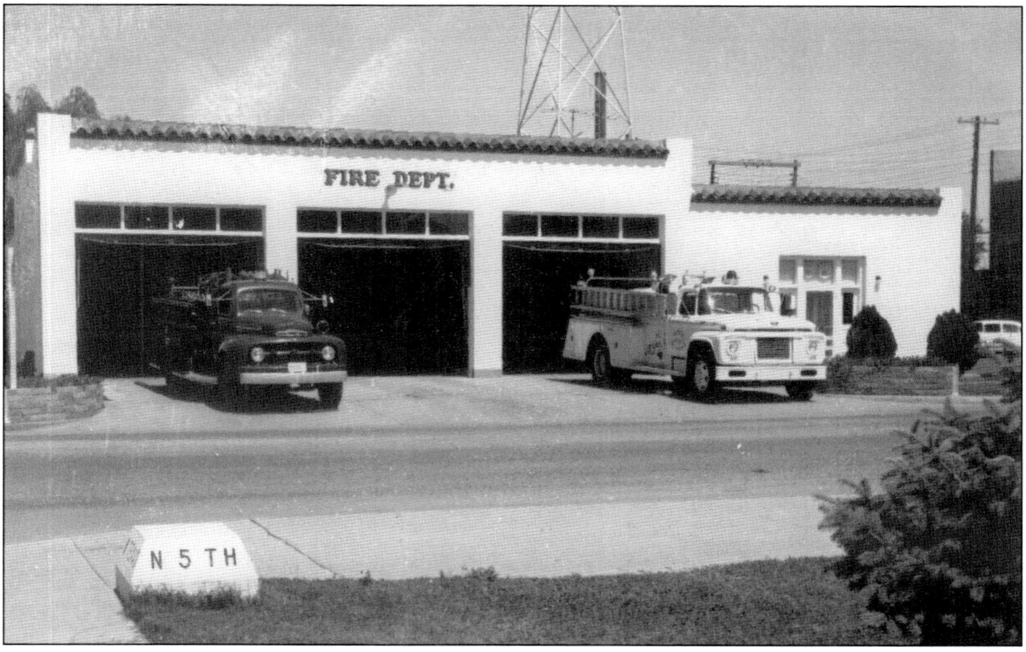

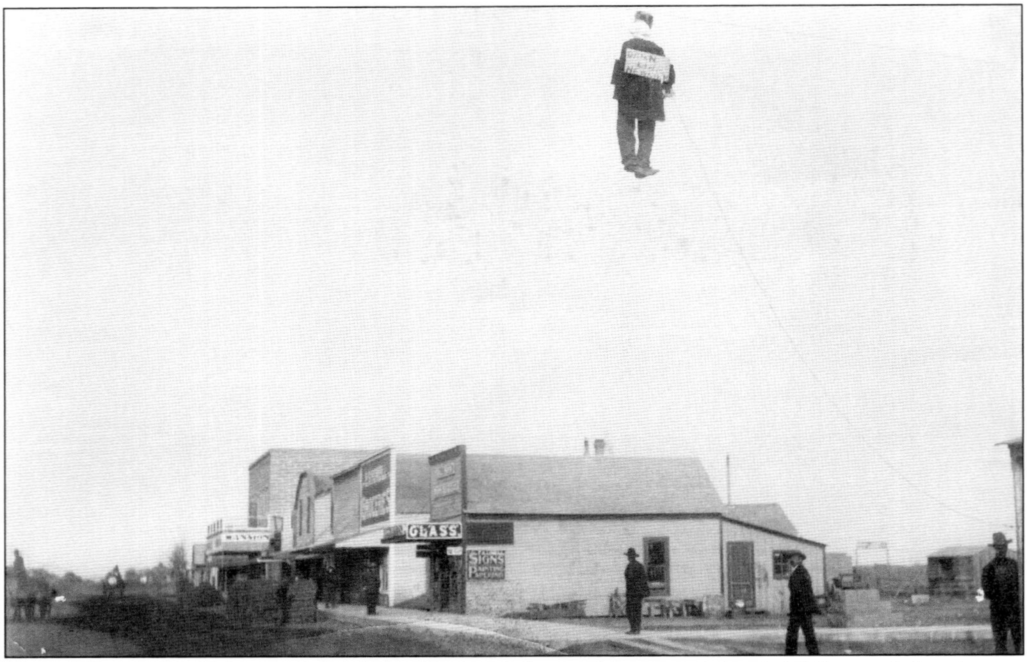

Early newspapers took on the personalities of their editors, and Gayle Talbot, of the *Artesia Advocate* (established 1903), had strong opinions. So did Daniel and Frank Newkirk, editors of the rival *Pecos Valley News*. An unfriendly competition existed between the two, with slams against the other appearing regularly. At some point around 1909, the Newkirks went too far, and Gayle Talbot hung "Damn Liar Newkirk" in effigy across Main Street.

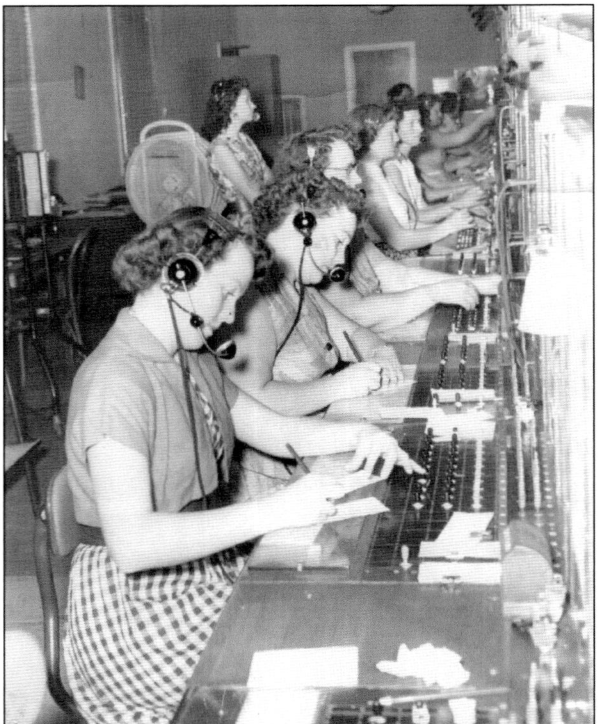

The Artesia Telephone Company started in 1905, and the first exchange office opened in 1910. As the town grew, the telephone company's service expanded greatly. In this photograph, Artesia switchboard operators are shown hard at work connecting calls around 1950. In 1955, the company became the Mountain States Telephone and Telegraph Company, and it switched over to the dial system.

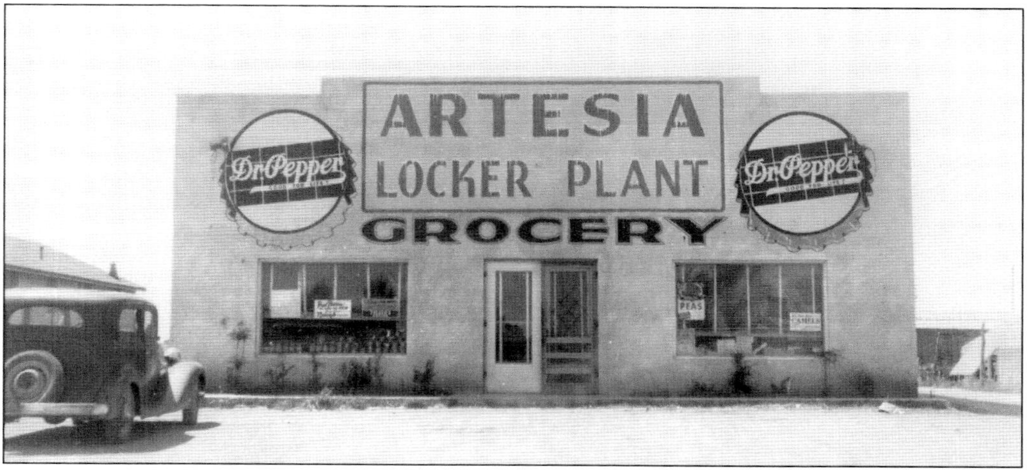

The Artesia Locker Plant and Grocery is pictured above. The locker plant was owned and operated by W.S. Hogsett and was located on Thirteenth Street at the end of Richardson. Dr. Pepper has always been a local favorite, and Artesia actually had a Dr. Pepper bottling plant, shown below, located at 611 South First Street from 1930 to 1967. Besides bottling Dr. Pepper, the plant also produced and distributed Squirt, Nesbitt's, and other sodas. Managers John and Thirza Parmer ran the facility in the early 1950s and produced their own brand of fruit-flavored soda, known as Parmers Pop, during that time.

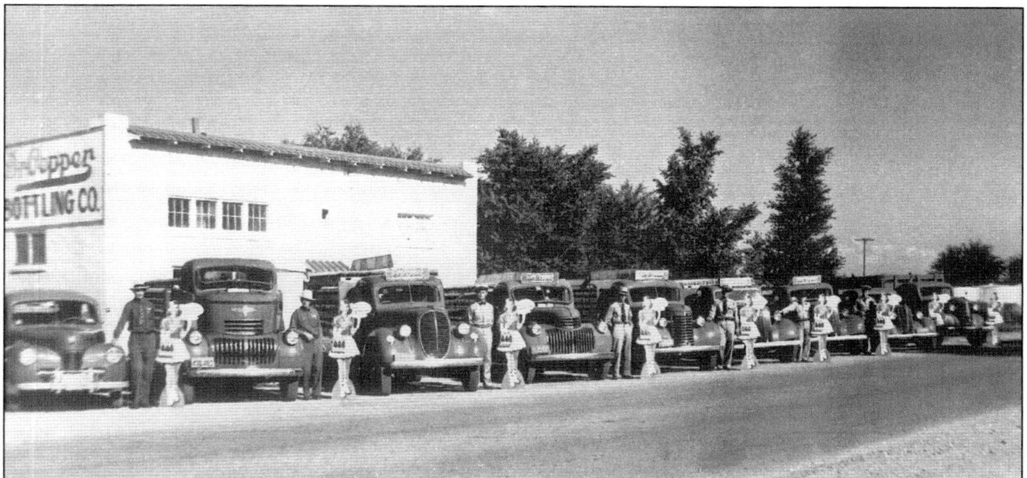

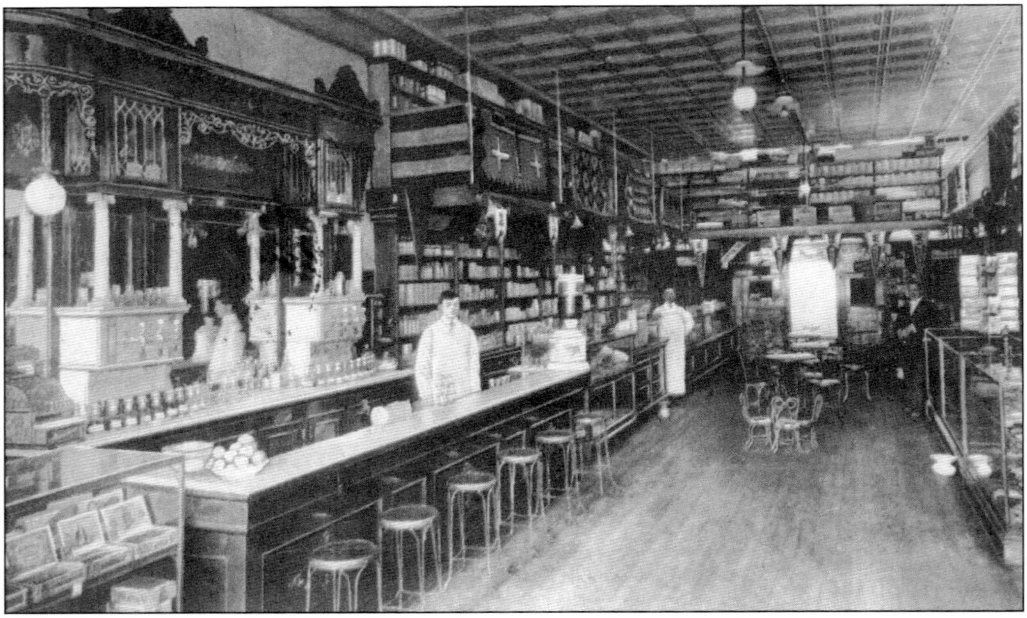

The local pharmacy/drugstore was a fixture in downtown Artesia from the earliest days. But it was much more than simply a place to fill a prescription. In a 1915 photograph above, employees pose in the Pecos Valley Drug Company. This drugstore not only met community medical needs, but it was also a place to enjoy an ice cream soda or snack or to purchase a variety of goods, ranging from cigars to shaving needs. It was torn down in 1935. Below, the Artesia Pharmacy on Main Street is shown in the late 1940s. Like its predecessor, the Pecos Valley Drug Company, the Artesia Pharmacy also offered a variety of goods, such as jewelry, home appliances, food, soda—and even prescriptions.

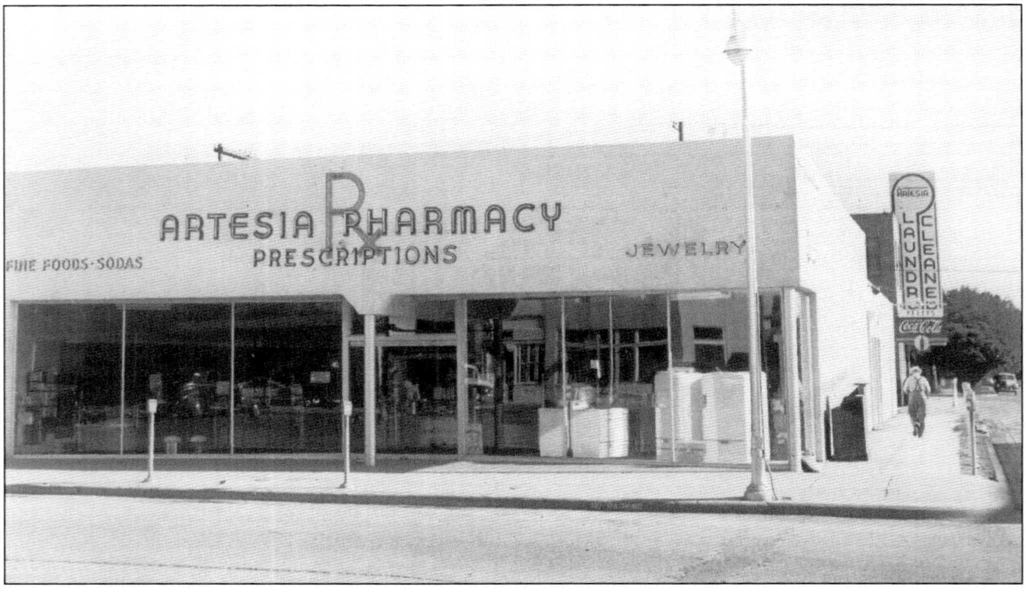

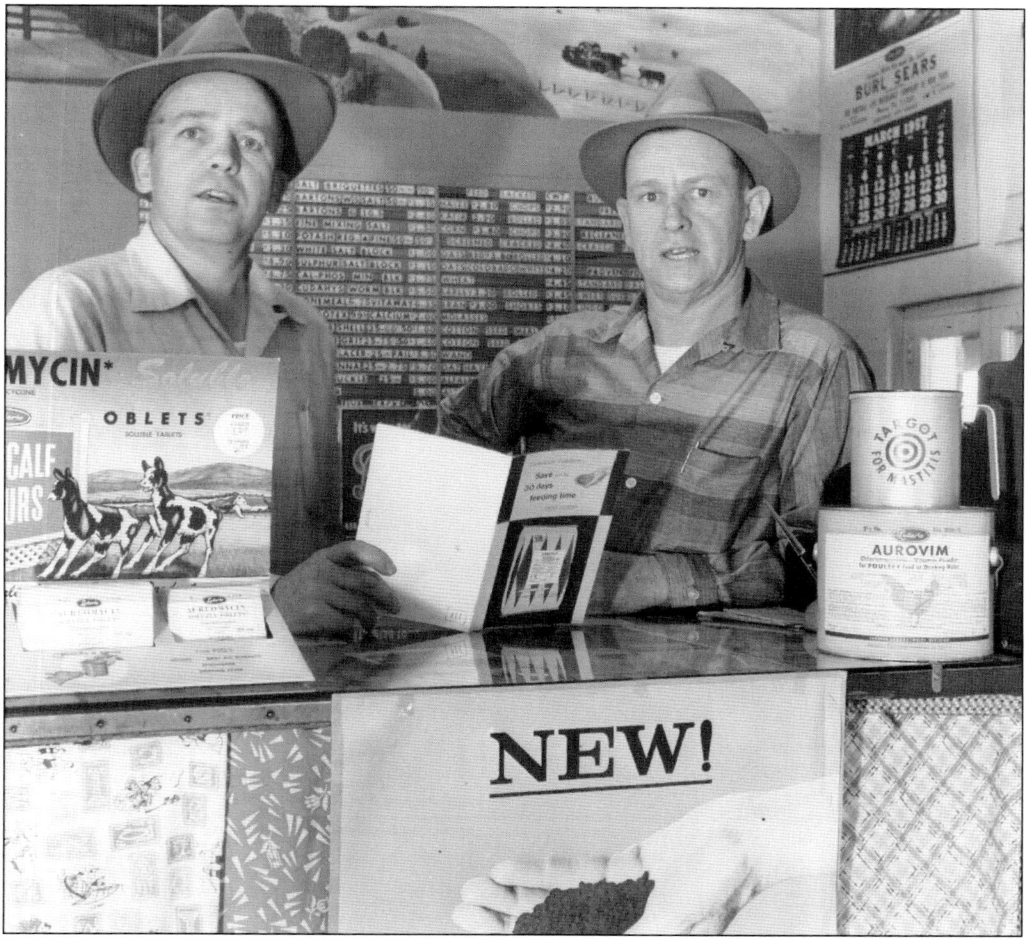

Bullock's Feed and Seed was Artesia's oldest family-owned business for many years, closing in the fall of 2011 a few months before its 100th anniversary. In the photograph above, William (left) and Charles Bullock look over a feed pamphlet in 1957. In the photograph below, the Park-Inn Grocery is shown in the late 1940s. The grocery was located on the northwest corner of Main and Thirteenth Streets and was owned by James Buck.

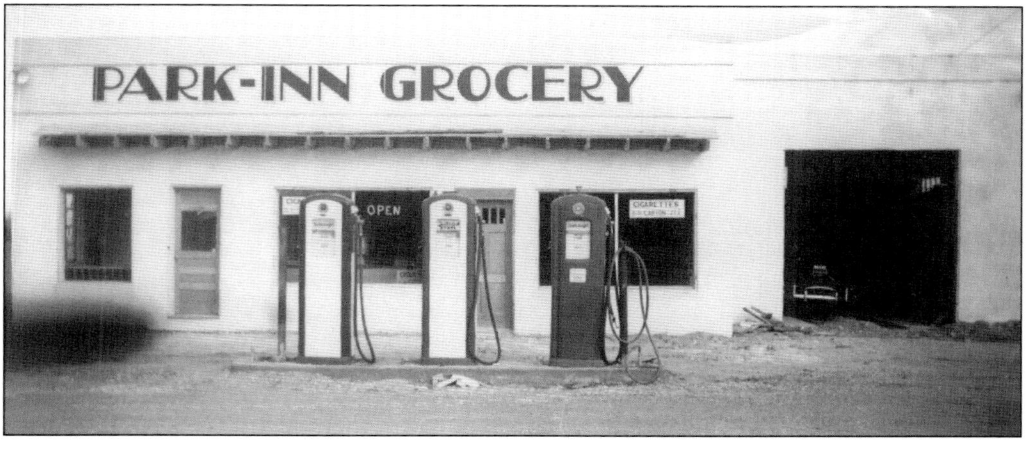

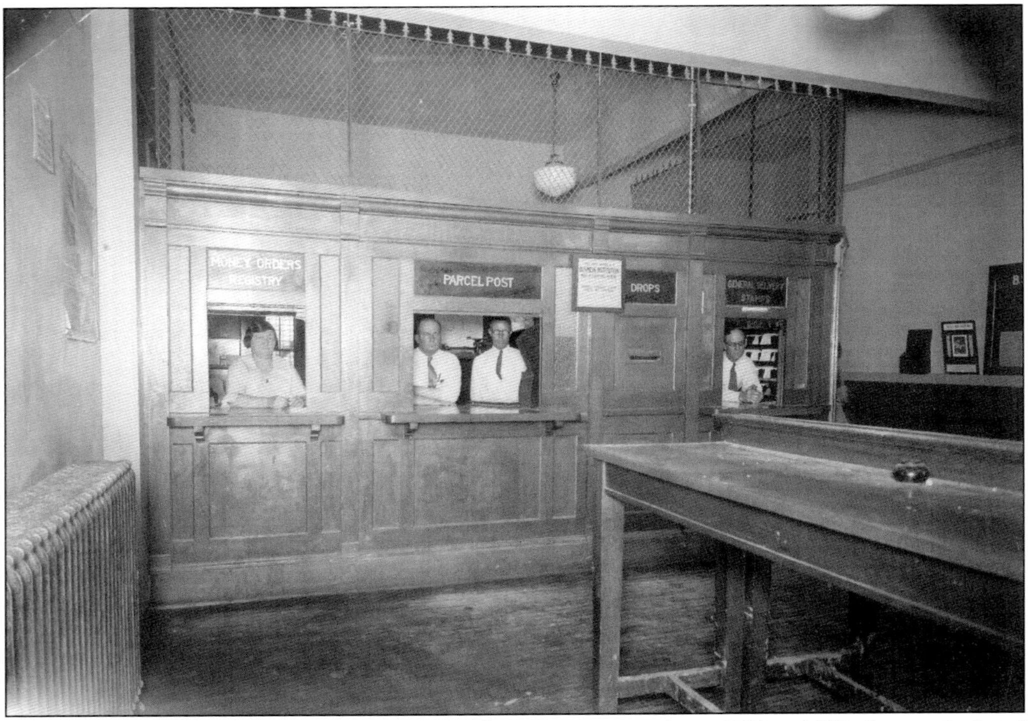

Sallie Chisum Robert Stegman was Artesia's first postmistress from 1899 to 1903, during the brief period when Artesia was known as Stegman. When Sallie divorced her husband, Baldwin Stegman, the name Stegman was dropped, and the town was renamed Artesia. In this 1934 photograph are, from left to right, Nellie Cogsdell, J. Austin Stuart, ? Duke, and Earl Collins.

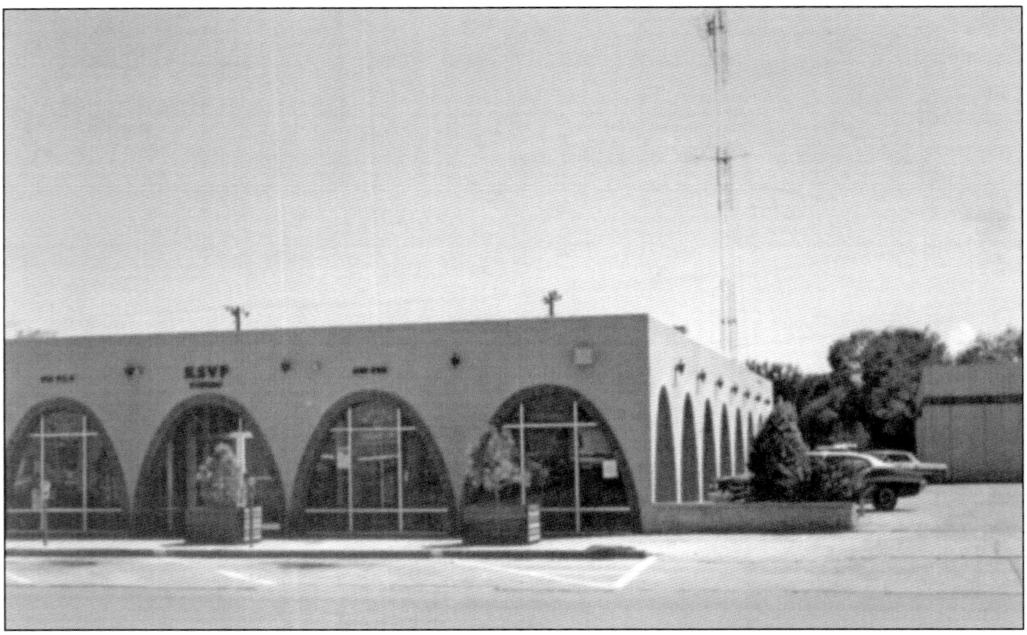

KSVP, Artesia's very own local radio station, went on the air for the first time on November 14, 1946, at 10:00 a.m. with longtime "voice of Artesia" Dave Button at the microphone. KSVP added FM in 1968; in 1979, the FM station received its own call letters: KTZA.

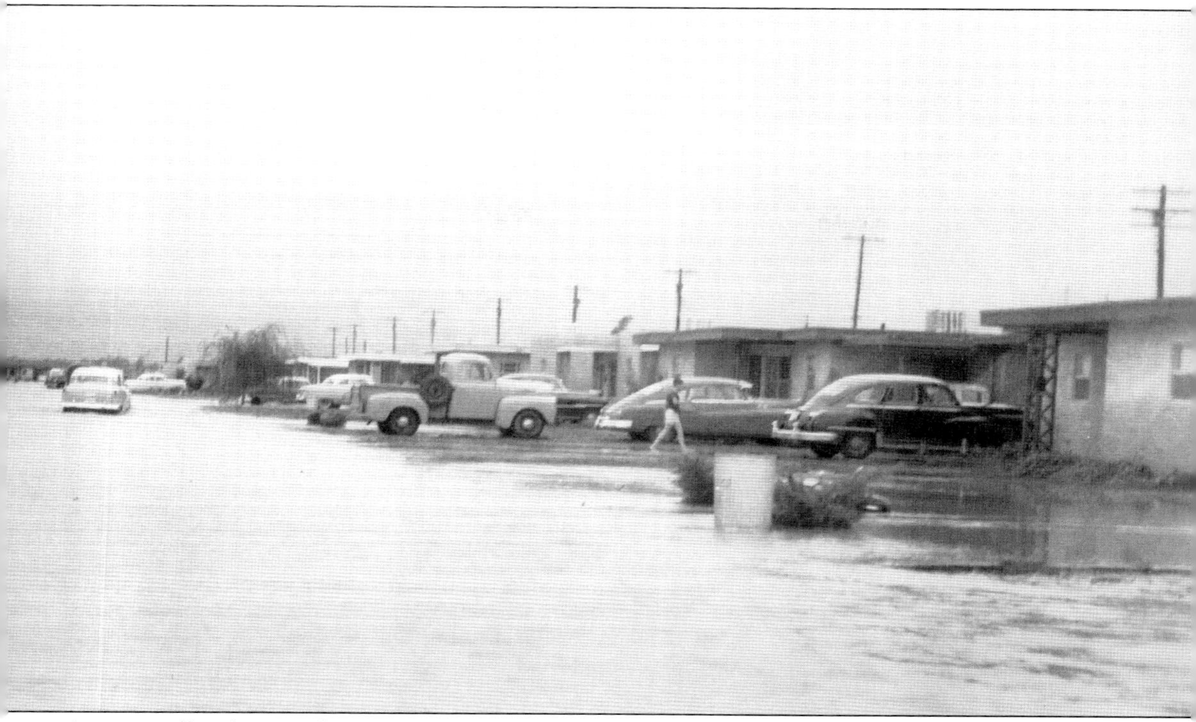

Artesia suffered many devastating storms and floods over the years, and by the early 1960s, something needed to be done to protect the residents and their property. The city opened a local urban renewal office and conducted an initial community survey in 1965, and by the middle of 1966, the Artesia City Council had approved plans to repair streets and construct several bridges over Eagle Draw. The Eagle Draw waterway was broadened and widened, and many residents were relocated to make room for this flood-control channel. Artesia's current 400,000-gallon-capacity water tower was constructed as part of this project in 1967. After completion, the Eagle Draw flood-control project was found to be effective; another severe storm hit soon after it was completed, and damage to Artesia was minimal.

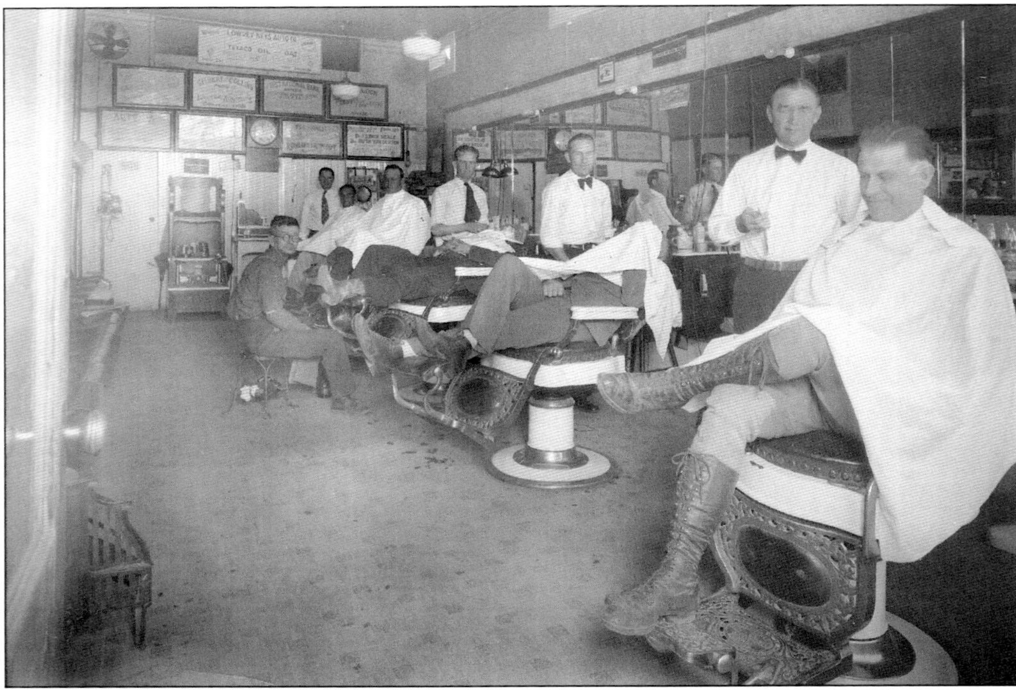

Early barbershops offered more than a fast haircut. Customers could also get a full shave (including a facial steaming to soften their beards) and a shoe shine. They could also catch up on the latest news of the day and town gossip. In the above photograph of an unknown early barbershop, customers Van Welch, Jess Truitt, John Prude (face lathered up), and Hugh Kiddy (face covered up) are shown along with porter and shoe-shine boy Joe Bates. No one else is identified in this image. When women started cutting their hair in the late 1920s, they also began frequenting previously all-male barbershops, as shown in the c. 1930 photograph below of the Sanitary Barber Shop.

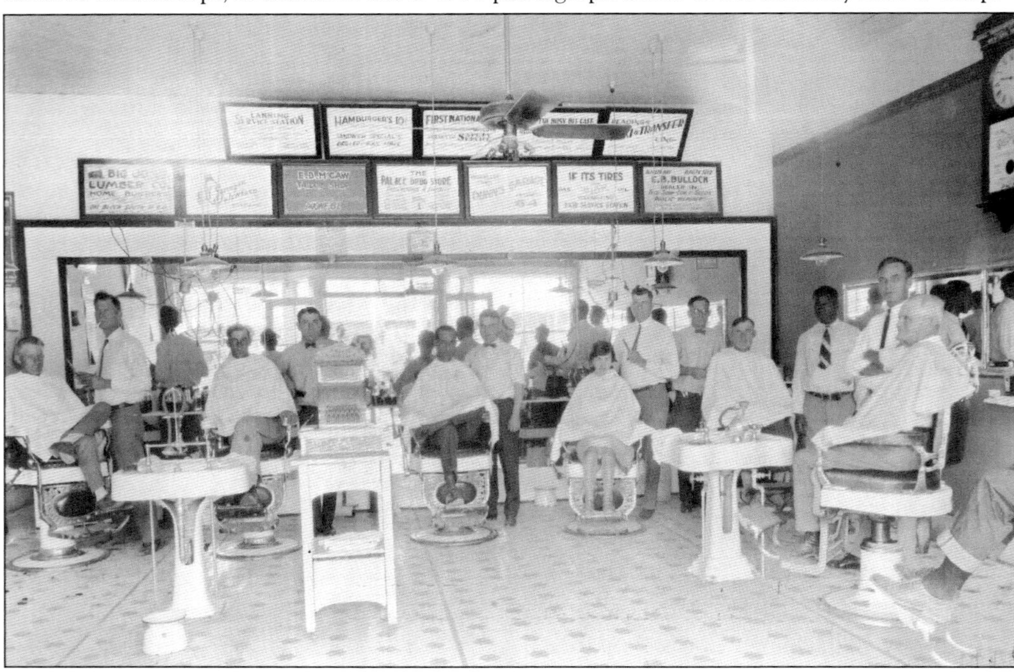

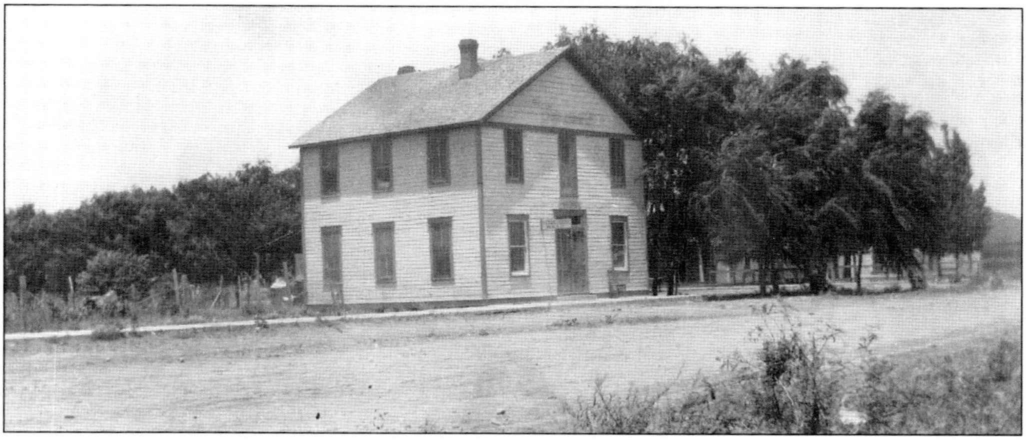

Prospective settlers needed a place to stay in early Artesia, and the Texas House (shown above) was an early choice. Built in 1904, the Texas House was also known locally as the D'Arcy Hotel, after the owners, and was the third lodging establishment built in Artesia. The sign on the front reads "Texas House Meals 25¢". The New Artesia Hotel (seen below) was owned and operated by the Rev. J.C. Gage until it burned down in 1916. The hotel was built in 1903 and was located on the north side of Main Street and Roselawn Avenue. Standing in front of the hotel are, from left to right, C.A. Sipple, Sheriff Jim Christopher, Letha Gage Christopher, and Nora Gage.

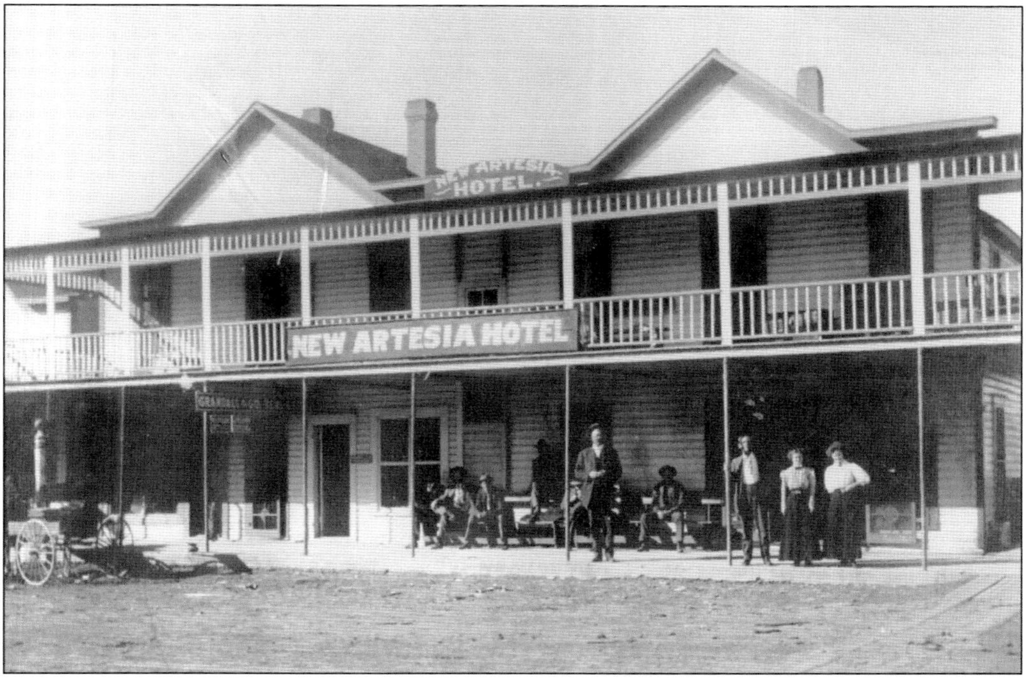

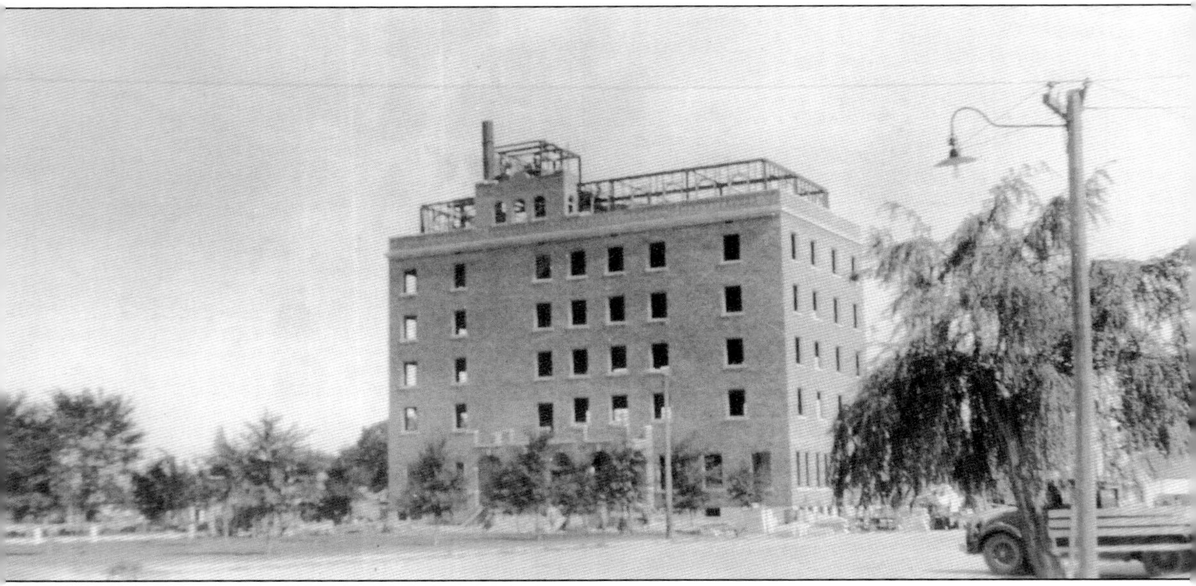

The Artesia Hotel was built in 1929. A group of local oilmen and businessmen subscribed to a building fund to finance the construction of a new lodging facility in Artesia. They felt that there was a need for a bigger, more modern hotel to accommodate the needs of visiting business executives and people traveling through Artesia. In this photograph, the Artesia Hotel is shown as its construction nears completion in the early fall of 1929. The fireproof building consisted of six stories built with steel framing. The exterior was made of artificial stone and tapestry brick. There were 60 guest rooms that included closets, their own bathrooms, telephones, running ice water, and even radio connections. Steam heat, soft water, and elevator and dumbwaiter service were provided to all floors. The ground floor had a large lobby, a dining room, coffee shop and kitchen, a drugstore, a barbershop, a ladies' parlor and dressing room, and there was a beauty shop on the mezzanine. The basement had a billiard room, sample room, and men's dressing rooms.

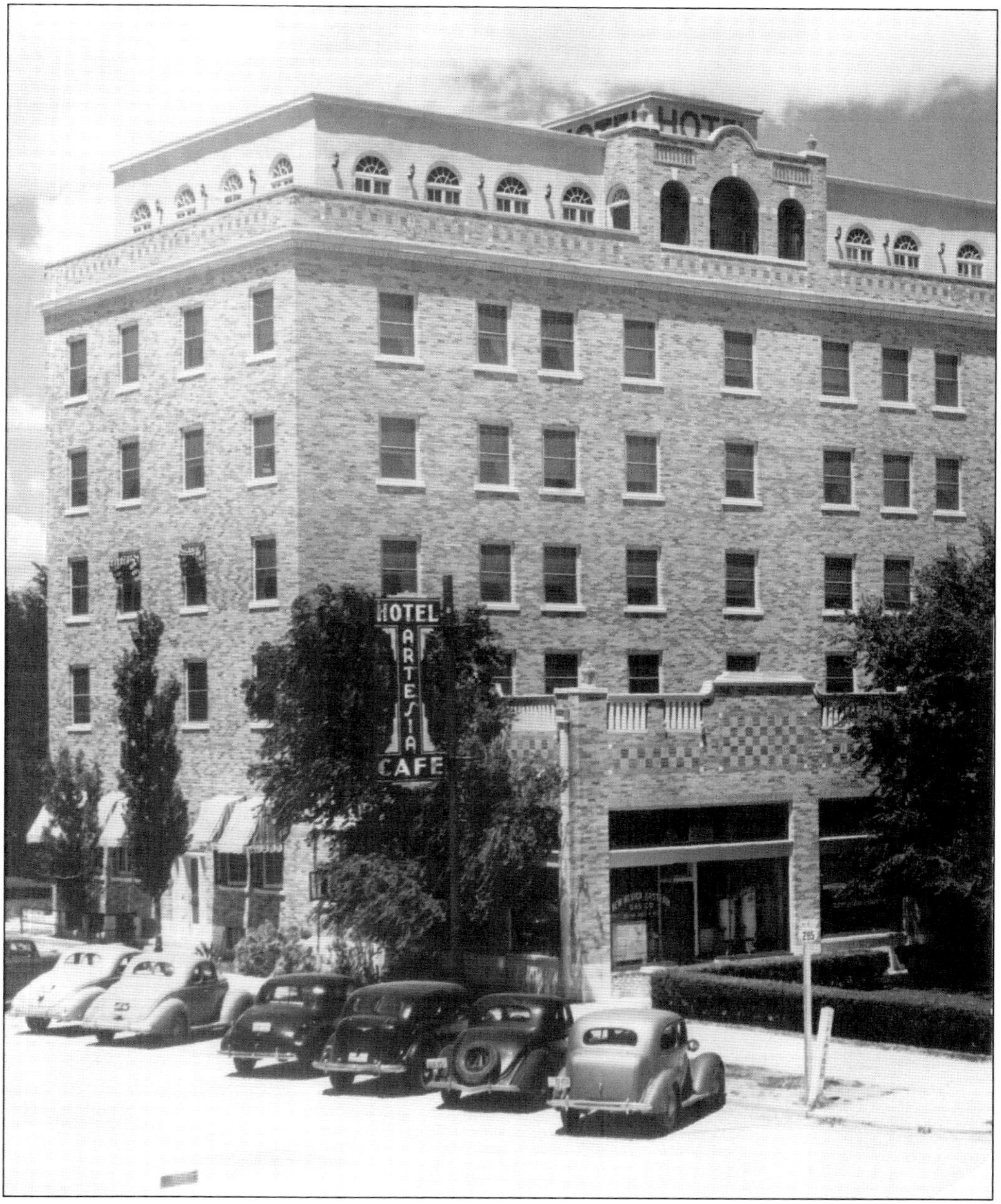

The Artesia Hotel is pictured in its heyday around the late 1930s. By this time, the hotel was in full operation and was well known all over the Southwest because of its central location in the heart of the Lower Pecos Valley at the crossroads of State Roads 83 and 285. The top floor of the structure had a roof garden and banquet room. The hotel hosted many events, including high school proms, public meetings, private business meetings, and many family affairs. Thanks to the spacious meeting rooms, civic groups held their meetings and functions there. The hotel's restaurant was considered the nicest place in town to dine, and the coffee shop was a favorite spot for locals to gather and socialize. Subscribers to the original construction fund were proud to see that the hotel was so successful.

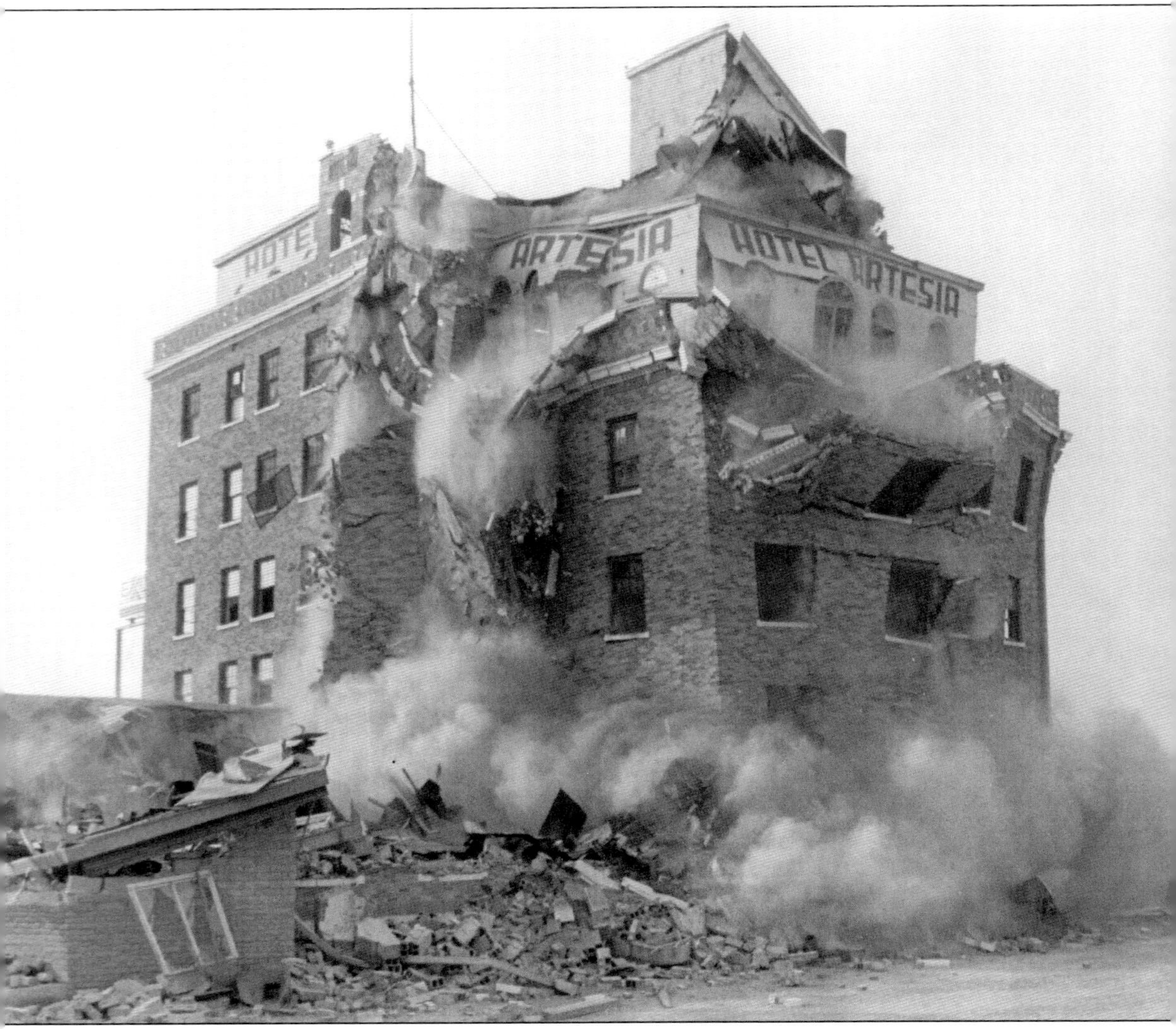

The Artesia Hotel had a number of owners over the years, but by the early 1970s, it was starting to show its age. The electrical, heating, and cooling systems were all out-of-date and in need of repair, and the rooms needed redecorating. Efforts to sell the hotel were unsuccessful—local and area businesses did not have the capital to make the necessary renovations to make the building usable. One of the last uses of the hotel was also one of its most enduring: in 1975, British director Nicholas Roeg filmed part of *The Man Who Fell to Earth* in Artesia, and stars David Bowie, Candy Clark, and Rip Torn all spent time in town. Many locals served as extras in the movie, and several scenes were filmed at the hotel. Although it took several building contractors and thousands of dollars to construct the hotel, it only took explosives two days to completely demolish it. The Artesia Hotel is missed to this day.

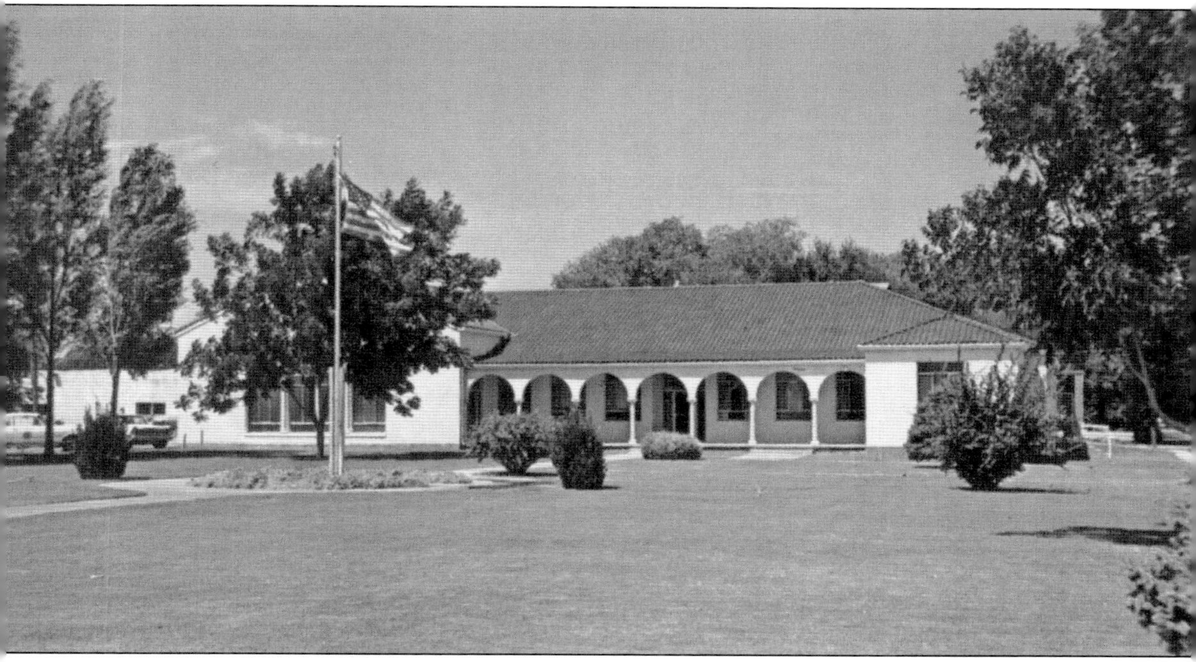

The City of Artesia's offices moved into the former Veterans' Memorial Building in 1965. The structure that was formerly known for its fun dances and veterans services became the new city hall, and the dance area became the city council meeting room. The new city hall quickly became the go-to spot for residents to pay utilities, find answers to their inquiries about city services, and attend city council meetings. Adjoining city hall, Baish Park remains a focal point for community veteran memorials today. Artesia MainStreet Inc. and the City of Artesia have finalized plans to expand the memorial in Baish Park as part of New Mexico's Statehood Centennial celebration. As of the beginning of 2012, the park will have undergone a complete face-lift. Since New Mexico became a state in 1912, many businesses have come and gone through the years, and many changes have taken place in Artesia.

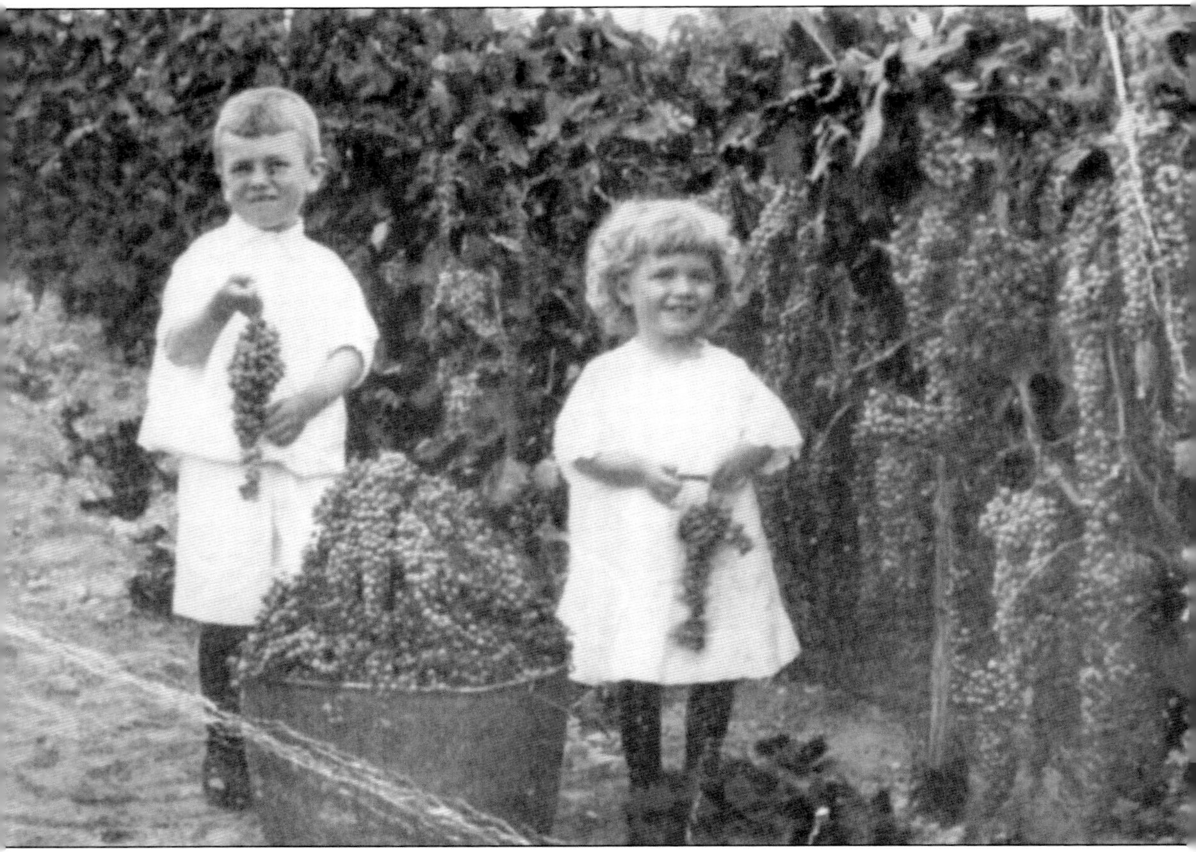

Many early farmers experimented with a wider variety of crops than are seen today. Grapes, apples, peaches, and apricots were among those that flourished in local orchards. These early gardens fell victim to record-low temperatures in 1933, when several days of below-freezing weather killed many of the crops in the Lower Pecos Valley. Most were not replanted because of problems with insect infestations, low prices at market, and economic hardships caused by the Depression. Local farmers and ranchers were reluctant to invest time and money into crops that had failed once already, and many former orchards were converted to pastureland. Other orchards were converted to hardier crops, such as pecans, chilies, beans, and melons, which could withstand more extreme weather conditions. Family-owned-and-operated farms traded their crops during the Depression, when cash was scarce.

Two

Farming and Ranching

Artesia's farming communities have been around since the very beginning of pioneer settlement. Many early farmers homesteaded on the outskirts of Artesia's town limits, and two early farming communities actually became known by separate names and had their own community stores, schools, and churches.

The Atoka community, about five miles south of Artesia, had both a store and a school at one time. A railroad siding there allowed farmers to load their alfalfa crops onto trains for shipment without having to transport the heavy bales into Artesia. Tomatoes and cantaloupes were also popular crops in the early years. The Sipple-Haney Company of Artesia laid out a townsite plan in 1920 in an effort to establish a separate municipality (in which the company would own and sell all the lots), but this did not work out. Atoka-area farmers were content with things the way they were.

The Cottonwood community, about five miles north of Artesia, was divided into the Upper and Lower Cottonwood areas. The community received its name from the large number of cottonwood trees that grew near a spring and creek known as Cottonwood Springs or Cottonwood Creek. Some early settlers also referred to the site as the Falls. Both Upper and Lower Cottonwood had community schools and general stores, and Cottonwood's church was located in the former Blackdom community church. Blackdom was an African American farming settlement located in Chaves County that was founded around 1900 and existed for about 20 years. A lack of water led to the abandonment of Blackdom, and the church (built in 1915) was sold to the First United Methodist Church of Cottonwood and moved to Cottonwood in the summer of 1922.

Along with farming and ranching, Artesia has also had many dairies since the earliest days. The Artesia Dairy was started in the early 1910s, and it became Price's Creamery in 1940. The Cole Dairy began operating around 1921 and closed down in the late 1930s. The Wilde Dairy was also started in the 1920s, but it was unable to make a profit and shut down after a few years. Many dairies were family businesses, and that tradition continues today.

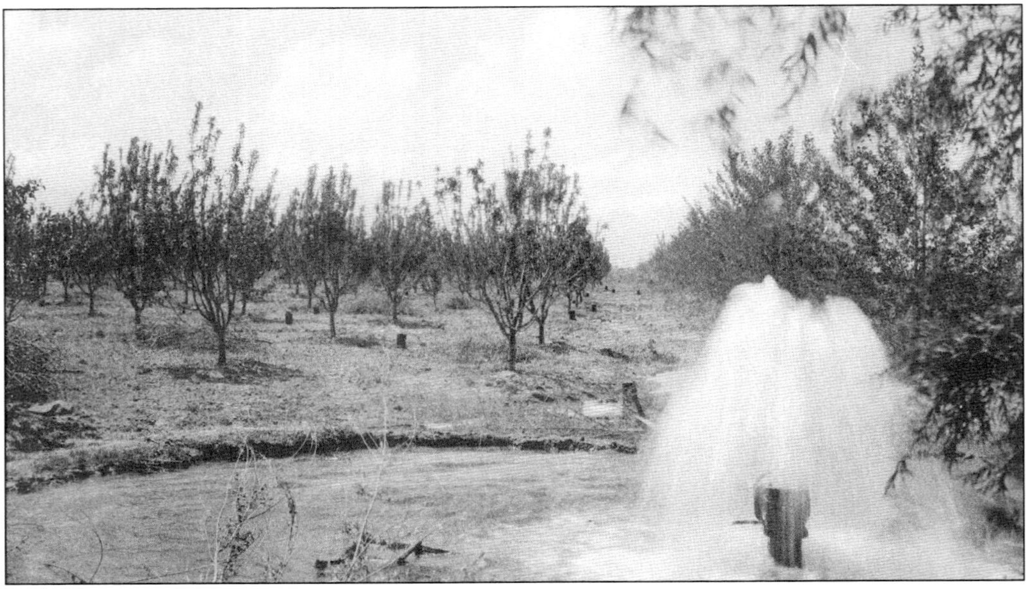

The artesian well, orchards, and smudge pots of the CAP Ranch are shown around 1910. The ranch was named for the three owners—John Cecill, T.C. Aldrich, and H.A. Porter—who established it in 1902. The spread was one of the most well-known ranches of its day because of its fresh produce and reliable service. It apples were shipped to Harvey Houses all over the Southwest.

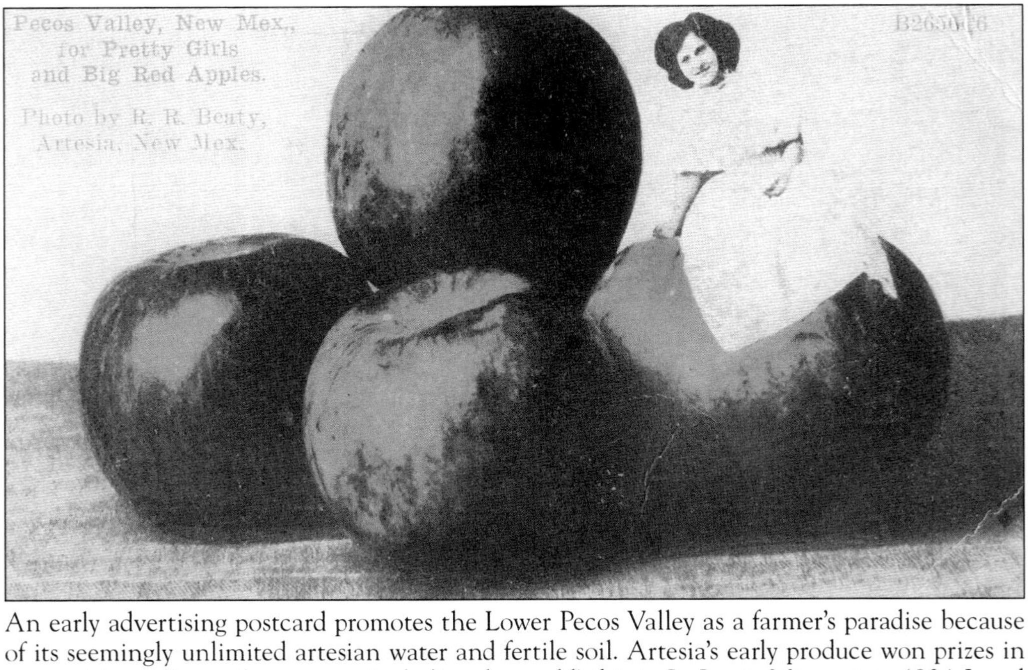

An early advertising postcard promotes the Lower Pecos Valley as a farmer's paradise because of its seemingly unlimited artesian water and fertile soil. Artesia's early produce won prizes in competitions all over the country, including the world's fair in St. Louis, Missouri, in 1904. Local beauty Sophie Bendel posed for this postcard around 1907.

In the photograph at right, a water well rig is drilling on the Rohrbough hog farm around 1917. In the image below, J.T. Collins is shown next to his artesian well in the early 1900s. Early pioneers discovered a vast supply of artesian water when they drilled their early wells, and the town's name was quickly changed to Artesia to capitalize on this resource. Real estate promoters used this as a way to lure settlers to this area. These early artesian wells were allowed to flow unchecked, and as the water table lowered, area springs dried up. By the early 1920s, many artesian wells were also beginning to run dry, and the first water-conservation measures were established and enforced. Today, area farms still water their crops from artesian wells, but they no longer flow freely.

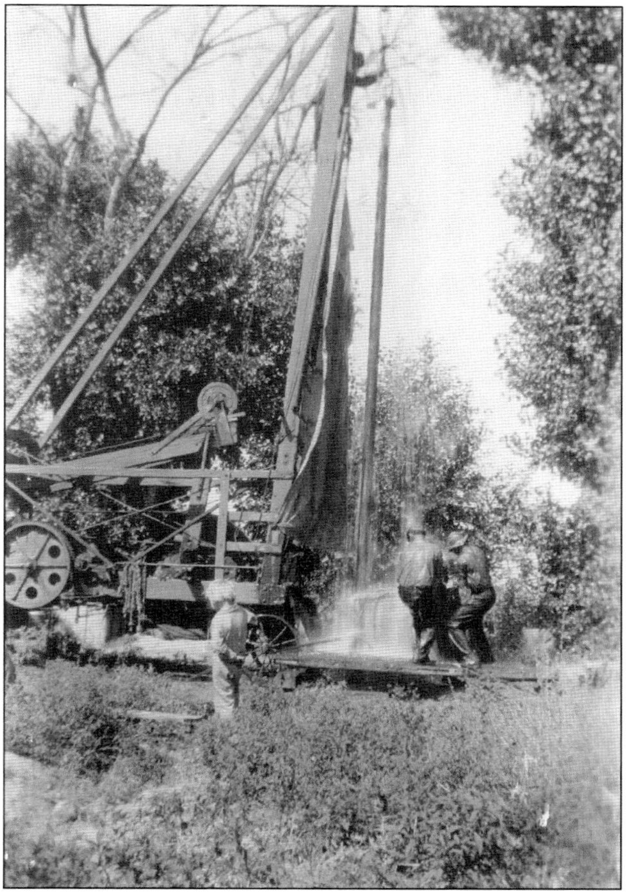

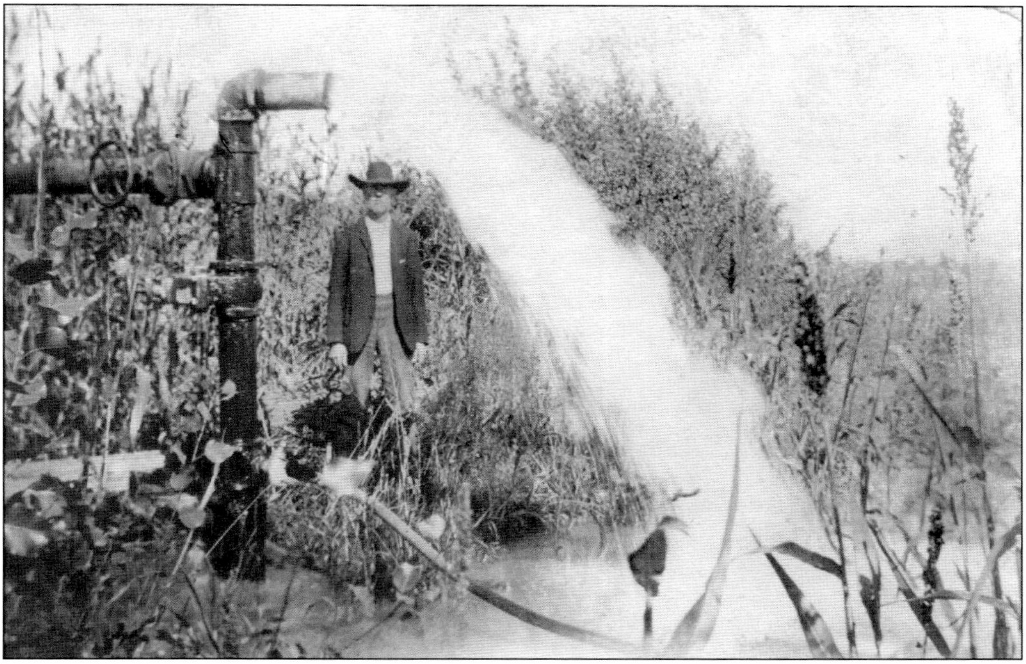

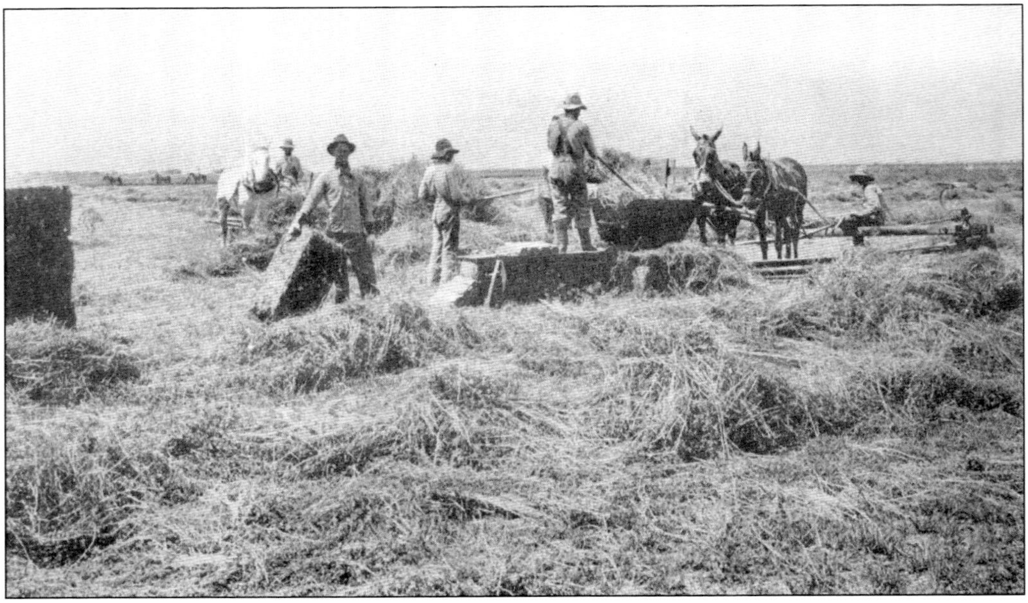

Alfalfa has been an important crop in the Lower Pecos Valley since the earliest days of farming and ranching. Local and area farmers grew enough to feed their own animals and sell their remaining crops locally; they also shipped bales of Pecos Valley alfalfa all over the country. Alfalfa from the Artesia area was especially prized for its hardy texture and nutritious qualities. As the photograph above shows, baling alfalfa in the 1900s by hand was a time-consuming, labor-intensive, but ultimately profitable job, even in extreme summer temperatures of over 100 degrees. Bales of alfalfa were then taken by wagon to the railroad depot where they would be packed into boxcars for shipment. In the photograph below, a line of wagons waits to unload alfalfa bales for shipment to New Orleans around 1910.

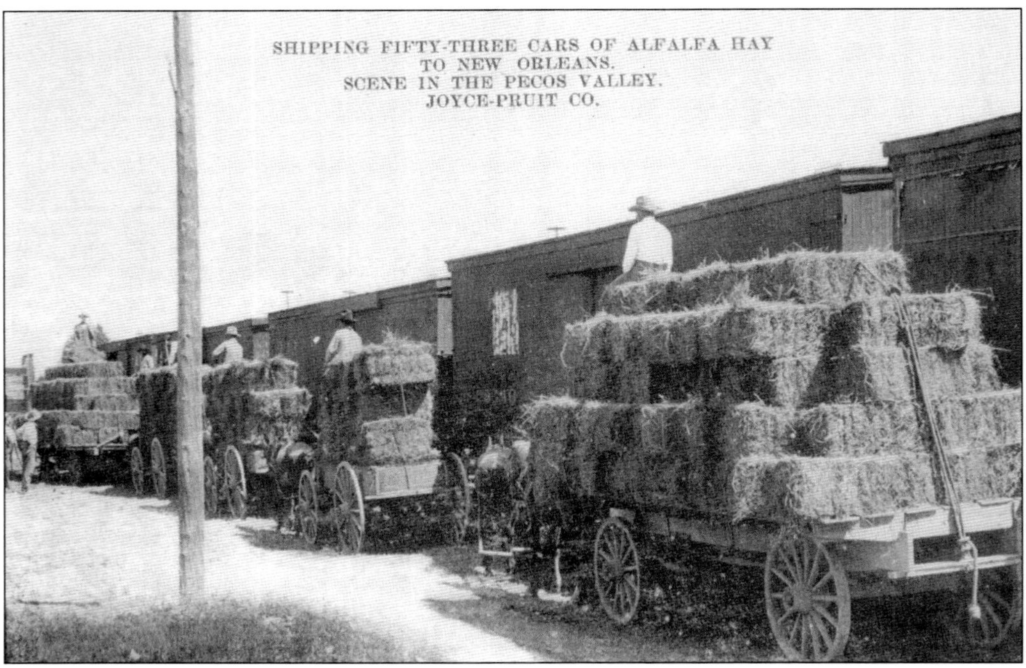

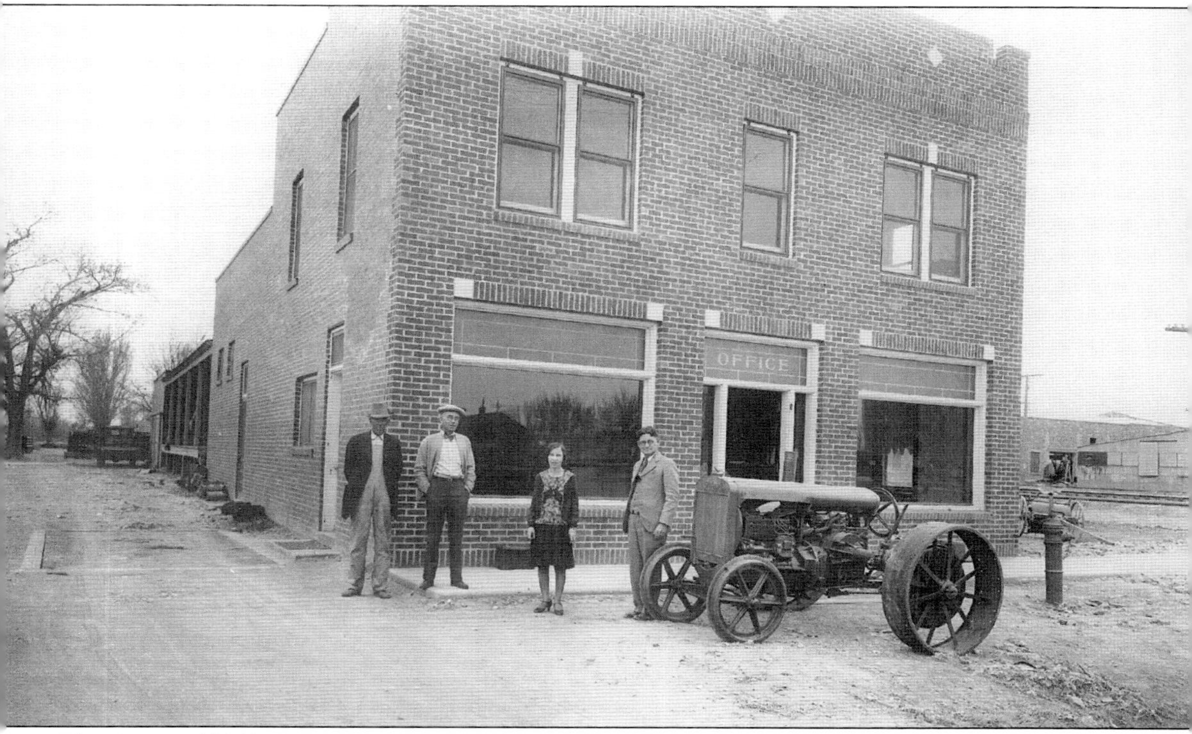

The Artesia Alfalfa Growers Association (AAGA) was formed in 1920. In this photograph, office staff members are shown in 1929 in front of their new office building and hardware store. They are, from left to right, unidentified, Noel Meeks, Juanita Cobble, and W.R. Hornbaker. The AAGA shipped area alfalfa for local growers for $17 per ton, saving farmers from having to broker their own alfalfa sales. Some growers were reluctant to turn their sales over to the AAGA, but they ultimately realized that their profits were greater when they sold as a united group. As more and more farmers began growing cotton, the AAGA purchased a cotton gin in 1923 so that cotton farmers would no longer have to transport their crops out of town for ginning, which ultimately became the biggest moneymaker for the AAGA each year.

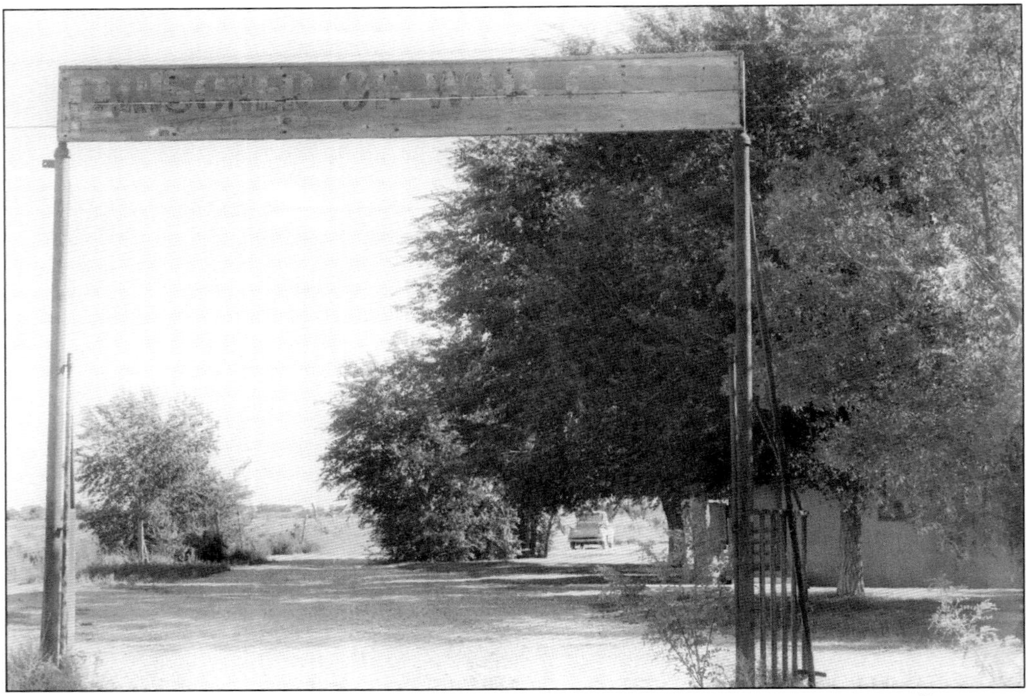

Citizens on the home front during World War II experienced many shortages: sugar, coffee, meat, canned foods, gasoline, and even shoes. But as the war progressed, it quickly became apparent that the most critical shortage was in labor. With so many men away fighting, there were not enough left at home to harvest the much-needed crops being grown. Another problem produced a solution: the United States had many prisoners of war (POWs) but nowhere to house them, so the obvious solution of using POW labor to harvest farm crops was born. New Mexico had prisoner-of-war camps in Roswell and Lordsburg. Each of these sites had many side, or branch, camps, and one of these camps was in Artesia. These 1964 photographs show the ruins of Artesia's POW camp entrance gate and barracks.

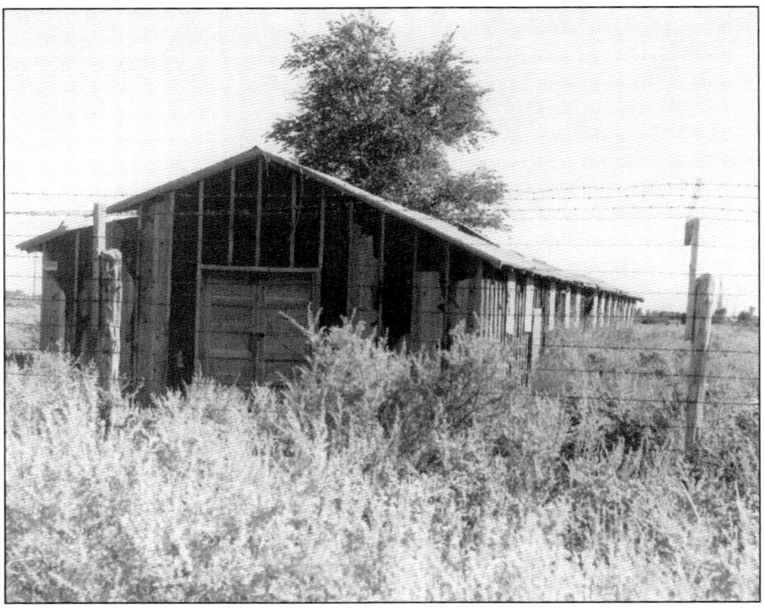

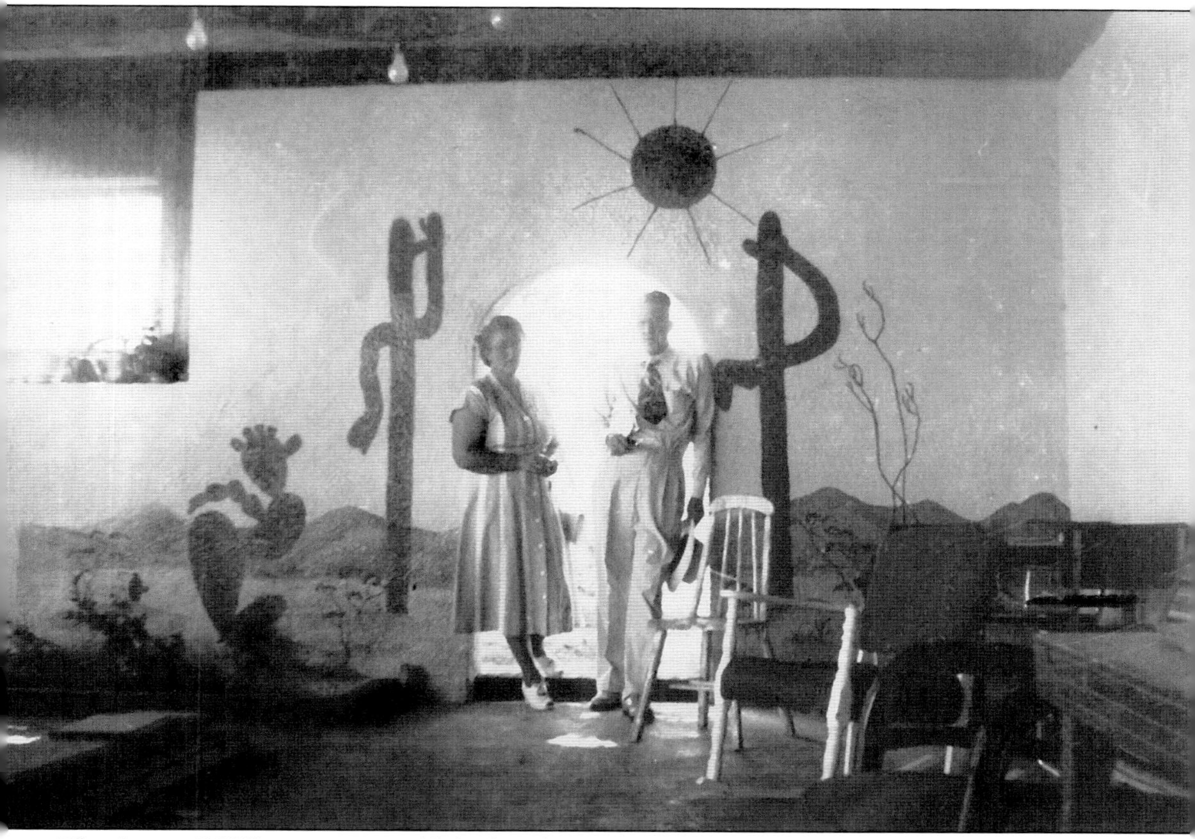

The Artesia POW camp was established so that prisoners could be housed closer to their work sites. Mainly Germans from General Erwin Rommel's elite Afrika Korps, the prisoners in Artesia's camp felt that manual labor was beneath them. The camp housed between 300 and 500 men, who were first used for the fall 1943 harvest. The prisoners turned out to be good workers. The original German prisoners were later joined by some Italian POWs, and the Germans were judged to be much better at picking cotton than the Italians. Escape attempts were few thanks to the geography, although two escapees were shot by a farmer while trying to steal laundry from his clothesline. On the whole, most POWs in Artesia and throughout New Mexico had relatively positive experiences. Many former prisoners kept in touch with the families they had worked for, exchanging letters and visits over the years. In this 1940s photograph, Vernie (left) and W.T. Haldeman are shown in their solarium; the mural was painted by a POW.

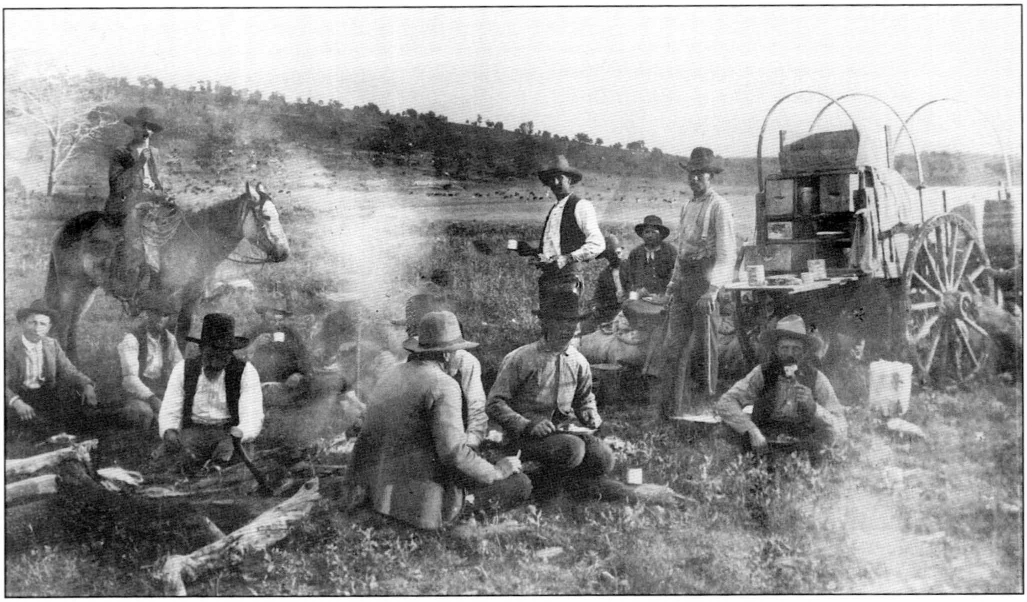

Before Artesia was founded, this area was part of John Chisum's cattle ranching empire. Ranching continued to be an important part of life, and helping local cowboys with the annual roundup gave some men a nice break from town life. In the photograph above, several cowboys enjoy their chuckwagon meal in 1904. In the image below, the Felix Cattle Company cowboys celebrate the end of the annual roundup in 1921. The Felix Cattle Ranch was located in the mountain foothills about 70 miles northwest of Artesia.

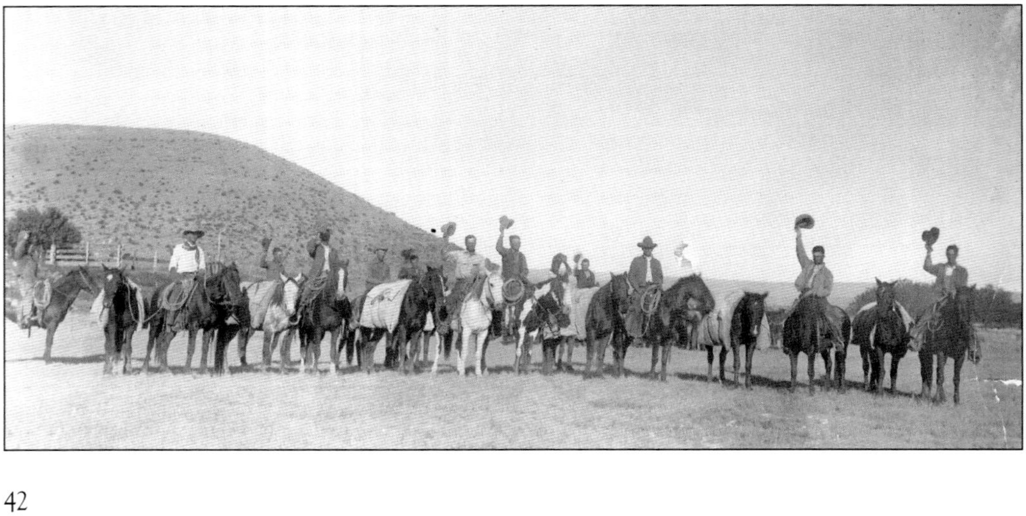

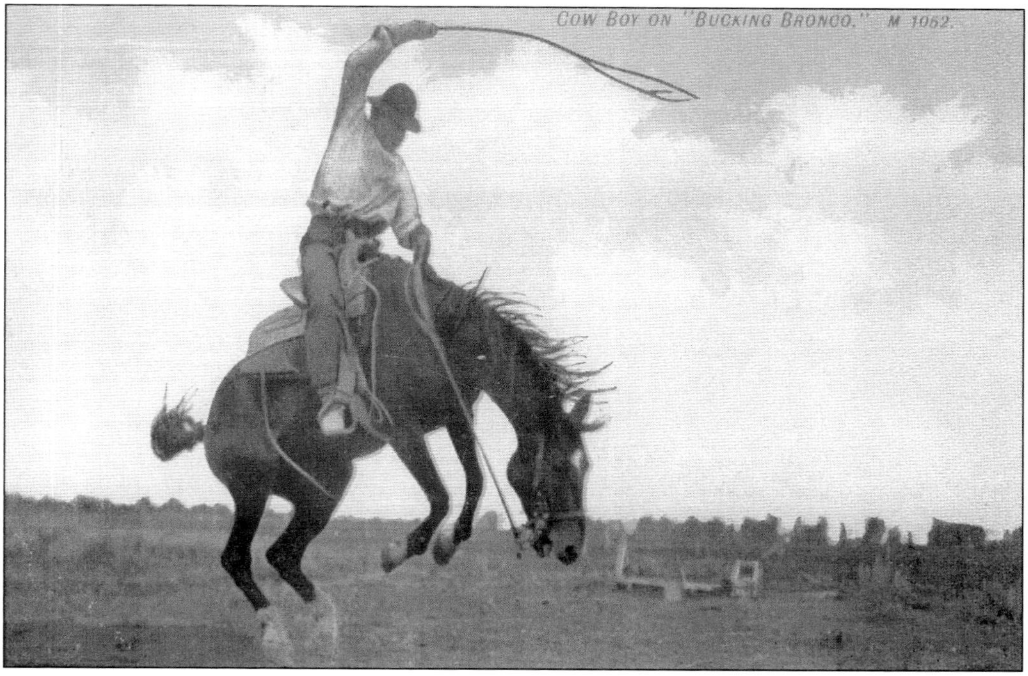

The rodeo competition grew out of the annual cattle roundup with different events based on the various duties of a cowboy during this time. There is some dispute as to when and where the first rodeo was held, but by the early 1900s, rodeos were a popular sport in Artesia. Above, an early rodeo rider shows off his skills in 1907. Below, a group of cowboys poses before competing in a rodeo on a Saturday afternoon in Cottonwood in 1913.

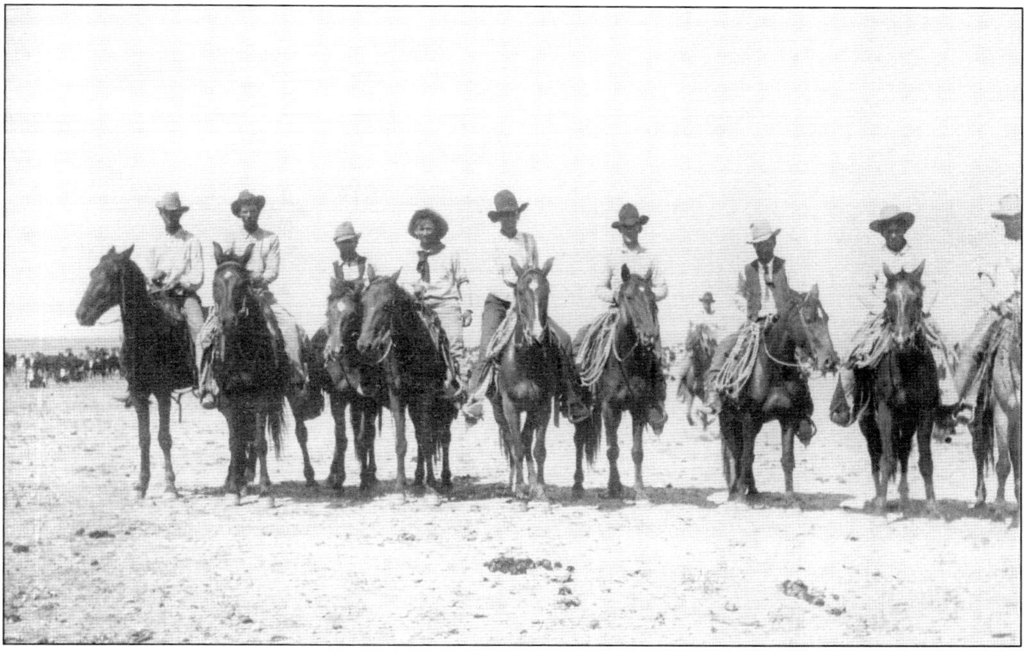

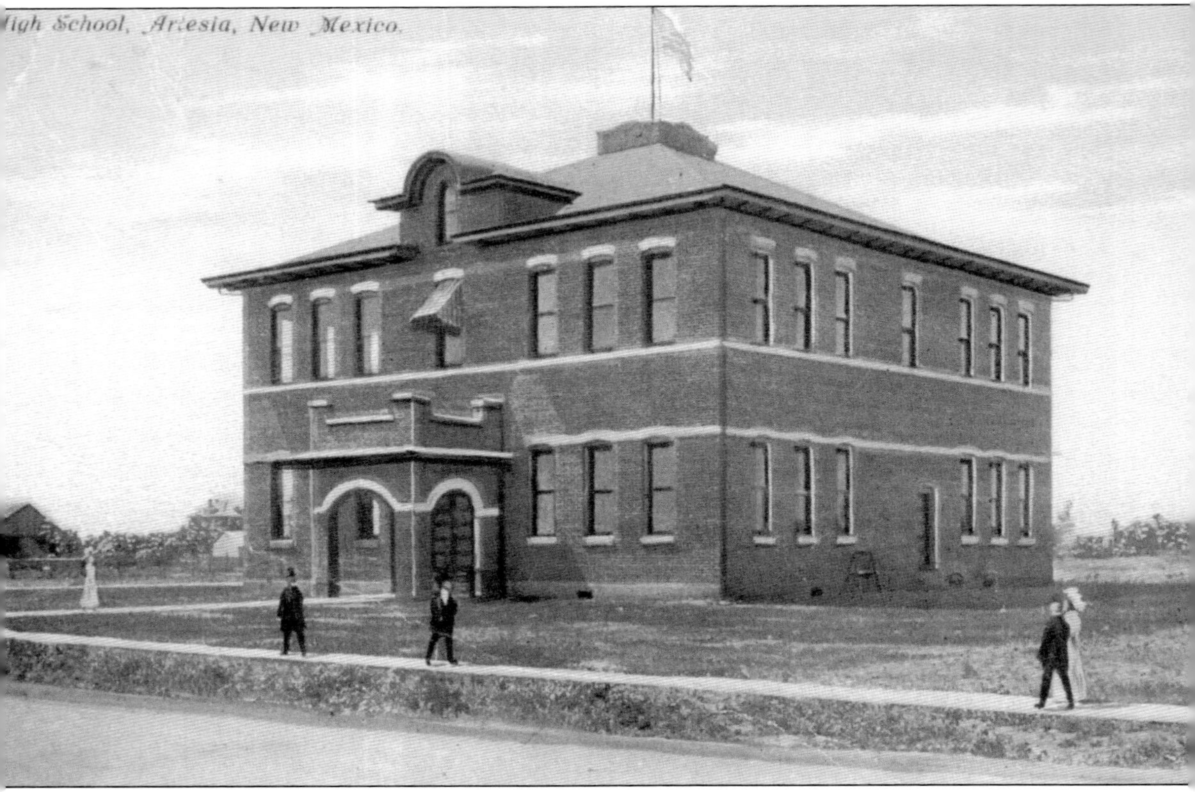

Artesia's first high school was established in a building that had previously served as the short-lived McIlhany College (1907–1908). Soon after the college closed, the structure became Artesia's first junior and senior high school in 1909. The students attended classes together in this building until 1921, when the senior high school students moved into another structure, the former Western College. The junior high school students continued attending classes at this site until 1938. Artesia High School's first graduating class of 1909 had three students—Ruth Brainard, Theodore Martin, and Rosa Wettig. Class sizes were small in the early years. But the town was still growing, and the graduating classes were larger year after year. Many early students in Artesia were not able to attend school full-time because of duties on family farms.

Three

Schools and Churches

Early residents of Artesia were eager to establish schools for their children and places of worship for their families. Most of the earliest children in Artesia received some sort of homeschooling before a tent school was set up near First Street and Richardson Avenue in 1902. Some students attended classes at the Red Top School, which was located a few miles south of Artesia in the Atoka farming community. Lessons were taught at Artesia's tent school until a small, two-room building was completed. The structure was paid for by popular subscription, as there were no tax funds available yet in the new town. Classes began in the newly built school in the fall of 1903. Artesia's first elementary school, Central School, was built in 1905. As the years went by, many more elementary schools were established to accommodate Artesia's growing student population.

Artesia has a strong tradition of supporting its students and schools. When the College of Artesia needed funds in the 1960s, every club and organization in town banded together to hold a huge community barbecue fundraiser—a wonderful example of cooperation between groups for the greater good. Today, the town's Chase Foundation offers scholarships to every Artesia high school graduate who qualifies.

Artesia's earliest worship services were held in homes, outdoor arbors, or tents until more permanent structures could be built. Several congregations shared these sites, taking turns with their service schedules. Rev. J.C. Gage was one of Artesia's first settlers and a circuit rider for the area. Being a circuit rider meant that Reverend Gage traveled throughout the mountain and the Lower Pecos Valley towns holding services in each community—sometimes, a given town might have only had a Sunday service once a month. Some of Artesia's earliest churches were the First United Methodist Church (1903), the First Presbyterian Church (1903), the First Christian Church (1903), the Church of Christ (1904), the First Baptist Church (1904), St. Paul's Episcopal Church (1905), and St. Anthony's Catholic Church (1905). Of course, many other churches have been established in Artesia since then, and today, Artesians have many worship choices open to them.

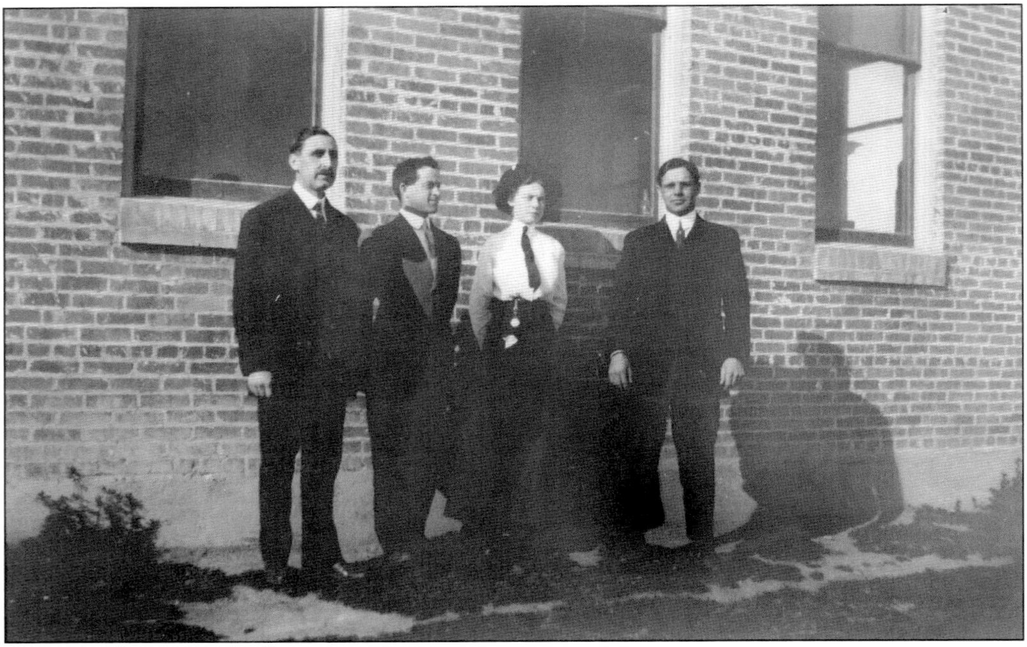

In a photograph taken in 1915, four Artesia school employees are pictured. They are, from left to right, superintendent C.E. Grover and teachers John Van Hay (eighth grade), Artie McMahon, and R.L. Paris. They are standing in front of Artesia's first junior and senior high school building. Below, Artesia's third high school is shown in the early 1940s. This structure was built in 1938 and was partially funded by the Works Progress Administration. The new Park Junior High School was constructed across the street, and junior and senior high school students again attended classes in the same vicinity after being separated for 17 years.

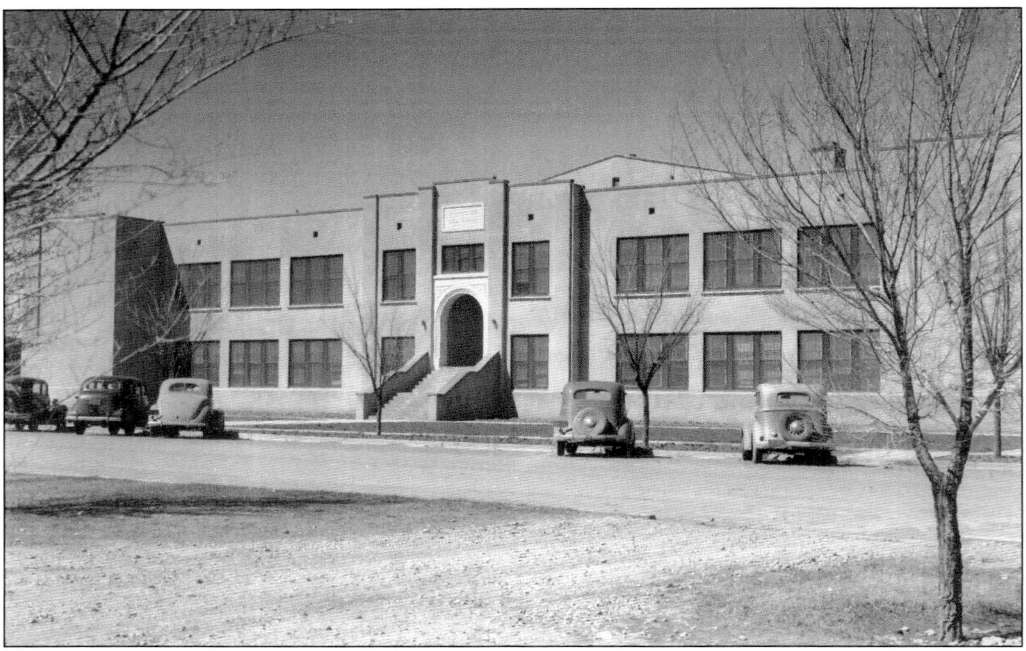

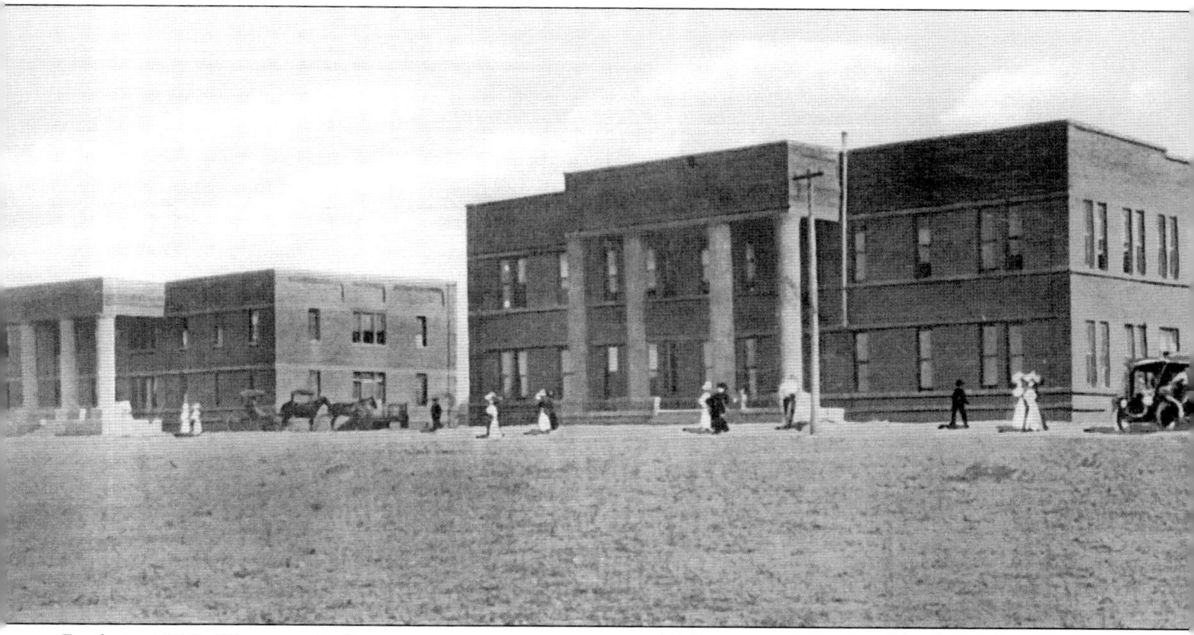

Built in 1909, Western College a serious attempt to establish an institution of higher education in Artesia. Unfortunately, the school was not able to support itself and closed in 1913. The buildings sat empty for eight years until Artesia's senior high school students were moved there to attend classes from 1921 to 1938. The Western College/Artesia High School buildings were torn down in 1938, and the building materials were used for Artesia's third high school. Other unsuccessful attempts to establish colleges in early-day Artesia included the Corrington College of Fine Arts, started by Professor Corrington in 1913, and the Southwestern College of Music, founded by ? McCrary in 1916. Both the Corrington College of Fine Arts and Southwestern College of Music used rooms in the Methodist Church for teaching, and neither school lasted for more than one year.

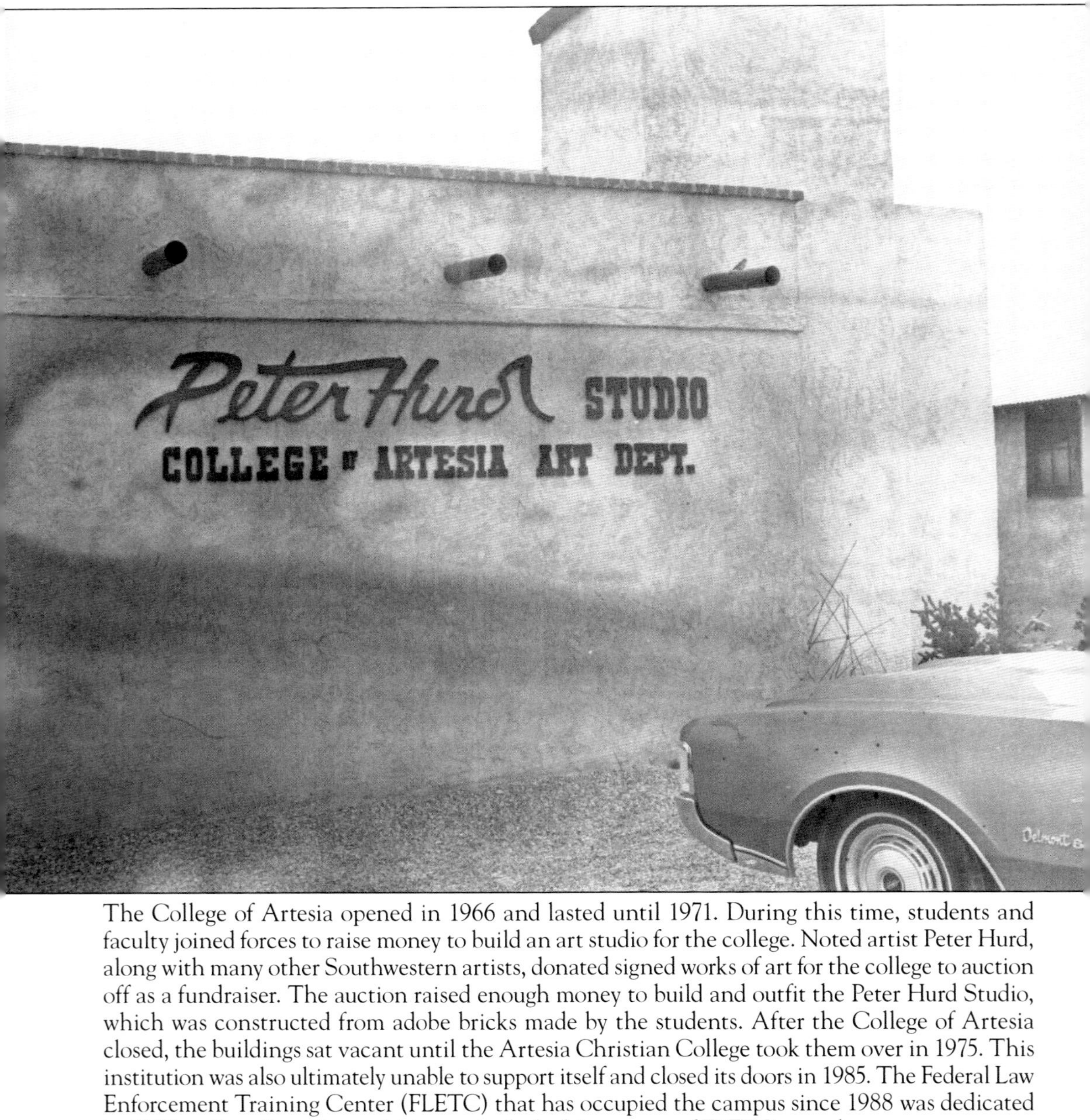

The College of Artesia opened in 1966 and lasted until 1971. During this time, students and faculty joined forces to raise money to build an art studio for the college. Noted artist Peter Hurd, along with many other Southwestern artists, donated signed works of art for the college to auction off as a fundraiser. The auction raised enough money to build and outfit the Peter Hurd Studio, which was constructed from adobe bricks made by the students. After the College of Artesia closed, the buildings sat vacant until the Artesia Christian College took them over in 1975. This institution was also ultimately unable to support itself and closed its doors in 1985. The Federal Law Enforcement Training Center (FLETC) that has occupied the campus since 1988 was dedicated in 2008 to Sen. Pete Domenici in gratitude for his support of FLETC over the years.

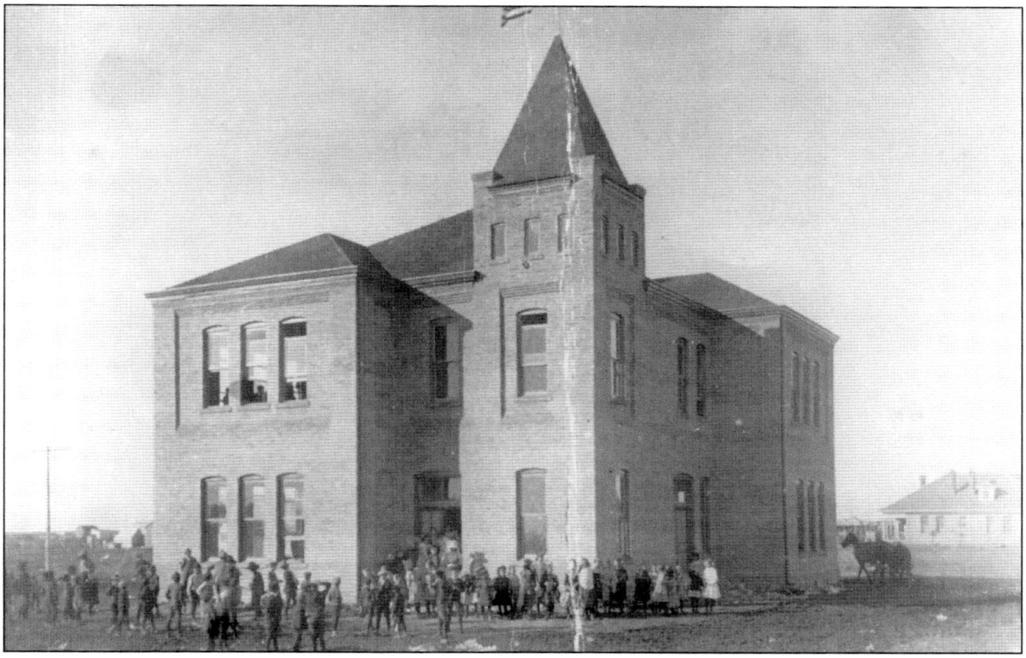

Artesia's first elementary school, Central School, was built in 1905. It was paid for by the passage of a bond issue and cost $10,000. Classes began in November 1905, and within a month, over 300 students were enrolled. Within a year, enrollment outgrew the school. Because of Artesia's rapid growth, students had to be at least seven years old to attend. In 1927, the original Central School building was condemned and torn down. A second Central School, built at a cost of $50,000, opened in 1928, and additional wings were added 10 years later as WPA projects. In 1980, this building was razed, and Artesia's third Central School was completed two months later at a cost of $726,000. The first Central School is pictured in 1906, and a 1910 photograph shows maypole dancers at the school.

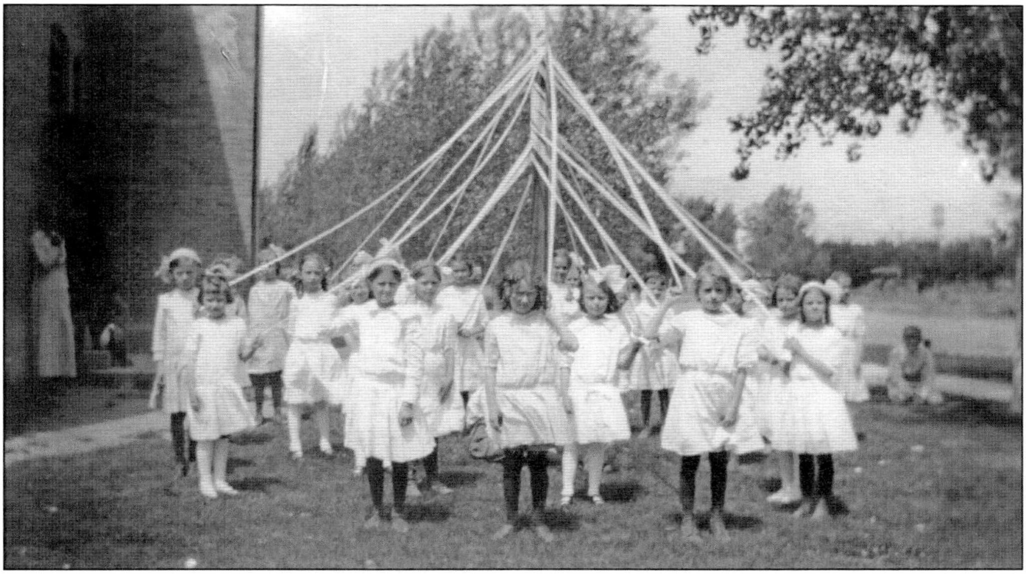

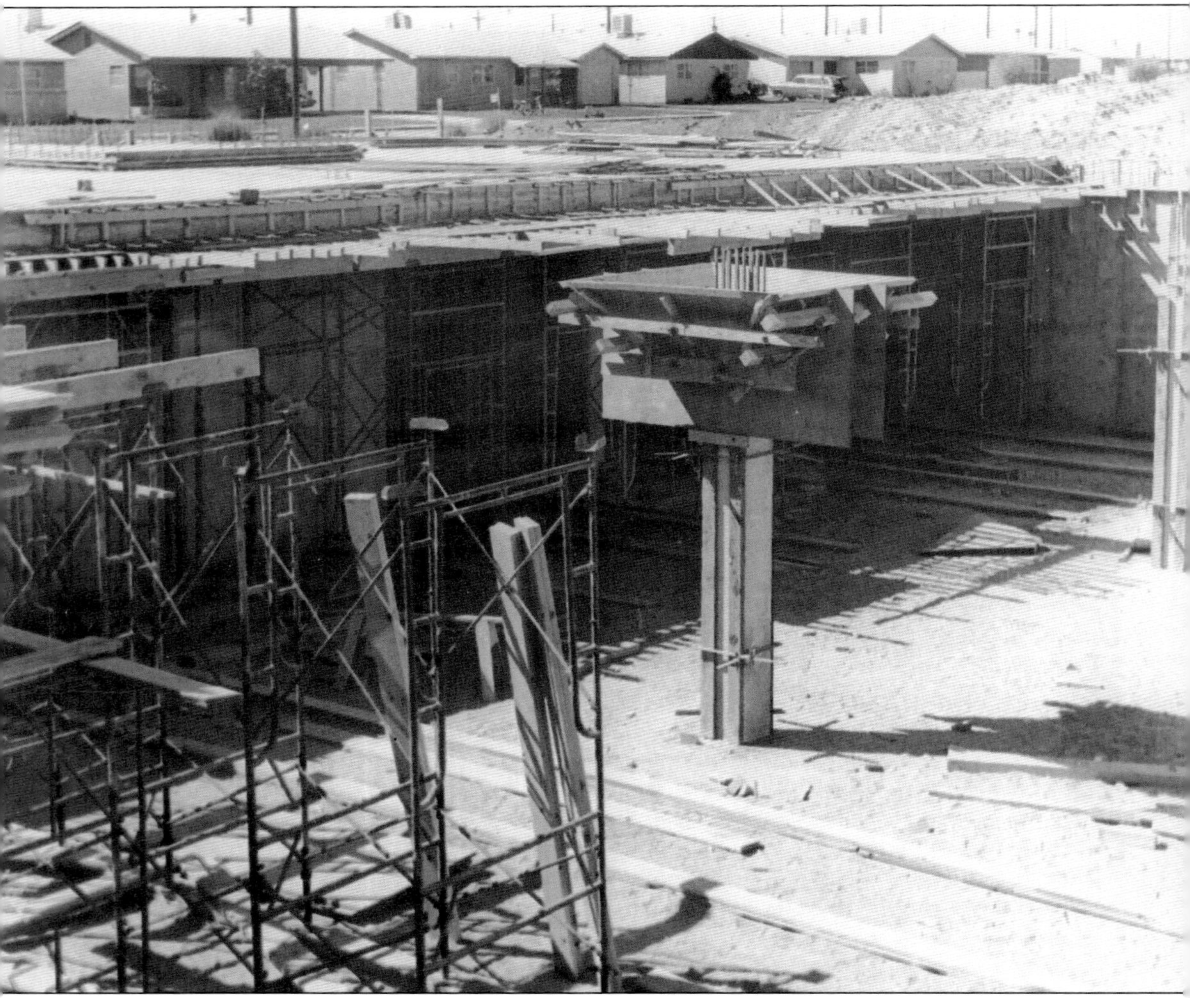

Artesia's most famous school is the Abo Elementary School and Fallout Shelter, which opened in 1962. Among the most unusual schools in the world, it was the first to serve as a combination school and fallout shelter. Conceived at the height of the Cold War and the era of bomb-shelter construction, the school was built 18 feet underground and covered by a 21-inch-thick, steel-reinforced concrete slab. Heavy steel doors said to be designed to hold up under a nuclear explosion were placed inside the aboveground entrances. The school's campus covered 10 acres, and the roof doubled as a playground. Besides having traditional school features, such as classrooms for 540 students, a cafeteria/multipurpose room, and modern restrooms, Abo School boasted an emergency entrance equipped with a shower to remove fallout particles, an air-conditioning system designed to filter out radioactivity, a generator to supply emergency power, and a morgue. Emergency rations were stored in the teachers' room. By 1989, the rations, outdated medical supplies, and body bags were discarded, and the morgue was used to store cafeteria supplies. Abo School was replaced by Yeso Elementary School in 1995.

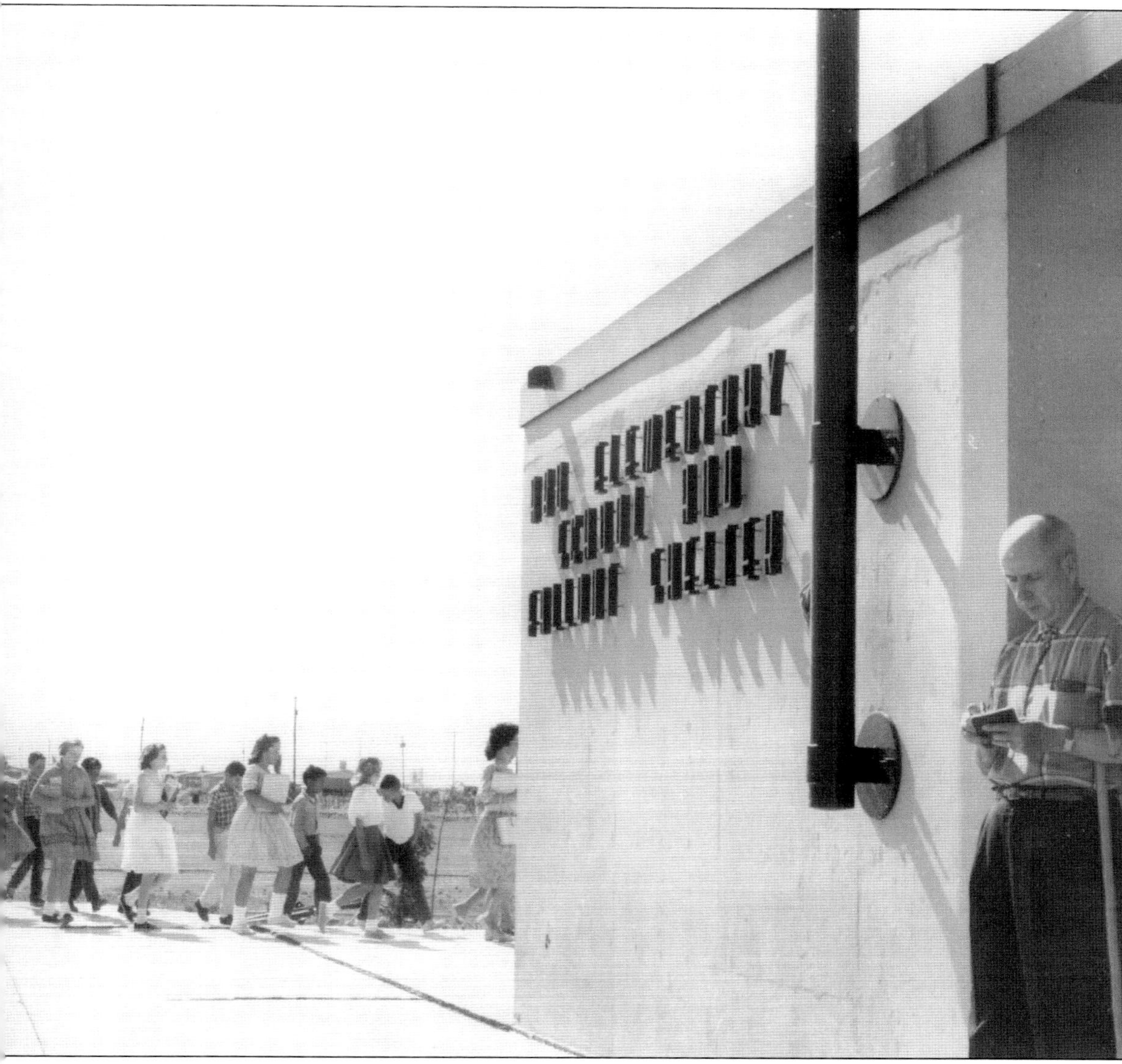

Abo School was a worldwide sensation when it opened in 1962. Architect Frank Standhart and Artesia Public Schools superintendent Vernon Mills were interviewed countless times as media representatives from all over the world descended on Artesia. Students from the early years became accustomed to having tour groups of curious visitors traipse through their classrooms. Because the school was underground, it was felt that students would be able to concentrate better on their lessons, as there were no windows to look out of, and the air-conditioning system was thought to help children with allergies and asthma. Named after the Abo geological formation, the school cost $468,623. Finances may have played a part in the final decision to build Abo School, as the Federal Civil Defense Administration paid $131,943 of the costs in return for the chance to test new construction technologies and experiment with new educational forms and functions. In this photograph, students perform a drill in May 1967 while Walter Short (at far right), director of the board of education, takes notes.

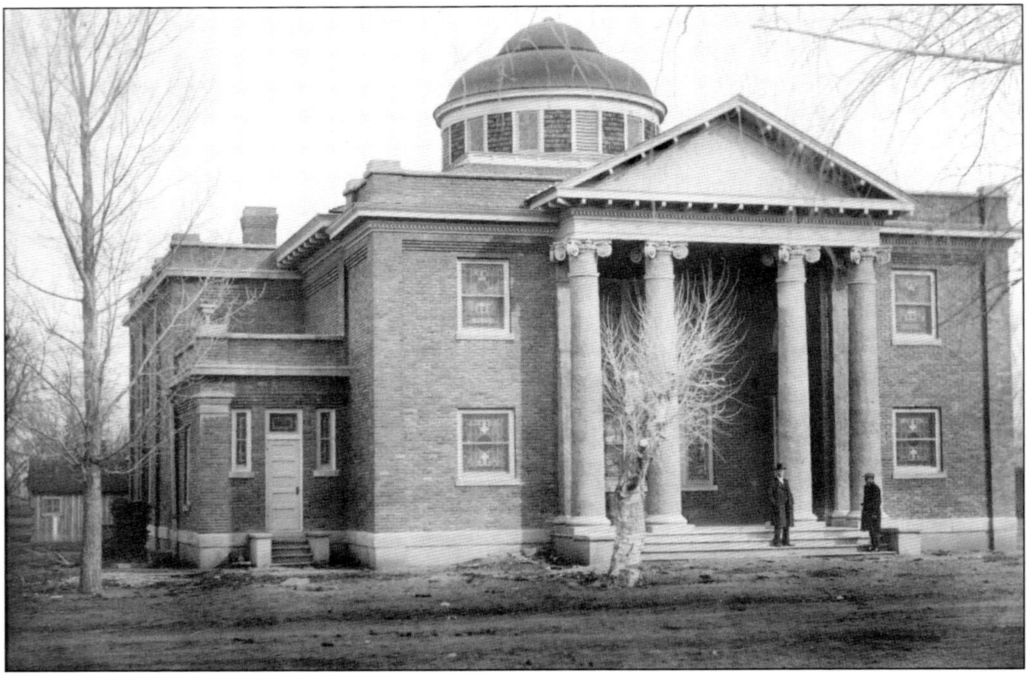

Construction of the First United Methodist Church building, shown above, began in 1916. Because of a shortage of building materials during World War I and afterwards, the structure was not completed until 1919. As the membership increased, the need for a new building became apparent. In 1968, the new church was opened. In the photograph below, Fannie Terpening's Sunday school class prepares for an outing in 1920. Identified are, from left to right, (first row) two unidentified, Bethelgene Stagner, Edna Dungan, unidentified, Lorene Kirkpatrick, and Vesta Frisch; (second row) Fannie Terpening, two unidentified, Irene Syferd, unidentified, Mildred Frisch, three unidentified, and Maurine Terpening.

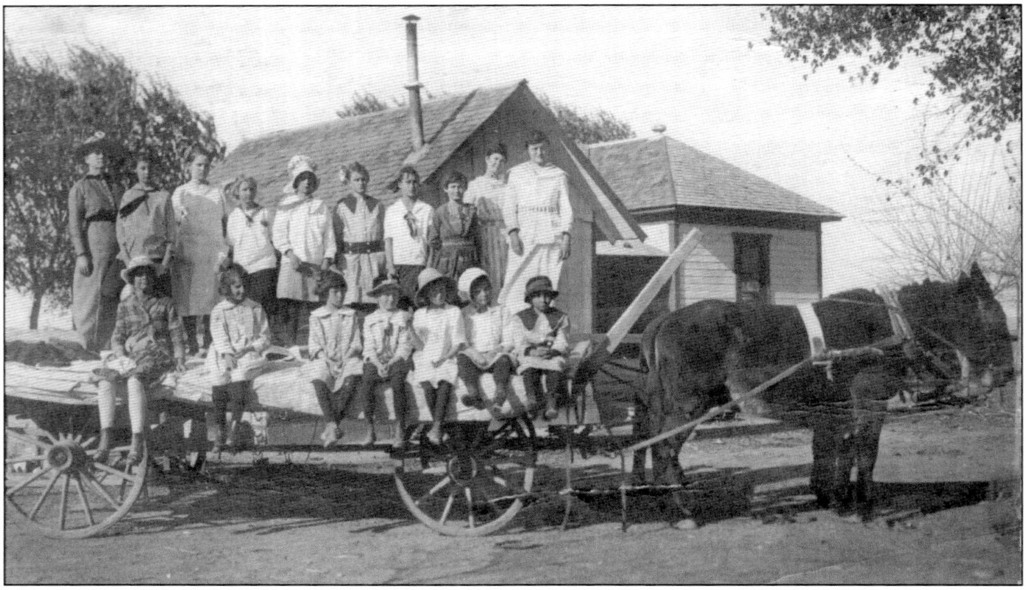

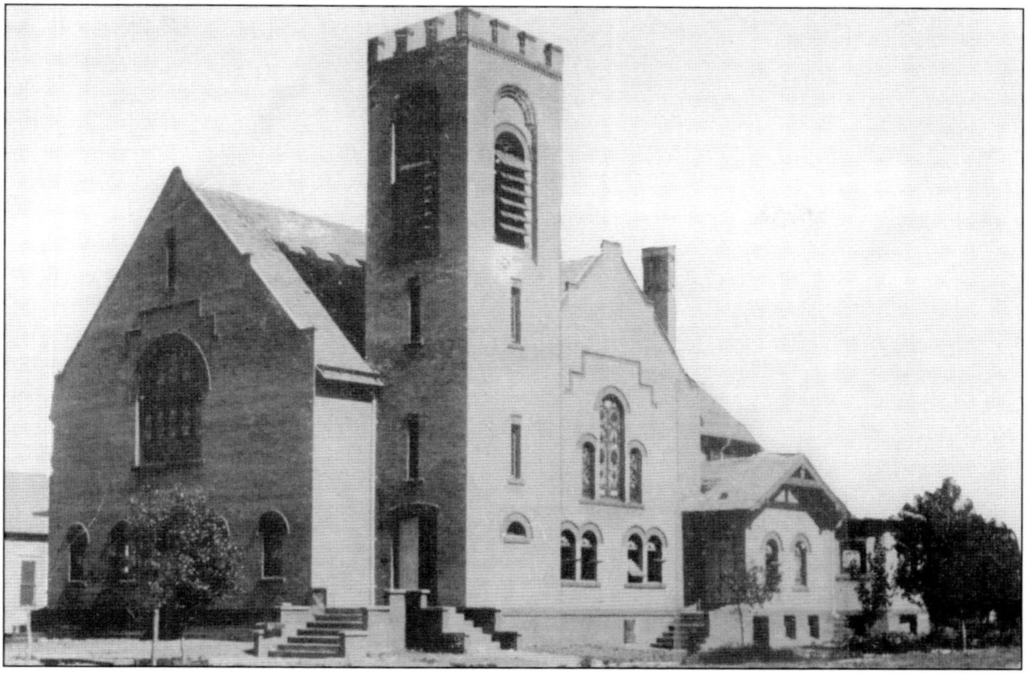

The First Baptist Church of Artesia is shown above in 1913. The church was organized in 1904, and its large brick church building was erected in 1910 at a cost of $23,000. Our Lady of Grace Catholic Church is pictured below in the mid-1940s. The church was built from adobe bricks made by Hispanic parishioners who carried water and sand from the Pecos River. It took nearly a year to build the church, and when it was dedicated, a special luncheon was held—for Anglos only—to celebrate the dedication. Sadly, none of the devoted parishioners who had actually labored to build the structure were invited or even acknowledged in any way.

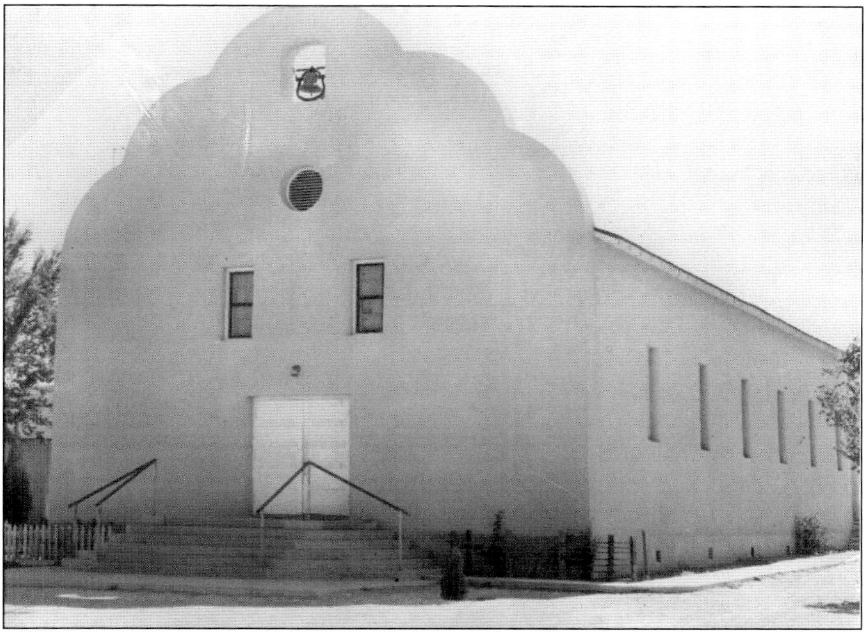

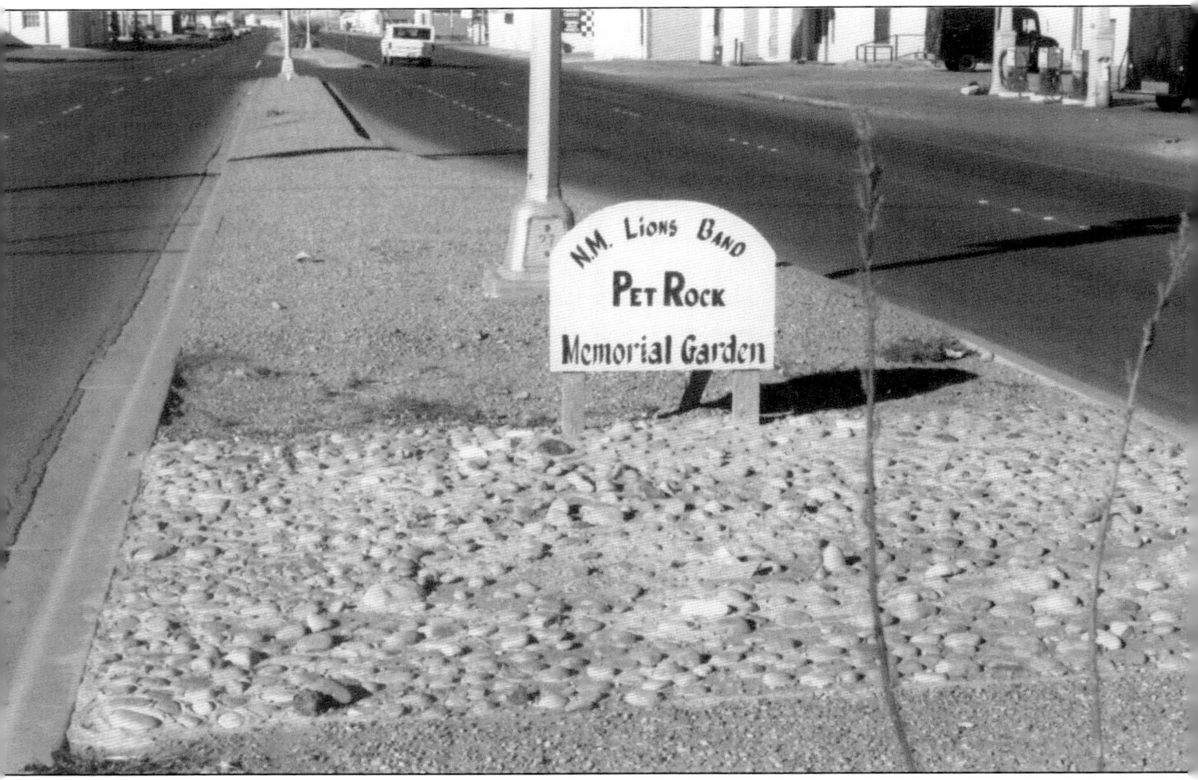

The Artesia Downtown Lions Club was chartered in June 1928. The club dissolved in the 1930s because of the Depression and was rechartered in June 1939. Through the years, the club has sponsored many school and community projects, with an emphasis on assisting the visually impaired. The Lions took on a tongue-in-cheek project in the fall of 1979 when they repaired a median on First Street (between Quay and Richardson Avenues) with a Pet Rock Memorial Garden. Pet rocks were a huge fad in the mid-1970s. They were marketed as the "perfect pet" because they required no care and were sold in a box with breathing holes, hay or straw bedding, and a 32-page care manual. As this photograph shows, many Artesians were initially caught up in the pet rock fad, which had run its course by 1979, when the Lions Club found a better use for the discarded pets.

Four

Clubs and Organizations

Artesians have been joining together for social purposes since the town was founded. Many early residents formed private and independent clubs and organizations based on mutual interests, professional goals, business promotion, community improvement, and recreation. Some have lasted for many years; others did not stand the test of time and disbanded as member interest diminished. The various groups served to bring the residents together and helped to create a sense of community for Artesia.

Some of Artesia's earliest clubs actually helped to nurture town amenities. The Artesia Woman's Club, founded in 1904, established and cared for city parks, organized community clean-up drives, and prepared and served hot meals to schoolchildren during the Depression. The Order of the Eastern Star (founded in 1906) raised funds for polio equipment for Artesia's hospital during the polio epidemic of the 1950s.

Today, organizations such as the Artesia Arts Council, Artesia MainStreet, and Artesia Clean and Beautiful continue the traditions started by Artesia's earliest clubs. These groups all have paid staff members, although they also rely on a large volunteer base to help with special events. And Artesians are always ready to pitch in and help when needed.

This chapter includes Artesia's clubs and organizations through the years. Unfortunately, space limitations prevented the inclusion of every group photograph from organizations that have helped the community of Artesia. Some other notable groups that have been active in Artesia through the years (with their years of founding) are the Girl Scouts (1925), the Artesia Garden Club (1940), the Square Dance Club (1946), the Kiwanis (1947), the Elks Lodge (1948), the Moose Lodge (1967), the Daughters of the American Revolution (1949), the Future Farmers of America (1948), Desk and Derrick (1956), numerous sports and recreational clubs, and many groups associated with churches.

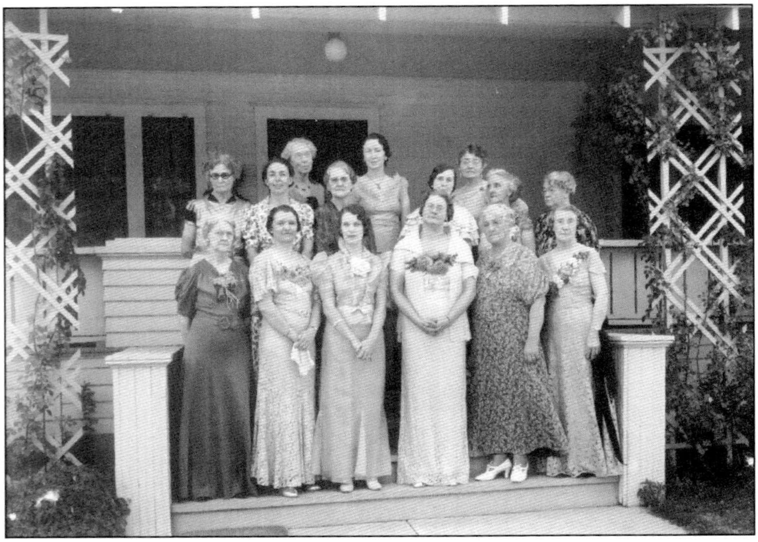

The Artesia Woman's Club evolved from the early Woman's Literary Club and was founded in 1904. The purpose of the group was to create an opportunity for women to socialize, explore culture and arts, and do civic work. In this photograph, Woman's Club members pose after a formal tea party on September 1, 1937.

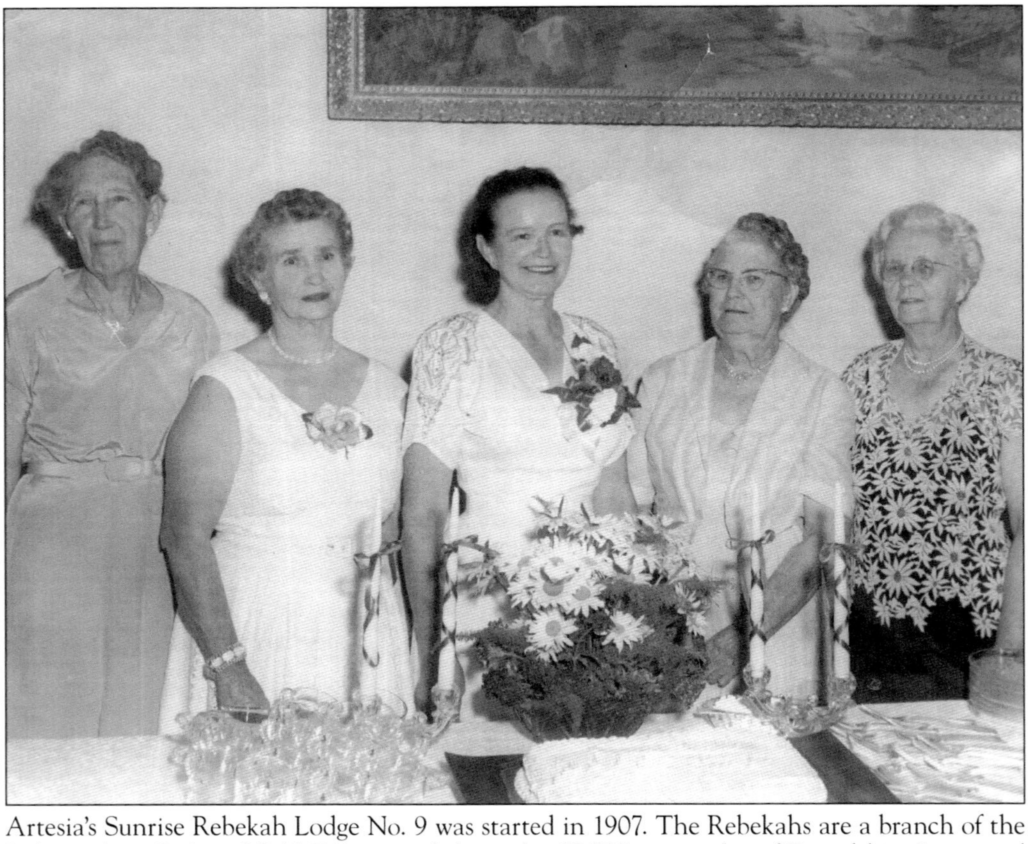

Artesia's Sunrise Rebekah Lodge No. 9 was started in 1907. The Rebekahs are a branch of the Independent Order of Odd Fellows and share the IOOF's principles of Friendship, Love, and Truth. The Rebekahs focus on social and charitable activities, and they support orphanages and provide funds for education. Rebekah Lodge in this 1958 photograph are, from left to right, Ethel Brandell, Lucille Green, Bonnie McKinstry, Effie Wingfield, and unidentified.

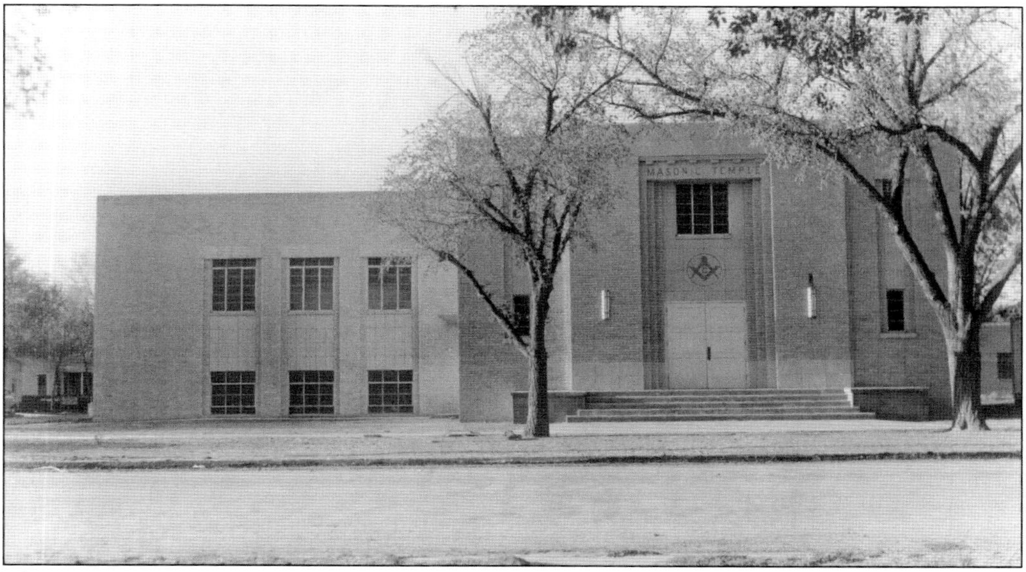

The Artesia Masonic Lodge No. 28 was chartered in 1903. Meetings were held on the first Saturdays of each month in the fraternal hall in the First National Bank Building. In 1947, the lodge completed a Masonic temple on the corner of Richardson and Roselawn Avenues, shown in 1949.

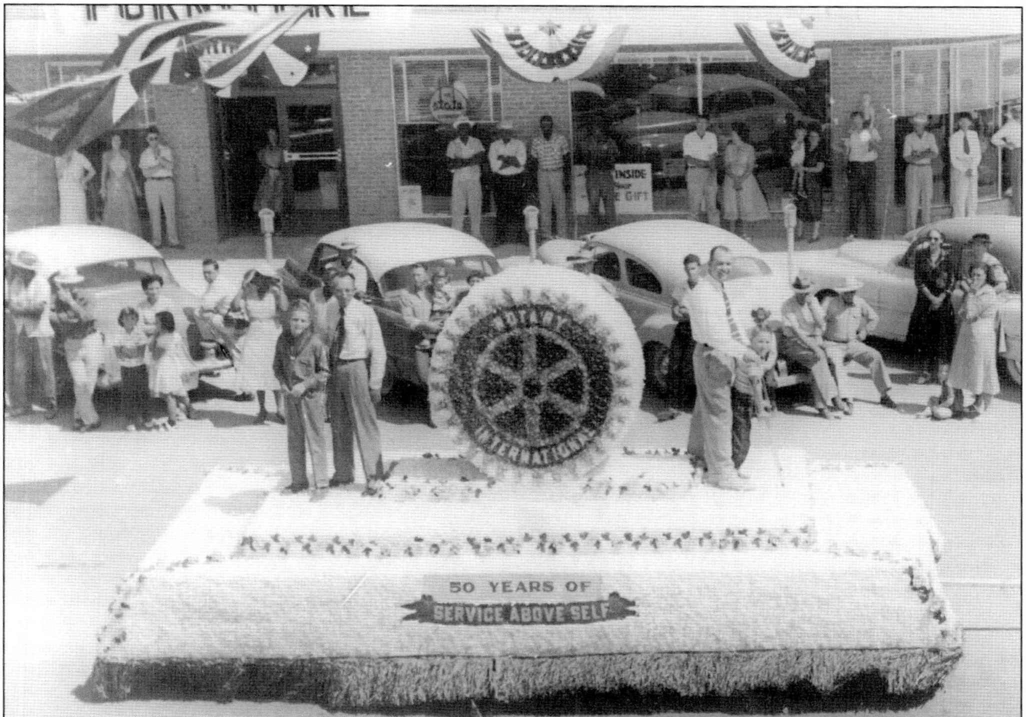

The Artesia Rotary Club was chartered in November 1923. The Rotary Club encourages high ethical standards and professionalism in business; its motto is Service above Self. Rotarians help with community projects as needed. In this photograph, a Rotary Club float is shown in a 1963 parade.

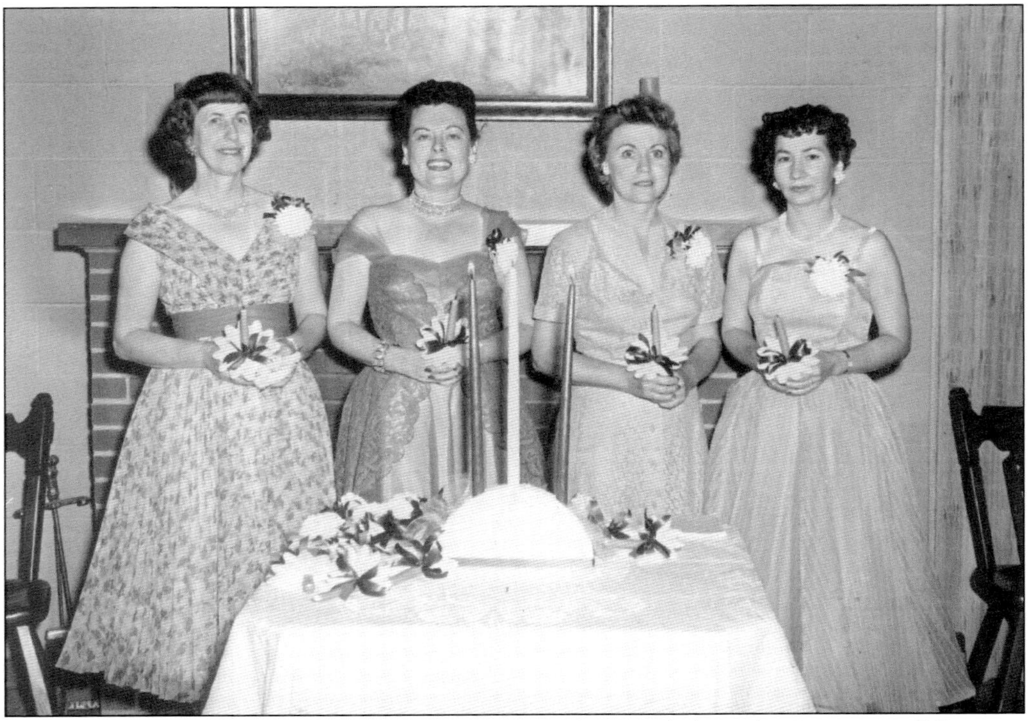

Artesia's Altrusa Club chapter was founded in 1953. Altrusa is dedicated to Patriotism, Efficiency, and Service, and members assist in a wide variety of community projects. The Artesia Altrusa Club's annual Smorgasbord feast is a highly anticipated event each year. In this photograph from their initiation ceremony in the 1950s are, from left to right, new club members Winnie Hensley, Eva Bryant, Thelma Gelwick, and Dorothy Stogner.

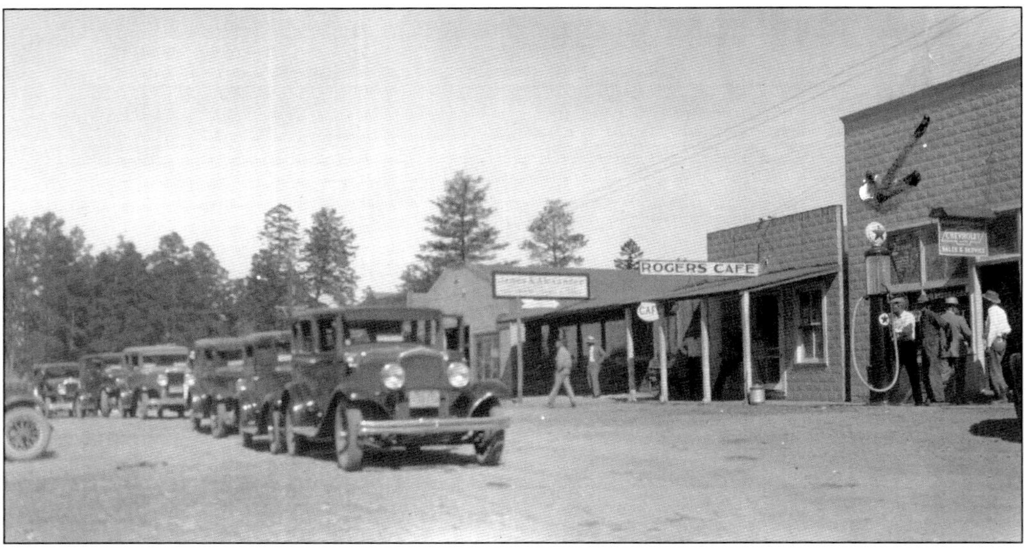

The Artesia Chamber of Commerce made Mountain Good Will Trips for many years to promote Artesia businesses to the mountain community residents. This photograph was taken in Cloudcroft, New Mexico, on the program's very first outing in 1929. The trip celebrated the completion of the new highway from Artesia to Cloudcroft, and it took two days for participants to complete their circuit of all of the Sacramento Mountain communities.

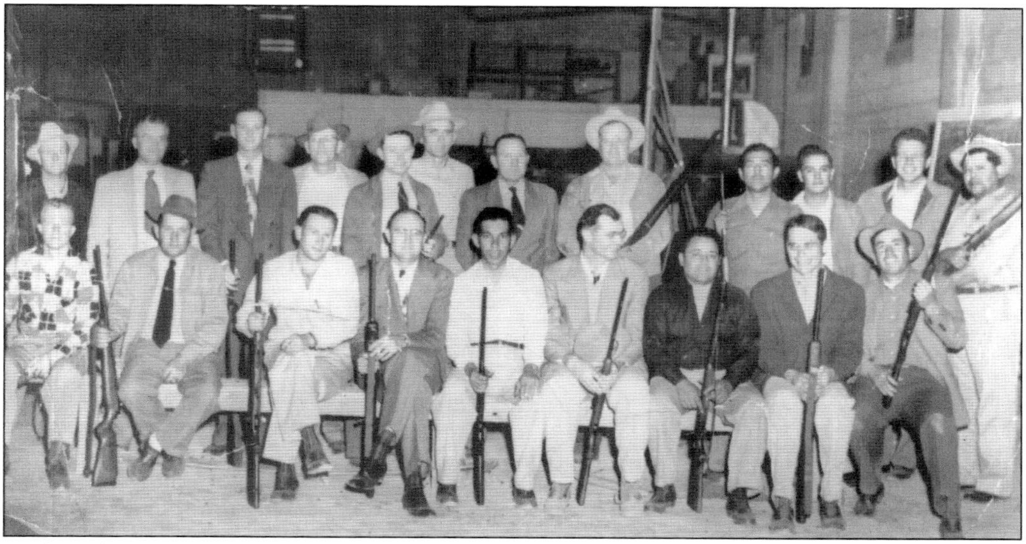

In this photograph, the Artesia Rifle Club members are shown around 1950–1951. From left to right are (first row) Tommy Brown, Sam Henderson, Vic Haldeman, Carl Foster, Manuel Rodriguez, "Preacher" Morgan, Fred Cota, Bill Jeffers, and Al Baca; (second row) Mark Walters, Mack McGuffin, ? Williams, Ted Maschek, Owen Hensley, Jim Buck, Hugh Kiddy, B.G. Robinson, Fred Lopez, Benito Gomez, Charles Mooney, and Ramon Hernandez.

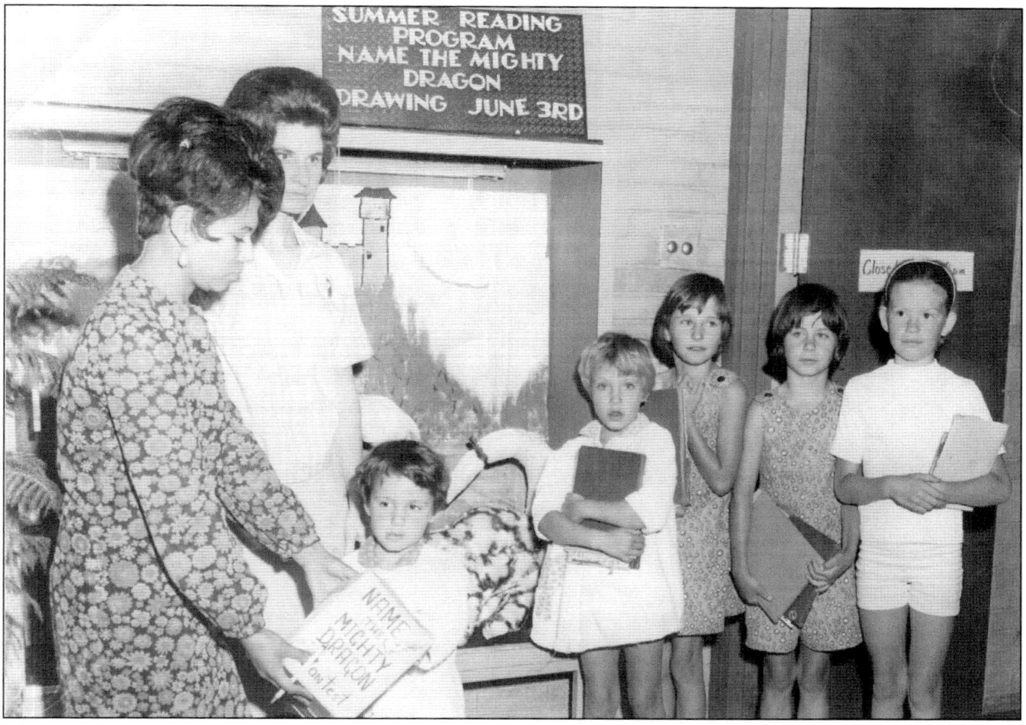

The Artesia Story League was started in 1942 to perpetuate and stimulate the art of storytelling as a vital educational force for the building of character and to foster work in the collecting and preserving of folklore and stories of our community. In this photograph, two Story League members hold a drawing at the Artesia Public Library for a Summer Reading Program contest to "Name the Mighty Dragon."

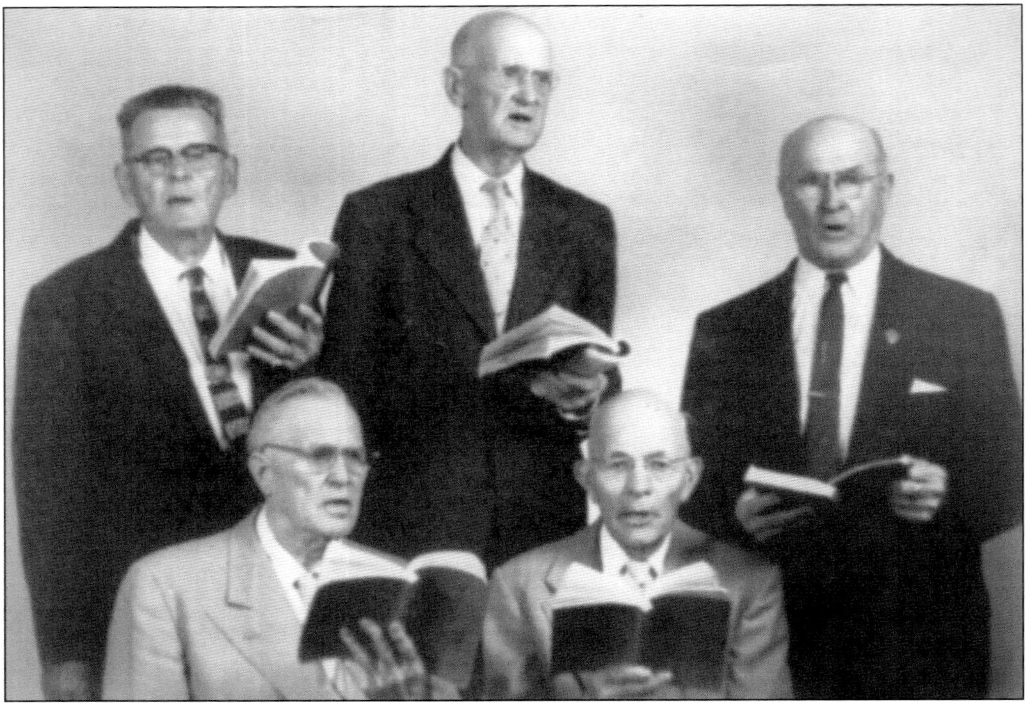

Sponsored by the Artesia Altrusa Club, the Golden Age Club was organized in 1957. The photograph above shows members of the Golden Age Quintet. They are, in no particular order, Rev. C.A. Clark, J.H. Jones, Robert Yeats, Vic Alexander, and Milton Sams. The men were all over the age of 80 and still in fine voice. In the photograph below, Golden Age Club members are shown at a banquet in 1957. The club evolved into the Senior Citizens Club. Today, Artesia's Commission on Aging continues to serve the needs of the area's older residents.

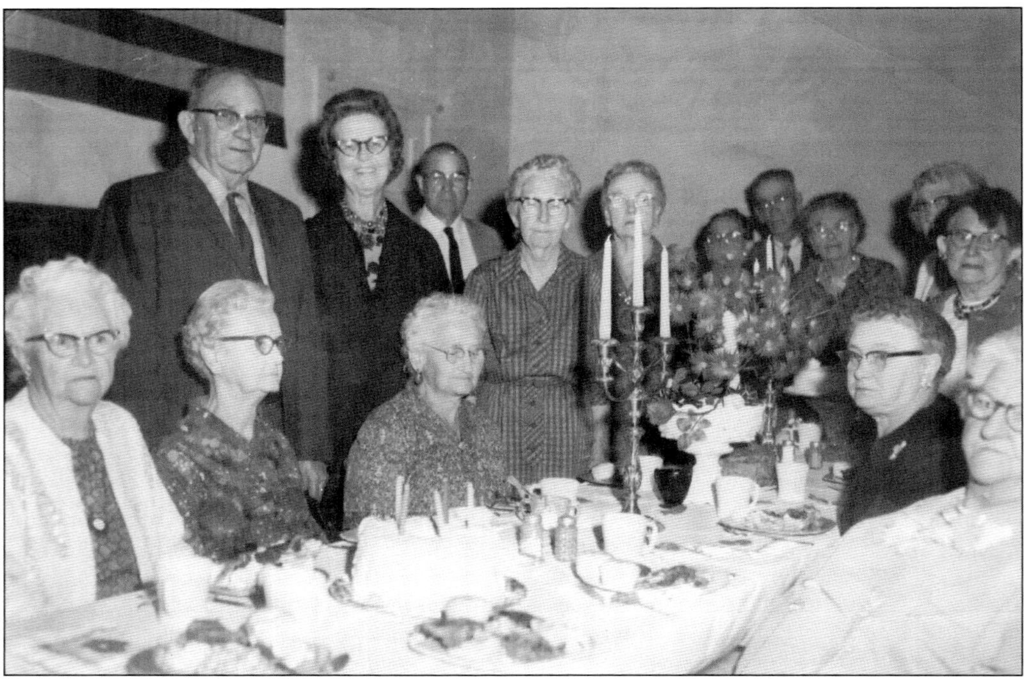

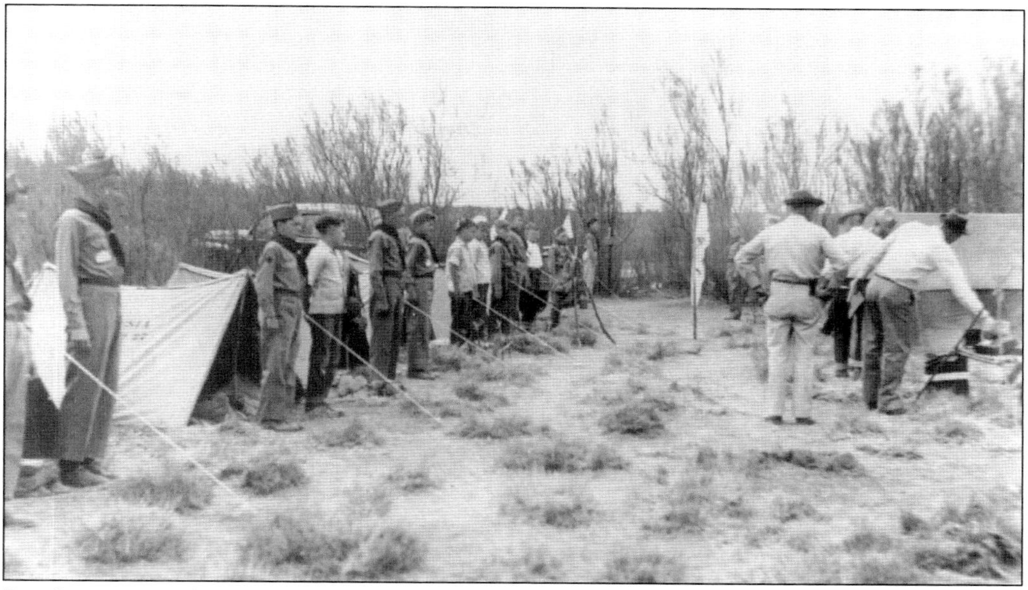

Boy Scouting in Artesia began in 1926, sponsored by the Artesia Rotary Club. The first Court of Honor was held in February 1926 and was presided over by E.B. Bullock. Many community groups, including the First Baptist Church, the American Legion, and the First United Methodist Church, have helped sponsor Artesia's Boy Scout troops over the years. In these photographs, Boy Scout Troop 28 is shown on a camping trip on the Pecos River, led by Ernest Thompson around the early 1950s. In the photograph above, the Scouts prepare for their inspection. At right, an unidentified Scout (left), Tom Myers (center), and Bobby McQuay cook a meal.

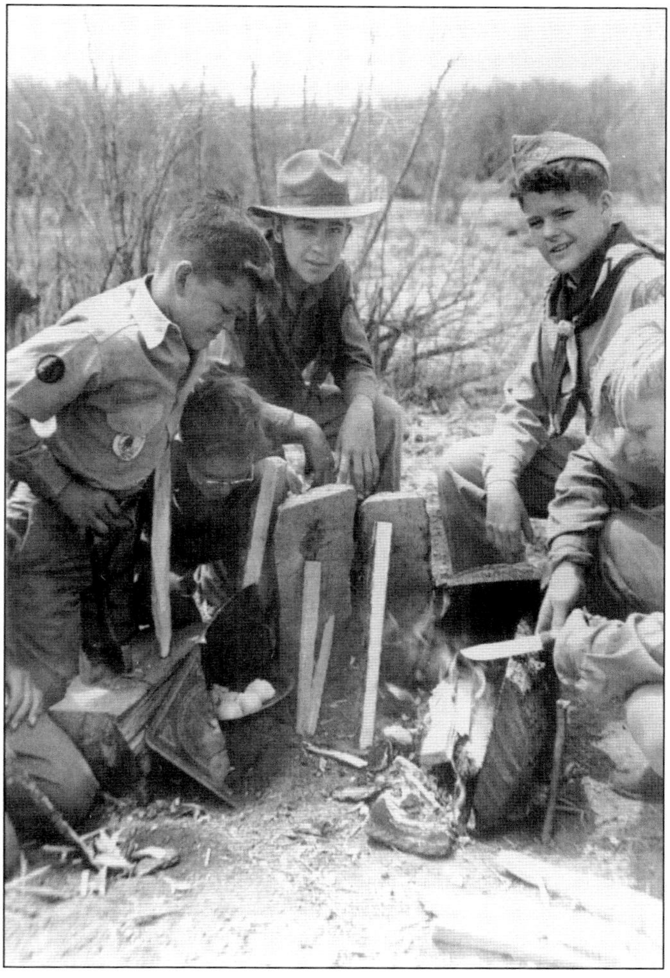

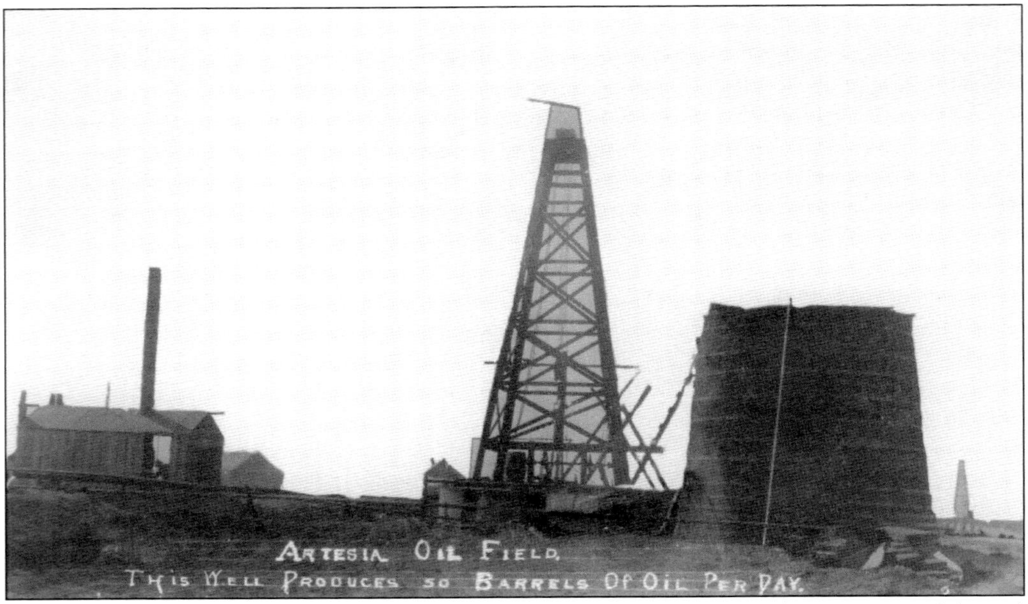

The Hammond-Brown well was originally drilled as a water well in 1909 by ? Hammond, but oil was struck at 947 feet. The water was cased off, and the well was quickly transformed into an oil source. Charles Brown purchased the property in 1912, and the well was a slow but steady producer until it was plugged in 1932.

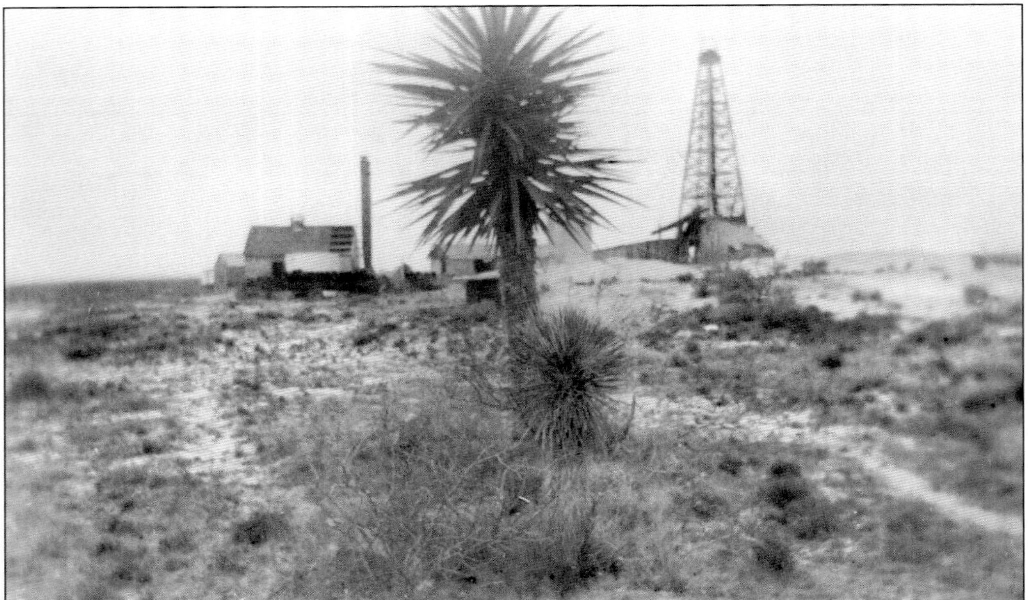
By the late 1910s and early 1920s, many wooden oil derricks, such as this one, dotted the landscape around Artesia. Many early oil-field investors hardly broke even with these first wells, but anticipation kept speculators hopeful that the big payoff would come in soon.

Five

The Oil and Gas Industry

In the early days of artesian well-drilling, drillers were frequently annoyed by the intrusion of oil into the water flow, and this leakage is what originally alerted people to the presence of oil in the area. It was hard to separate the flows of oil and water back then because the technology was still evolving. Sometimes, artesian wells had to be abandoned because of continued contamination by oil, and vice versa.

As early as 1904, local oil speculation had started. The Standard Oil Company sent a scout to file claims in the area. Within a month, Artesians had formed the Seven Rivers Oil Company, and the Artesia Oil Company was the first to get a drilling rig into the field. A small gusher near Dayton, eight miles south of Artesia, created a little excitement in February 1905, but most of the early enthusiasm died down pretty quickly because, according to the February 11, 1905, *Artesia Advocate*, "the good land near Artesia with its gushing fountains offers a much better and safer place for investment."

The Dayton Oil Company hung in there, and it struck oil in January 1908 near Dayton and Lakewood, 16 miles south of Artesia. A year later, in February 1909, the Dayton gas well came in, and the local boom was on. But these first area oil and gas wells were relatively small producers. Most of the early oil and gas produced by Artesia's wells went for local use. The CAP Ranch used local oil from the 1909 Hammond-Brown well to burn smudge pots in its apple orchards.

The Hammond-Brown well produced 25 to 50 barrels a day, which sold for $1.50 per barrel. Despite problems with water seepage and blowouts, the well and its potential kept speculators interested in Artesia's oil fields until April 1924, when the Illinois No. 3 Well, financed by early Hammond-Brown well investor Martin Yates Jr., came in with a bang as the first to produce in commercial quantities and started Artesia's oil boom in earnest.

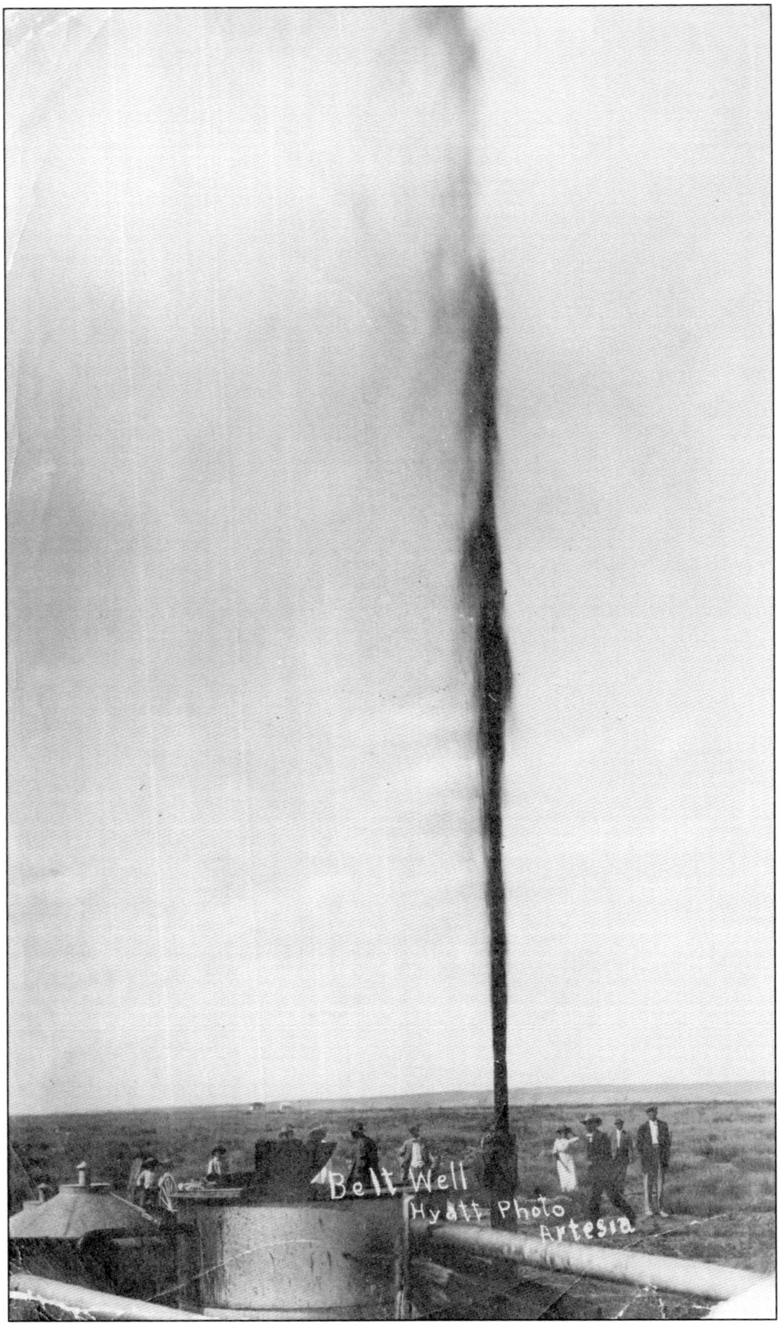

The Belt Well was drilled in 1913 as a water well, but the discovery of oil at 1,300 feet caused it to be quickly switched over to an oil well. Real estate promoters used the Belt Well to lure potential settlers and investors to this area by capping off the well for several days to allow pressure to build up. When a visiting group was on-site, the well was ceremoniously uncapped, and the resulting spectacular blowout would hopefully impress the visitors and motivate them to settle in Artesia and invest in the oil industry. The Belt Well was used for a series of these demonstrations throughout the spring of 1913, and it played its part in the earliest oil boom by bringing investors and independent oil drillers to the Lower Pecos Valley.

Thornton "Duke" Ferson drilled one of the first shallow wells in 1924. The Royal Duke No. 1 Well played an early part in opening up the Artesia Oil Field. Ferson died about a month after investing in and drilling this well.

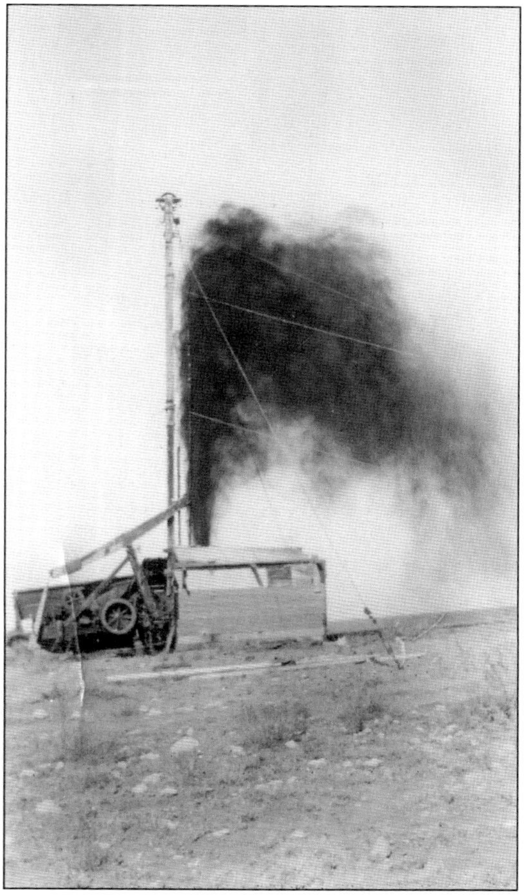

The Kansas–New Mexico Oil Company was created in 1919, and the company's first well was drilled in July 1919. The rig had mechanical problems, and it was not until November 1920 that oil was struck at 583 feet. The well was shot with nitroglycerine to increase productivity at 611 feet, but like many early wells, this one did not live up to investor expectations and was capped in the summer of 1922.

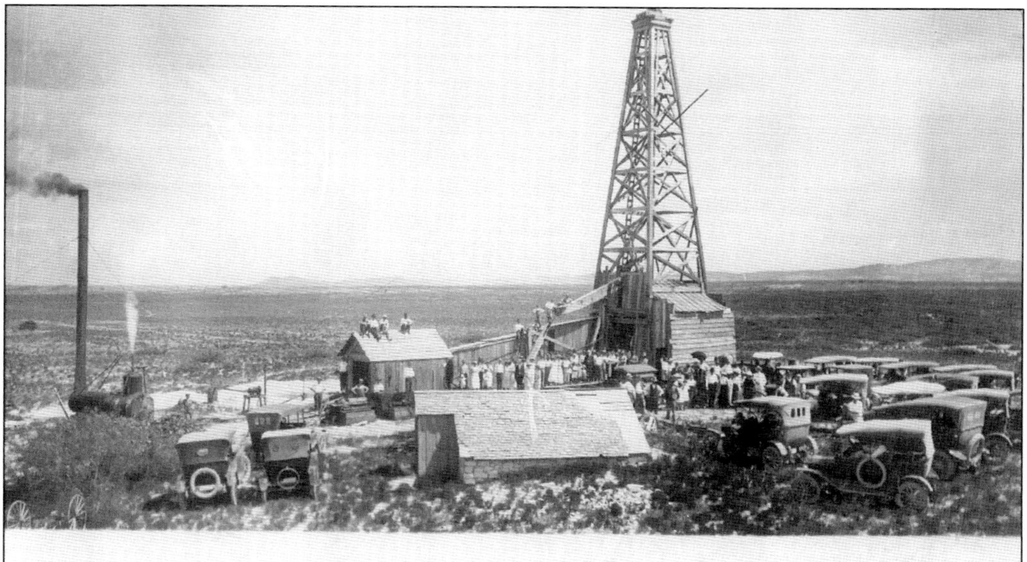

Kansas-New Mexico Oil Co. Well No.1
Now drilling seven miles S.W. of Lakewood, N.M.
August 19th.1920

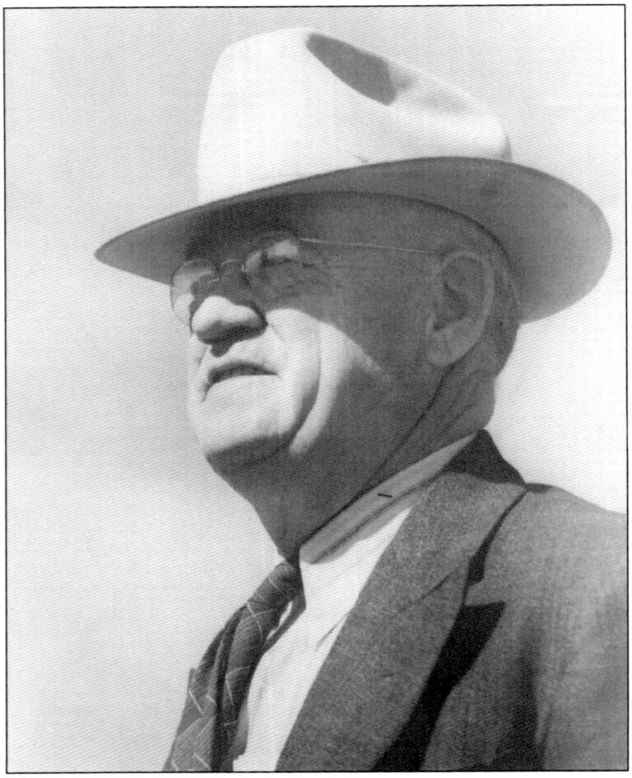

Martin Yates Jr. and his wife, Mary, were early settlers in the Artesia area. In the early 1920s, Martin and fellow Illinois Producers investors drilled the Illinois No. 1 Well east of Artesia. The No. 1 Well was commercially unsuccessful, but the Illinois No. 2 well produced natural gas. Company geologist V.H. McNutt was uncertain where to drill next, so Martin and Mary went for a drive, and Mary chose the site for the Illinois No. 3 Well based on her intuition. She marked the site with her heel. The Illinois No. 3 Well was drilled using gas from the No. 2 Well in the spring of 1924.

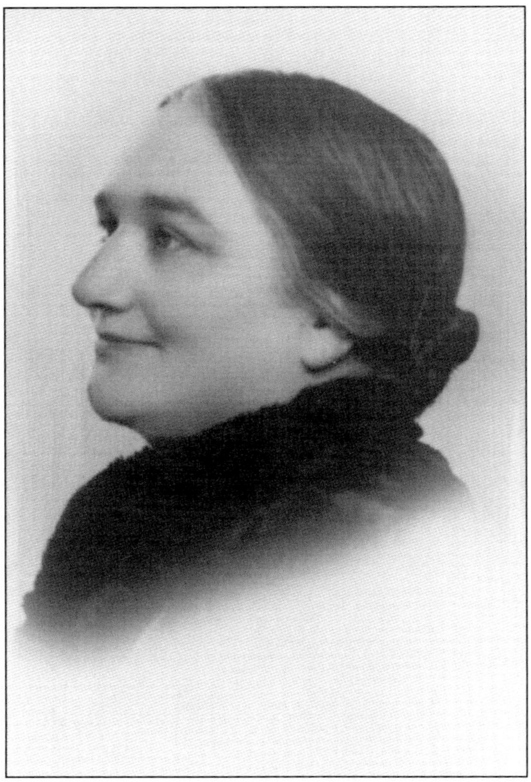

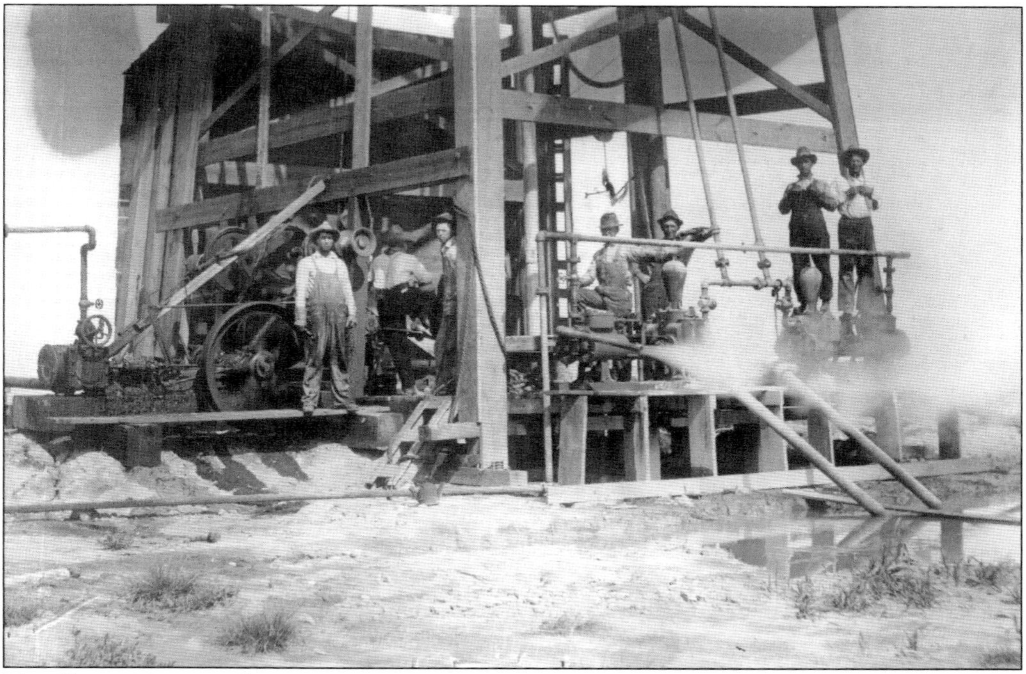

The Illinois No. 3 Well was a winner, striking oil at 1,947 feet. To increase productivity, the well was shot with nitroglycerine by Tex Thornton on June 29, 1924. As Tex lowered the nitro torpedoes into the well, a sudden flow forced the shells back to the surface. Tex caught the torpedoes as they surfaced one by one, preventing a catastrophic explosion. He later said that this was the scariest moment of his entire career as a nitroglycerine handler. The Illinois No. 3 Well was the first commercially successful oil well in the Artesia area, and it started an oil boom that resulted in the creation of the petroleum industry in Artesia. The photograph above shows the Illinois No. 1 Well floor and crew. The right photograph shows Illinois No. 3 Well on June 29, 1924.

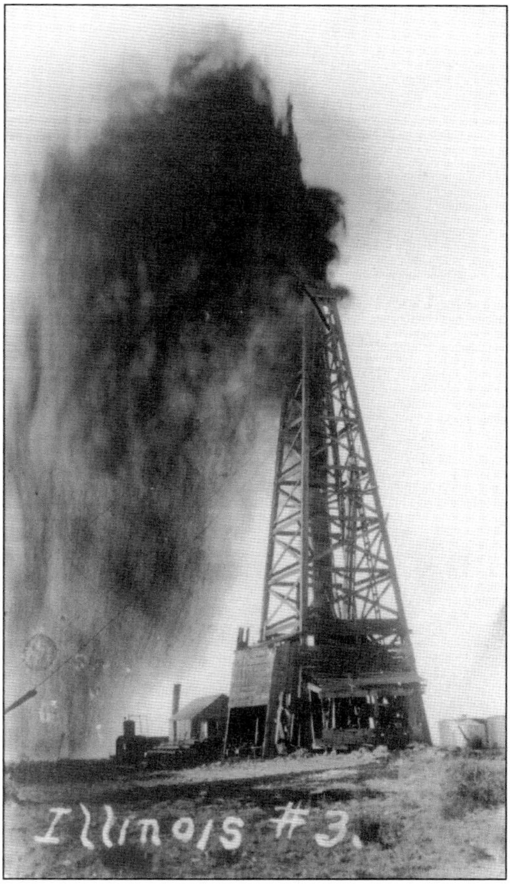

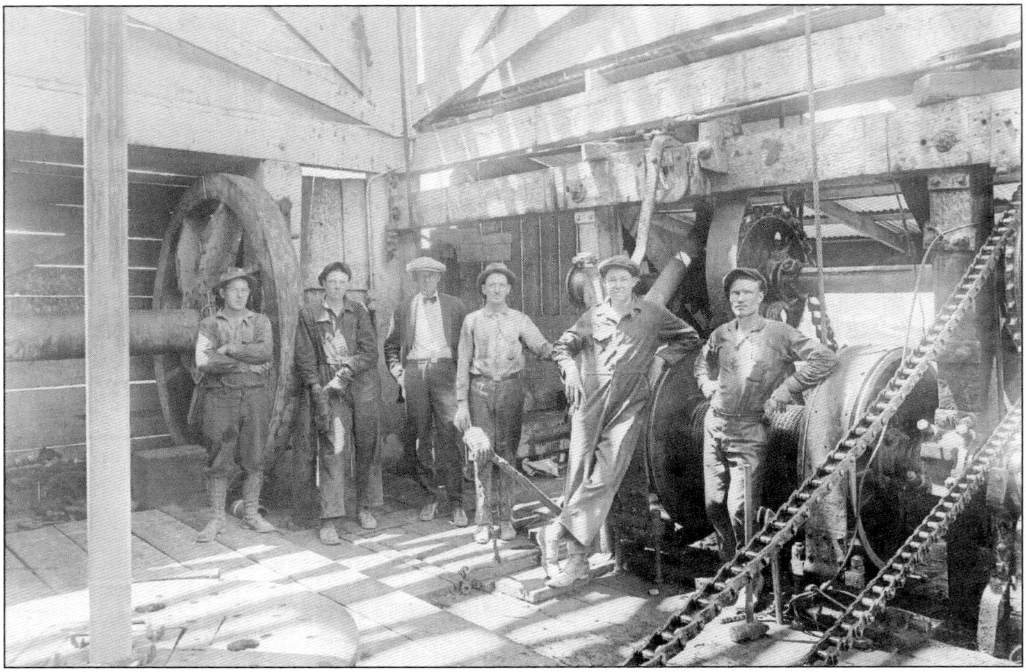

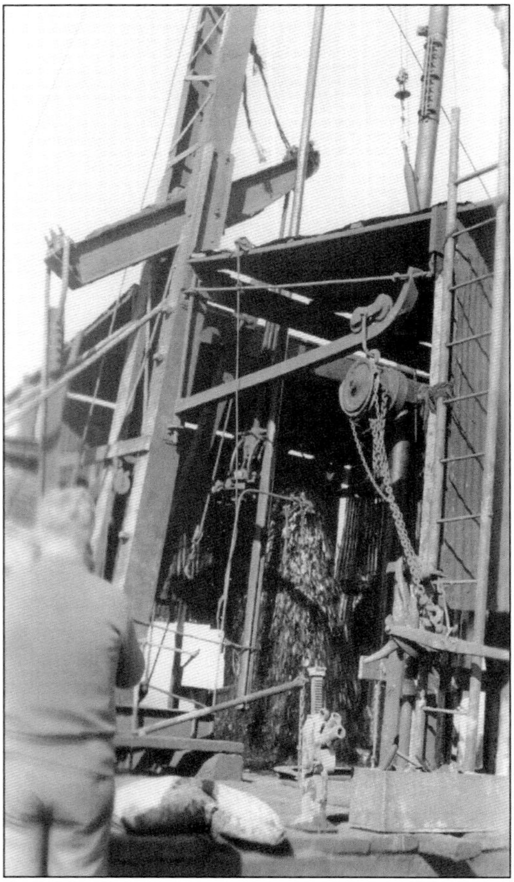

The growth of the petroleum industry created many employment opportunities, and Artesia's population nearly doubled by the end of the 1920s. Above, a drilling crew from the late 1920s takes a moment to pose at the well location. Ralph Shugart is third from the left (with the bow tie); he came to Artesia in 1926 as part of the oil boom. The drilling activity continued into the 1930s. At left, the Brainard No. 1 Well east of Artesia produces a flow of oil. Investor Fred Brainard was an original Bulldog football player in 1909, a World War I veteran, and former professional baseball player in the 1920s. Upon his retirement, he returned home to Artesia and speculated in the oil field.

The Artesia Oil Field had so much activity that many oil companies had their own employee-based communities near their well sites. The Illinois Camp and the Conoco Colony were two of the longest-standing company towns, although there were many others. The Conoco Colony was located a few miles northeast of Artesia and was noted for its fabulous Christmas-light displays every year. The Illinois Camp was located 22 miles southeast of Artesia. The community had a laundry facility, a pool hall, and a church/school building. In the photograph at right, Bill (left), Betty (center), and Lola Matthews are pictured at the Illinois Camp in 1938. In the photograph below are Jim Francis (left) and Claude Matthews alongside the Illinois Camp warehouse/office in 1938.

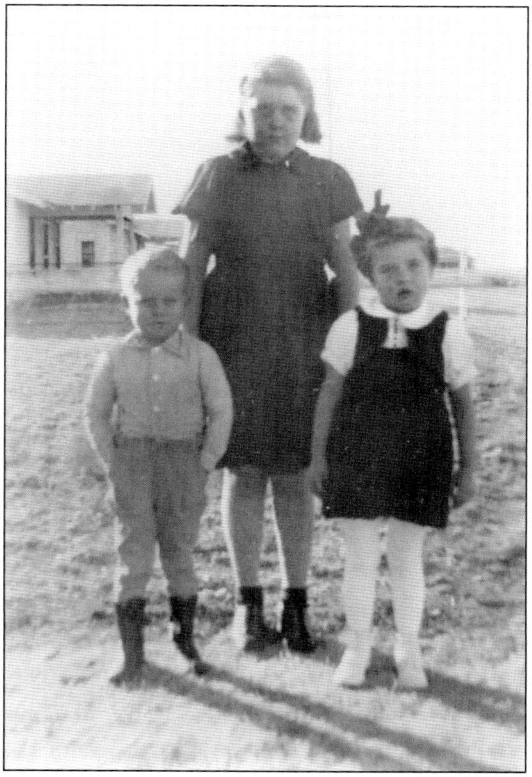

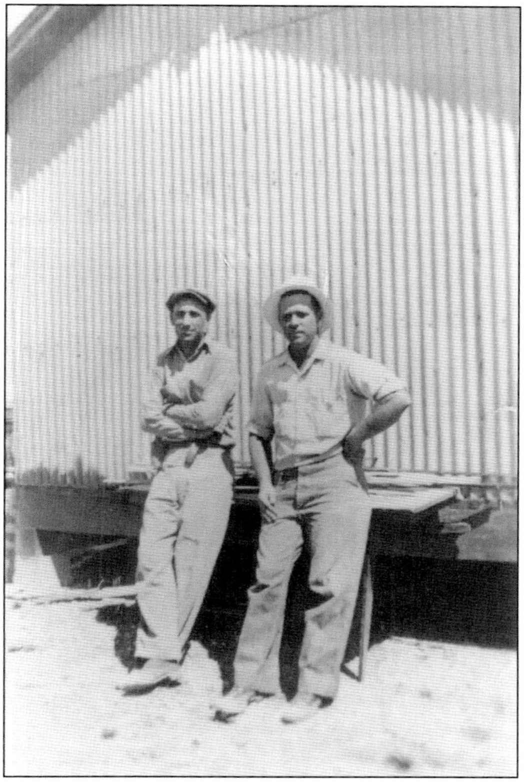

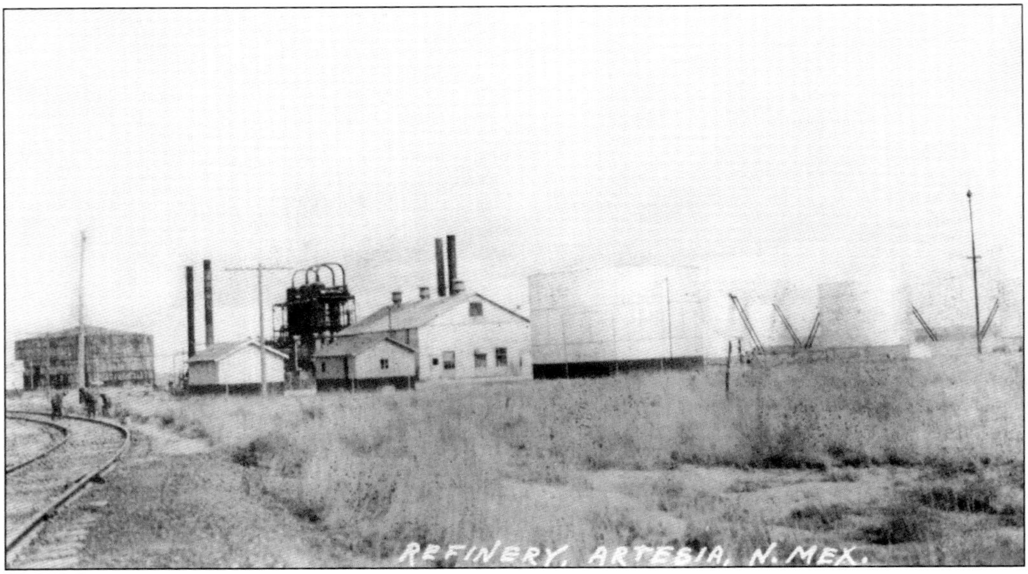

With the development of Artesia's commercial petroleum industry came the need for a local refinery. Artesia's original North Plant was built by the Illinois Oil Producers in 1925. The company also built a pipeline from its oil fields to the refinery. In 1931, the refinery was sold to the Continental Oil Company, and it was shut down and dismantled in 1946. The image above shows the original North Plant soon after being built in 1925. The plant is seen below in 1934, when it was operated by the Continental Oil Company; it had grown a lot in nine years.

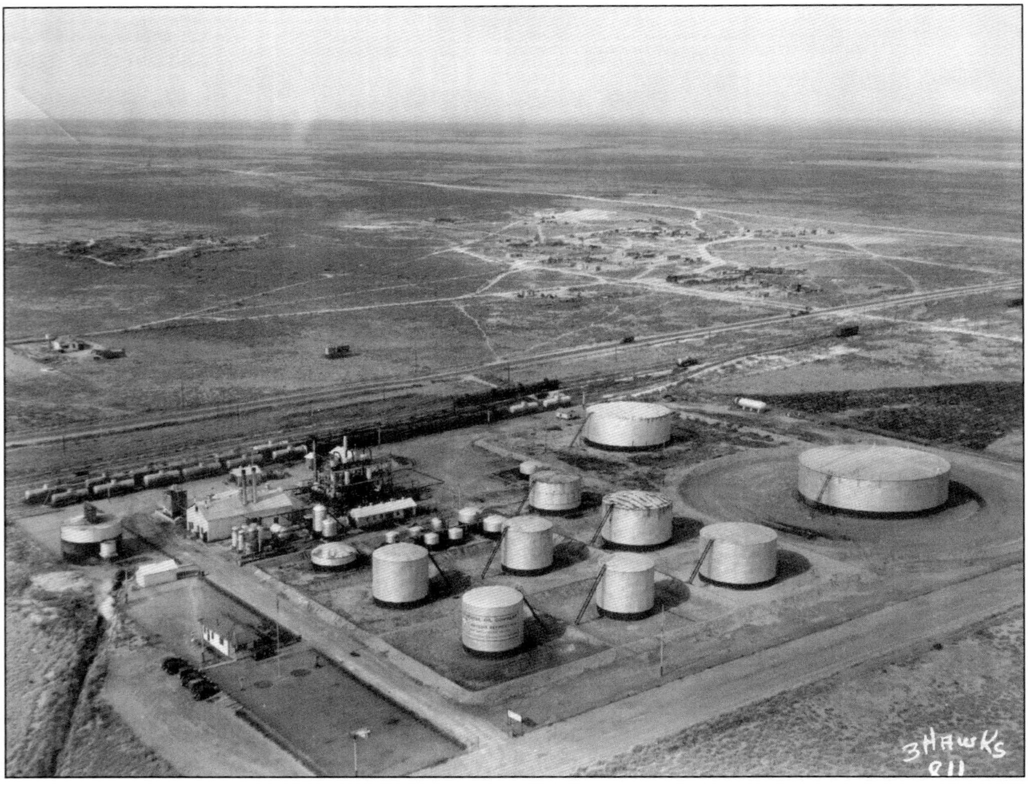

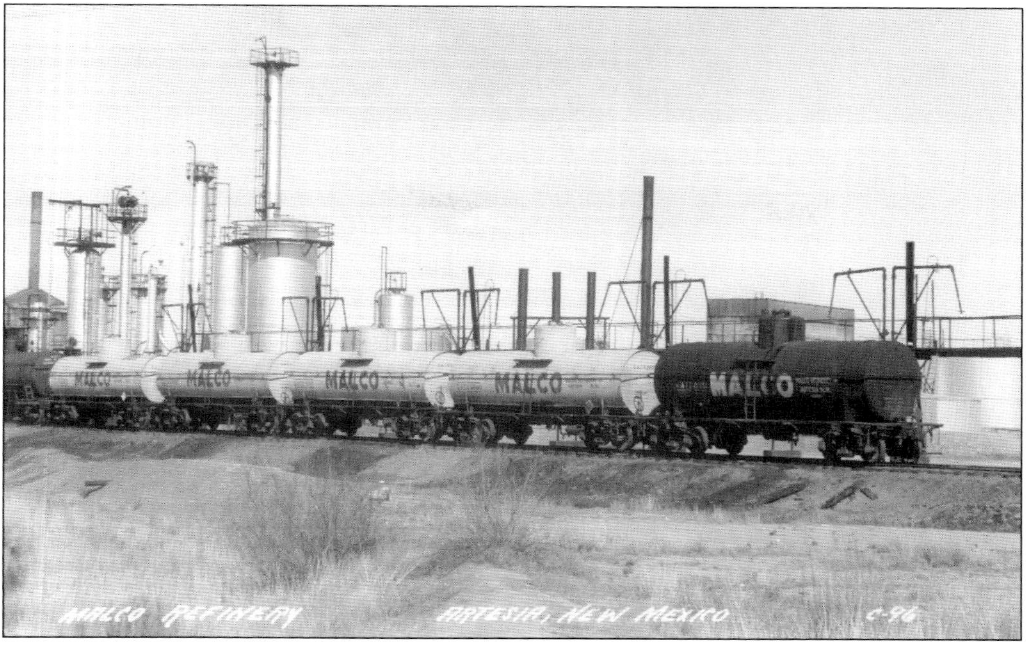

Artesia's second refinery was built in 1931 by the Maljamar Oil and Gas Company and was known as the Malco Plant. After 1934, it was served by a pipeline from the Maljamar oil fields east of Artesia. R.O. Anderson bought the plant in 1942, although the Malco name was retained. The Continental Oil Company purchased the facility in 1946 and renamed it the Conoco Refinery. The image above shows the Malco train and refinery around the late 1930s. The image below shows the Malco Plant at night in 1931. In 1939, Joe Head started the Nu-Mex Asphalt and Refining Company, located on East Main Street. The name was changed in 1941 to the New Mexico Asphalt and Refining Company, which was sold to R.O. Anderson in 1953 and renamed Malco, in memory of Artesia's former refinery.

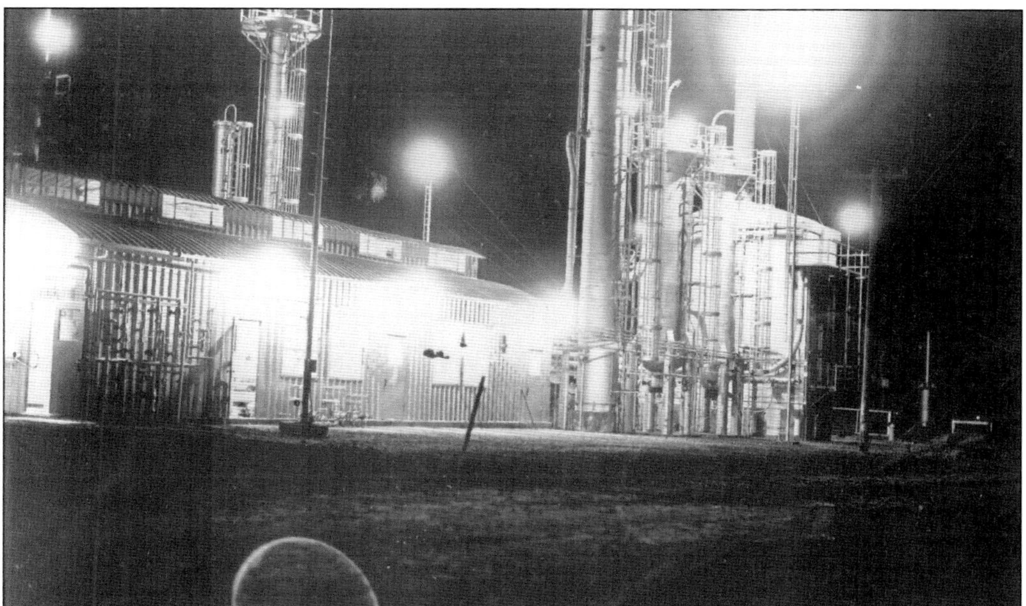

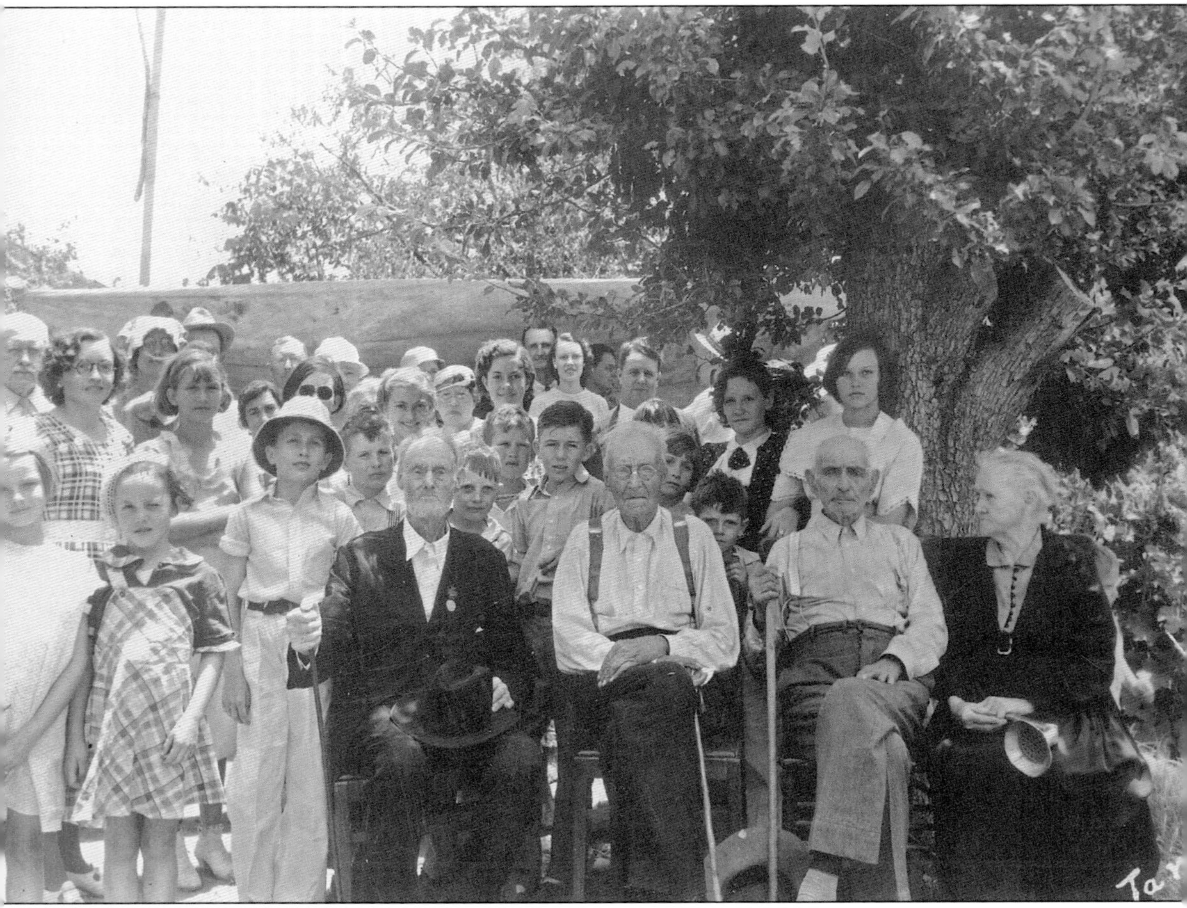

Artesia's last three surviving Civil War veterans gathered for a Memorial Day picnic in 1934. In the first row, from left to right, William Daugherty, T.H. Blakeney, and Rev. J.D. Terry all fought for the Confederacy. Daughtery joined up in 1861 with the 64th Virginia Infantry and was transferred to the cavalry in 1863. He was a prisoner of war at Camp Douglas in Chicago until June 1865. Reverend Terry enlisted in Louisiana in 1863 at the age of 16 as part of the Confederacy's last call for men and served in the cavalry until 1865. He never formally surrendered or received a discharge from the Confederate army. Blakeney enlisted in 1861 in the Confederate army of Texas. He was discharged in 1865 and joined the Texas Rangers. Blakeney always said that his years as a Texas Ranger and Indian fighter were much more interesting than his Civil War experiences.

Six

Artesia's Contributions to the Military

Artesia has a strong tradition of involvement in the military. Some of the earliest area settlers were displaced Southerners who had been in the Confederate army during the Civil War and were seeking new opportunities for themselves and their families. And Artesians have enlisted in every branch of the armed forces. In some cases, multiple generations of Artesians have served their country.

During World War II, many Artesians were with the 200th Coast Artillery, Battery F. It was this unit that helped defend Bataan and Corregidor against the Japanese from 1941 until 1942, holding out for over six months with little food and scant munitions. These defenders were eventually forced to surrender and subjected to the brutality of the Bataan Death March and subsequent imprisonment in the Japanese prisoner-of-war camps.

Memorials that have been established to honor Artesia's veterans include the Veterans of Foreign Wars Lloyd Walker Evans Post, named for Lt. Lloyd Walker Evans. Lieutenant Evans was killed in action in Europe in 1943, and the residents of Eddy County selected him as their representative namesake to honor all of the servicemen who have lost their lives in foreign conflicts. Local chapter No. 19 of the Disabled American Veterans is named for Pfc. Donald Simons, killed in action in the Pacific in 1944. American Legion Post No. 41 is named for Clarence Kepple, who died in combat during World War I. The Warren Brothers Army Reserve Center was dedicated in 1962 as a memorial for local brothers Roderick and Melvin Warren. Roderick was a casualty of the Bataan Death March; he survived the march itself only to succumb to disease in the Cabanatuan Prison Camp in July 1942. Roderick's family did not learn of his death until after the war ended. Originally, his brother Melvin had signed up to try to find him, and Melvin was killed in action in 1944 over the English Channel.

Artesia holds ceremonies to honor its veterans each year on Veterans Day and Memorial Day. Many other events throughout the community also recognize American veterans, including the annual Honoring Artesia's Veterans exhibit and reception at the Artesia Historical Museum and Art Center.

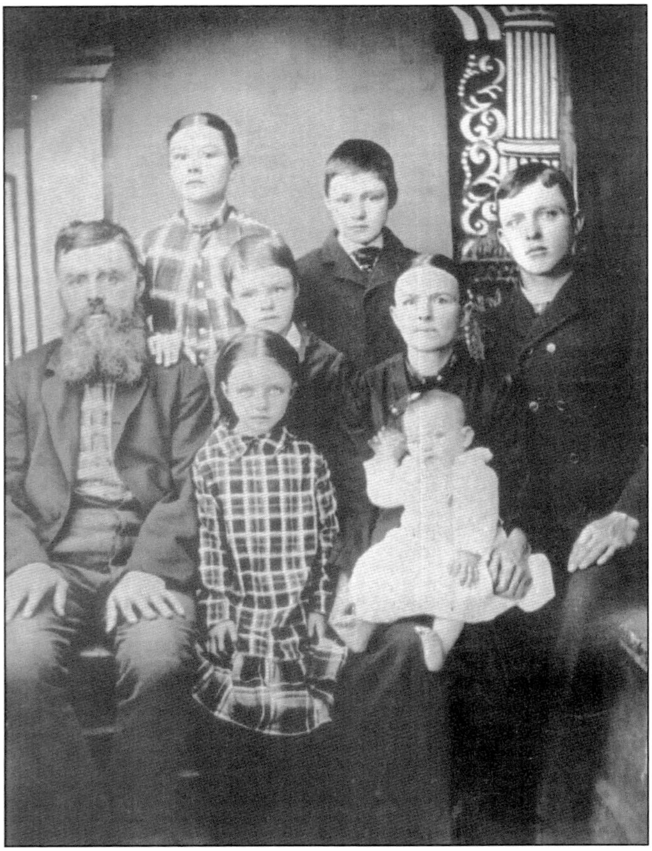

Silas Rogers served in the Union army during the Civil War, in Company B of the 18th Regiment of the Kentucky Infantry. After the war, his wife Elizabeth made his uniform jacket into the regular-style one pictured here. Silas and his family settled in Lakewood, New Mexico, in 1905 and later moved to Artesia. They are pictured around 1886, when they were living in Missouri.

Area Spanish-American War veterans gathered for annual reunions in Artesia each year. This group poses in 1940. Pictured are, from left to right, (first row) Loren Neeley, Jack Kennedy, and Joe Schuff; (second row) George Frisch, John Vandergriff, and Jack Hastie.

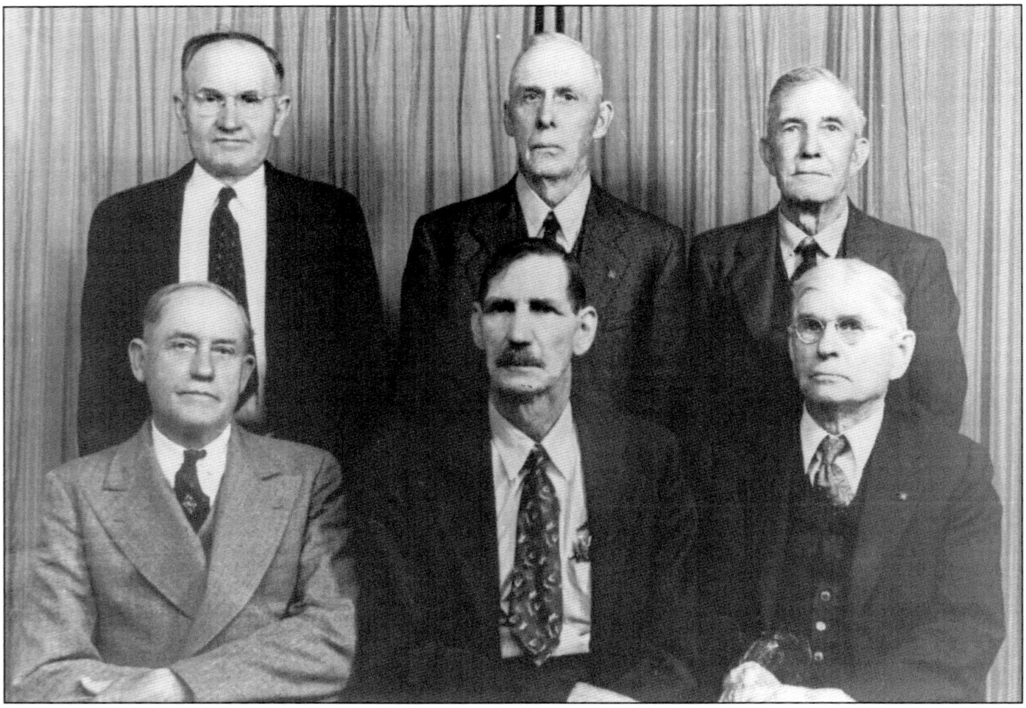

Fred McIlwain's family moved to Artesia in 1915, and he started school here that fall at age 13. He also joined the National Guard that year, with his father's consent, becoming a member of Carlsbad's Company B. Fred is shown on the first day of school in September 1915, six months before Pancho Villa attacked Columbus, New Mexico, on March 9, 1916.

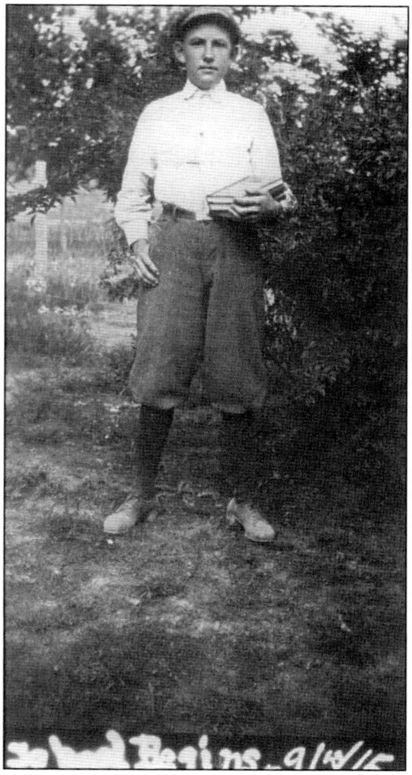

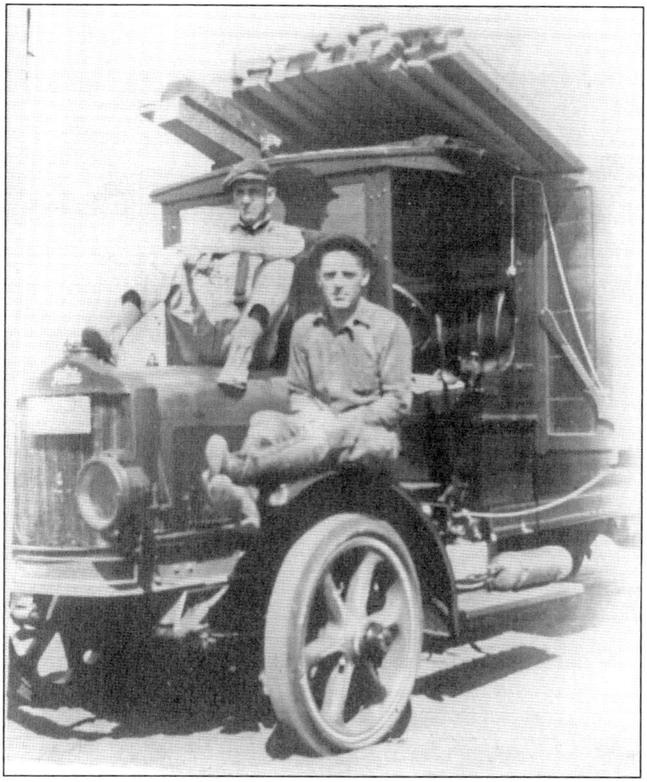

Fred McIlwain's National Guard, unit under the command of Gen. John "Black Jack" Pershing, was dispatched to Columbus, New Mexico, to take part in the punitive expedition into Mexico to capture Pancho Villa after his attack on Columbus. Here, Fred and his friend John take a break before their 11-month pursuit of Pancho Villa.

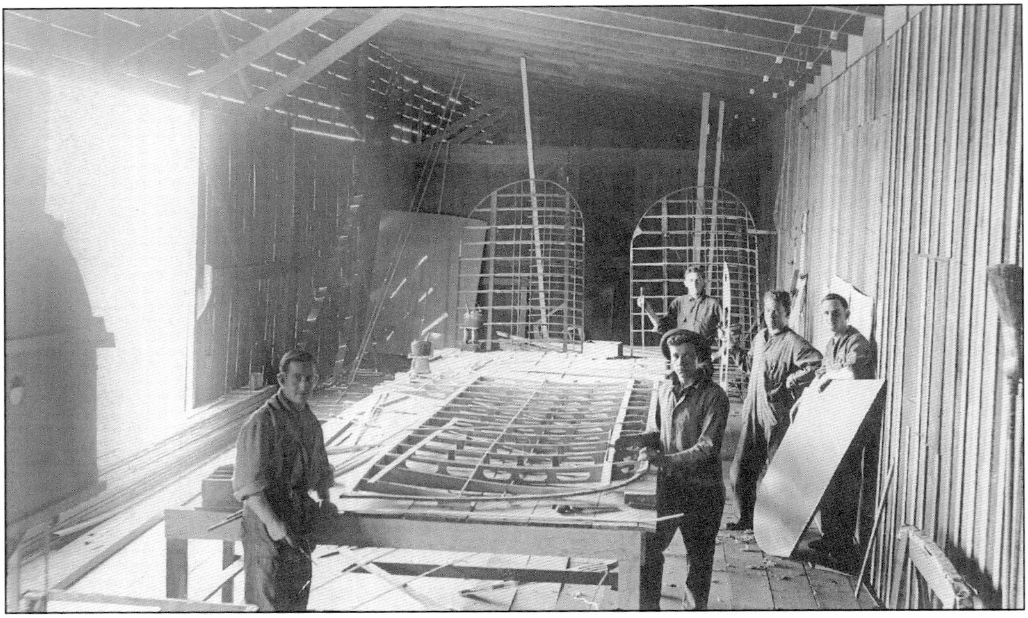

While Fred McIlwain served in Columbus, he worked in the airplane shops that prepared General Pershing's 1st Aero Squadron's Jenny biplanes for flying reconnaissance missions into Mexico in search of Pancho Villa. This was the first time airplanes were used in a military operation in the United States. Fred's story concluded in February 1917 when he returned home to Artesia; his experience was one that possibly no other 14-year-old boy could match. The image above shows the airplane hanger in Columbus, New Mexico; the men appear to be building wings. Fred's friend James Eisenhunt, from Ohio, is on the front right. The photograph below shows the aviation machine shop in Columbus, New Mexico. Both photographs were taken in March 1916.

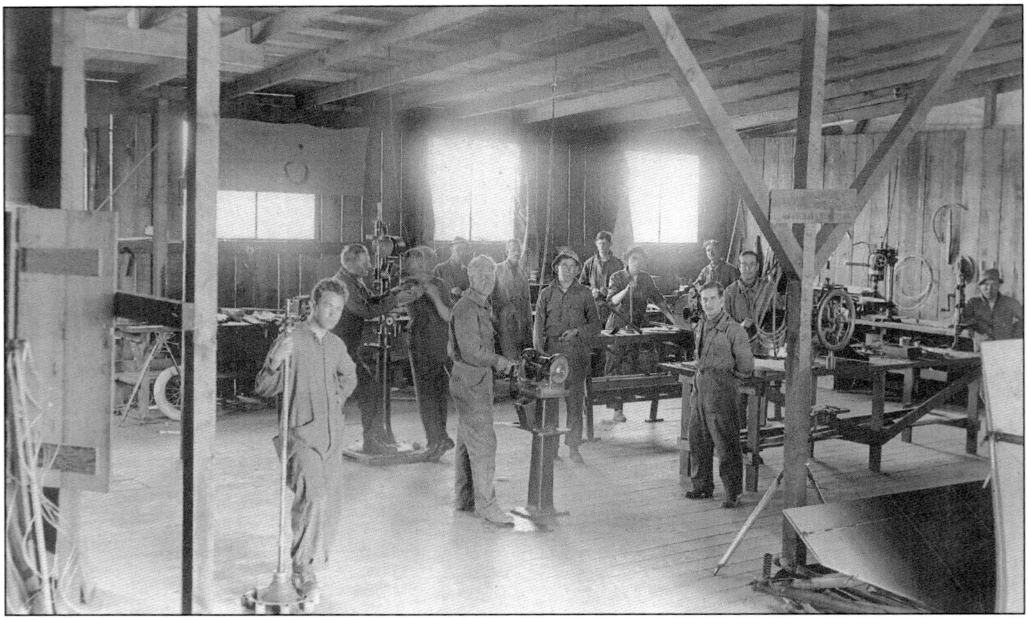

Sgt. Allen Warnock (left), of Artesia, and an unidentified friend also served in the National Guard under Pershing's command chasing Pancho Villa. After 11 months of Villa constantly slipping away, the expedition was recalled, and the troops returned to Columbus, New Mexico.

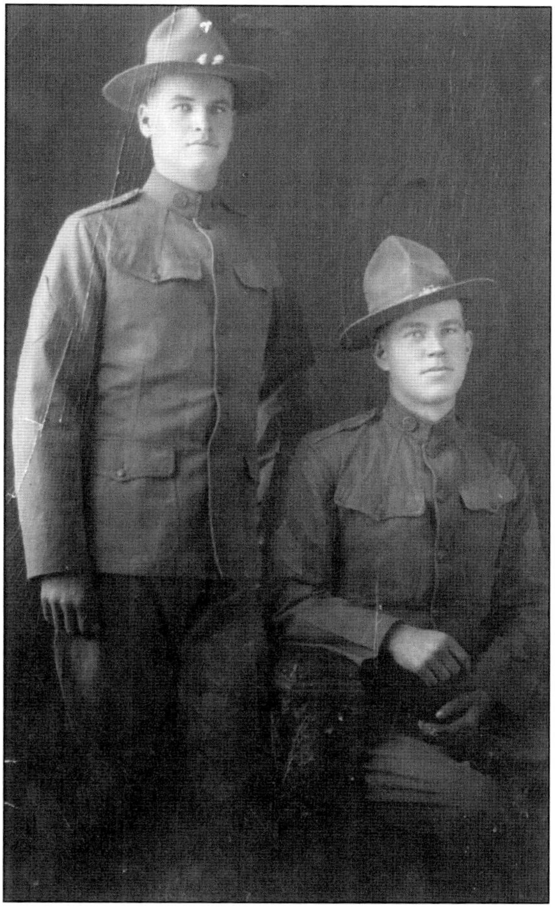

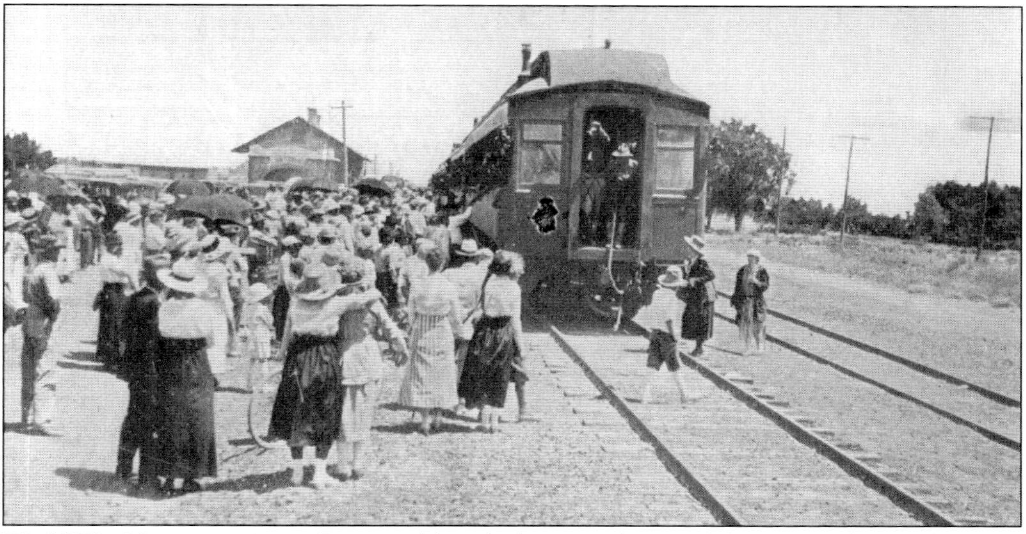

World War I began in 1914 in Europe, although the United States did not enter the conflict until 1917. Many Artesians enlisted then. In this 1917 photograph, members of Carlsbad's B Company and Artesia's C Company say goodbye to family and friends as they depart for Fort Kearney, Nebraska, en route to France.

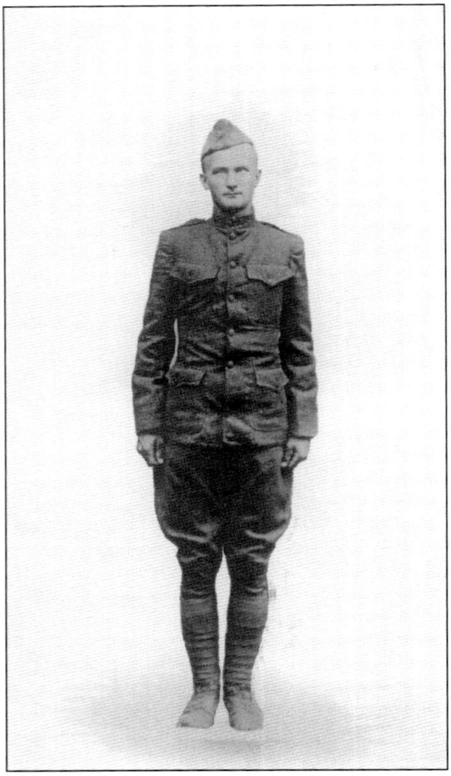

Clarence Kepple was a member of the first Bulldogs football team of 1909 and enlisted in the Army during World War I in April 1918. He was killed in France in September 1918 during a raid. The American Legion Post 41 in Artesia is named for him.

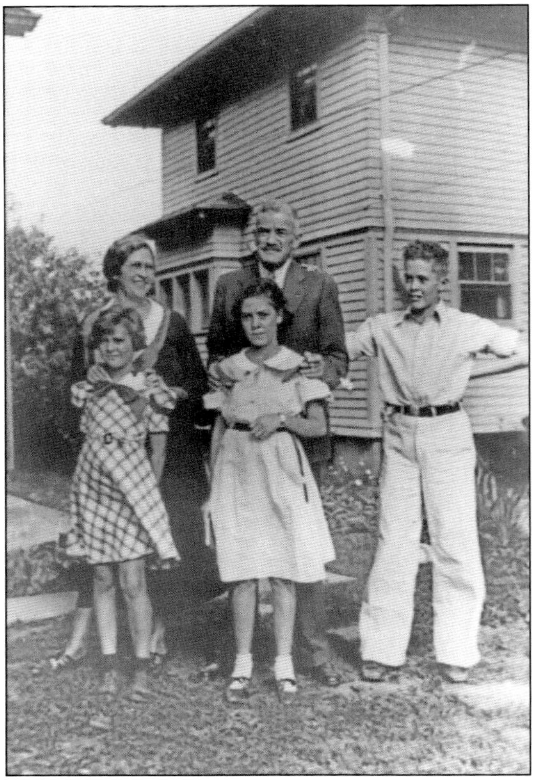

Lloyd Walker Evans, shown at age 15 with his family in Artesia in 1935, was killed in action in October 1943 in Europe during World War II. Artesia's Veterans of Foreign Wars Post 8145 is named for him, although it honors all northern Eddy County men who lost their lives in foreign conflicts. From left to right are (first row) Helen Keys and Mary Evans; (second row) Mary Evans, L.P. Evans, and Lloyd Walker Evans.

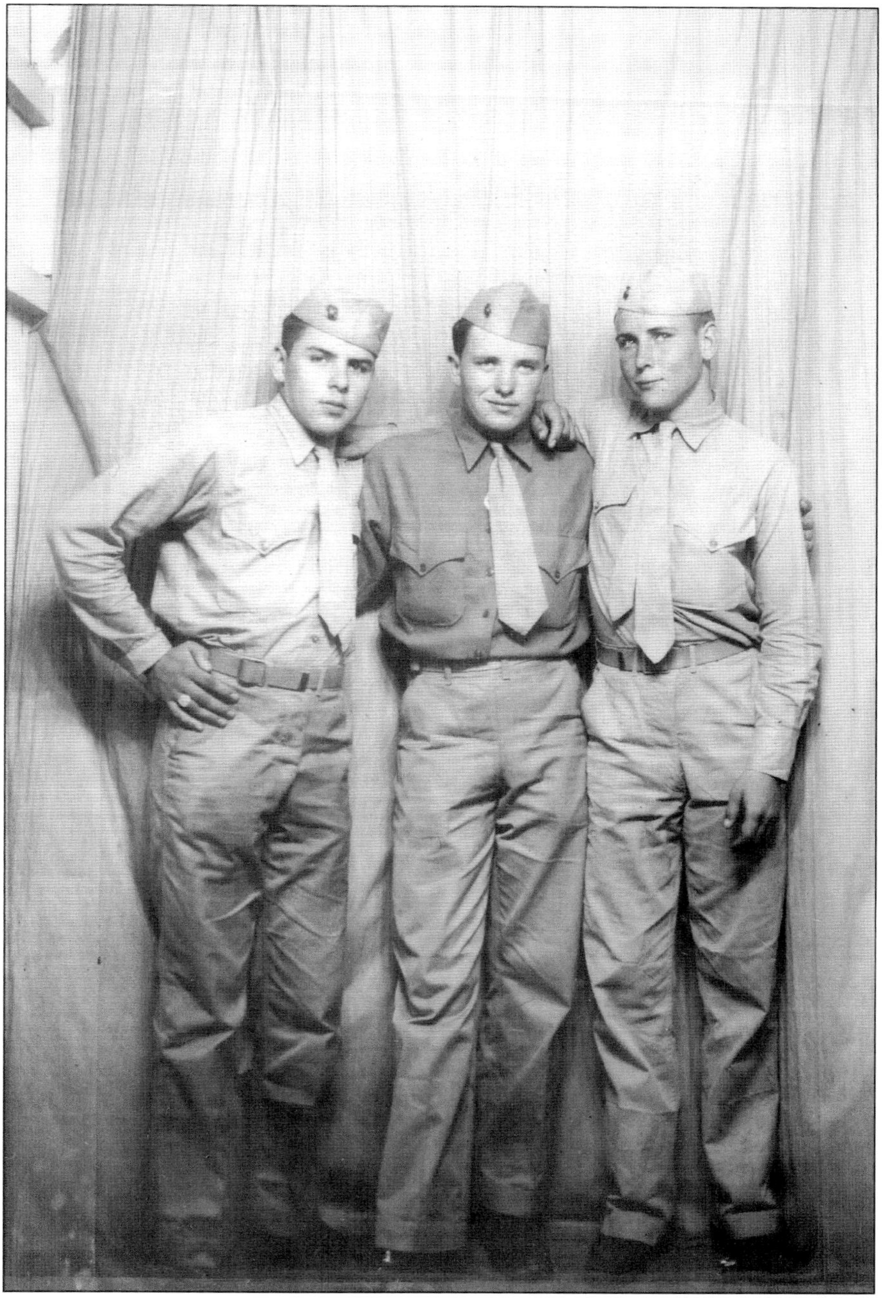

Roy Reyes (left), Donald Simons (center), and Avery Gray are shown on leave in Hawaii in 1944 during World War II. Donald wrote to his family on May 26, 1944: "Roy and I went on liberty today and ran into Avery . . . We had our picture taken. It is not so good, but was the best we could do in a short time. We had three hours together. We will not see Avery for some time. We are in the same fix, only we are a little worse off than he is. I don't guess you know what I mean, but one of these days, if God is willing, I'll tell you. I'll send you the picture . . . It is not much, but we are proud of it and have our own feeling about it." Soon after writing this letter, Donald was killed in action on June 14, Roy was wounded in battle on June 16, and Avery was killed in battle on June 18, 1944. Artesia's Chapter 19 of the Disabled American Veterans in named for Donald Simons.

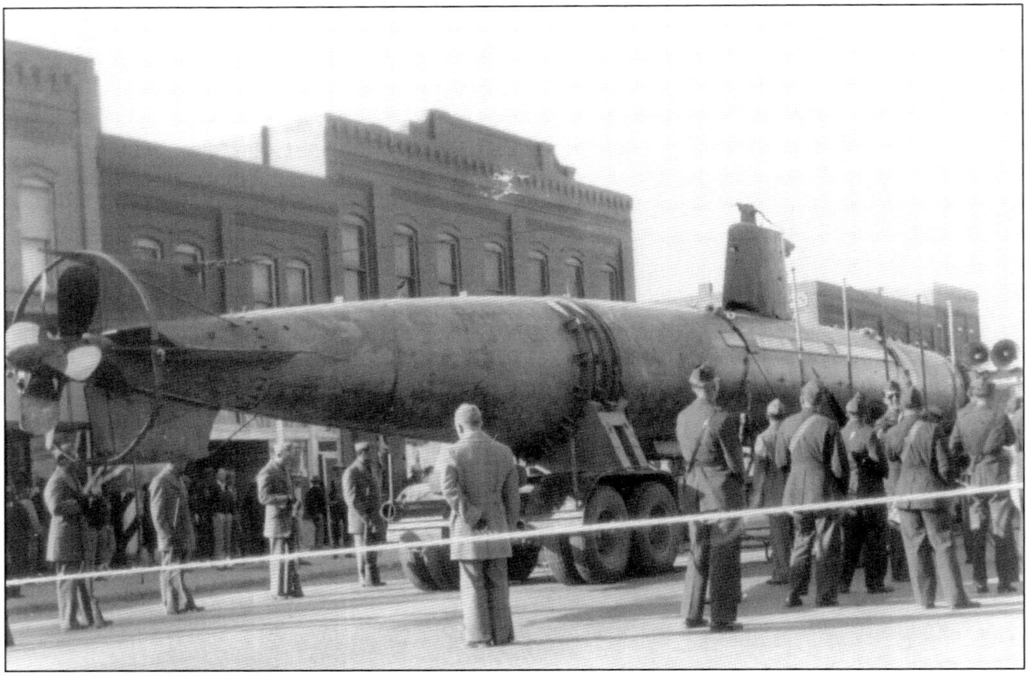

In January 1943, a two-man Japanese submarine captured on the island of Oahu, in Hawaii, during the Pearl Harbor attack on December 7, 1941, was exhibited in Artesia on Main Street. The submarine was used by the Treasury Department to stimulate the sale of war savings bonds and stamps. Parts of the submarine were cut away to allow the public to view its interior, admission for adults was the purchase at least $1 in savings stamps; children's admission cost 25¢. The submarine was 81 feet long and weighed 80,000 pounds. It was originally going to be exhibited in Albuquerque only, but the chief of the War Savings staff of New Mexico felt that the Lower Pecos Valley deserved to host the submarine because area residents had surpassed their quota in war bond sales.

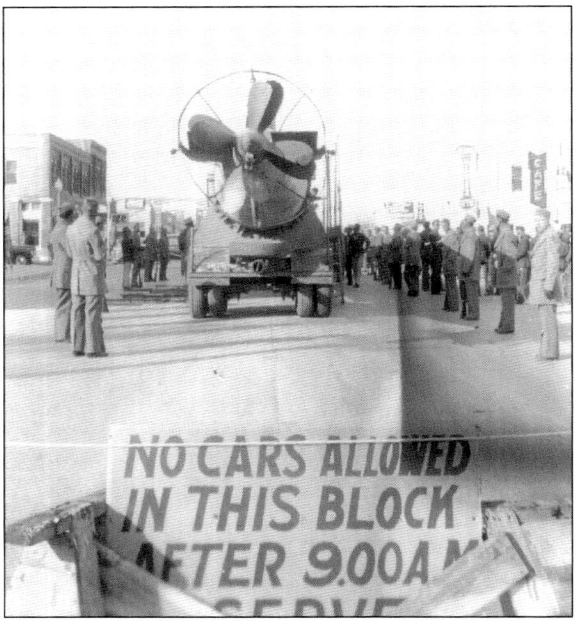

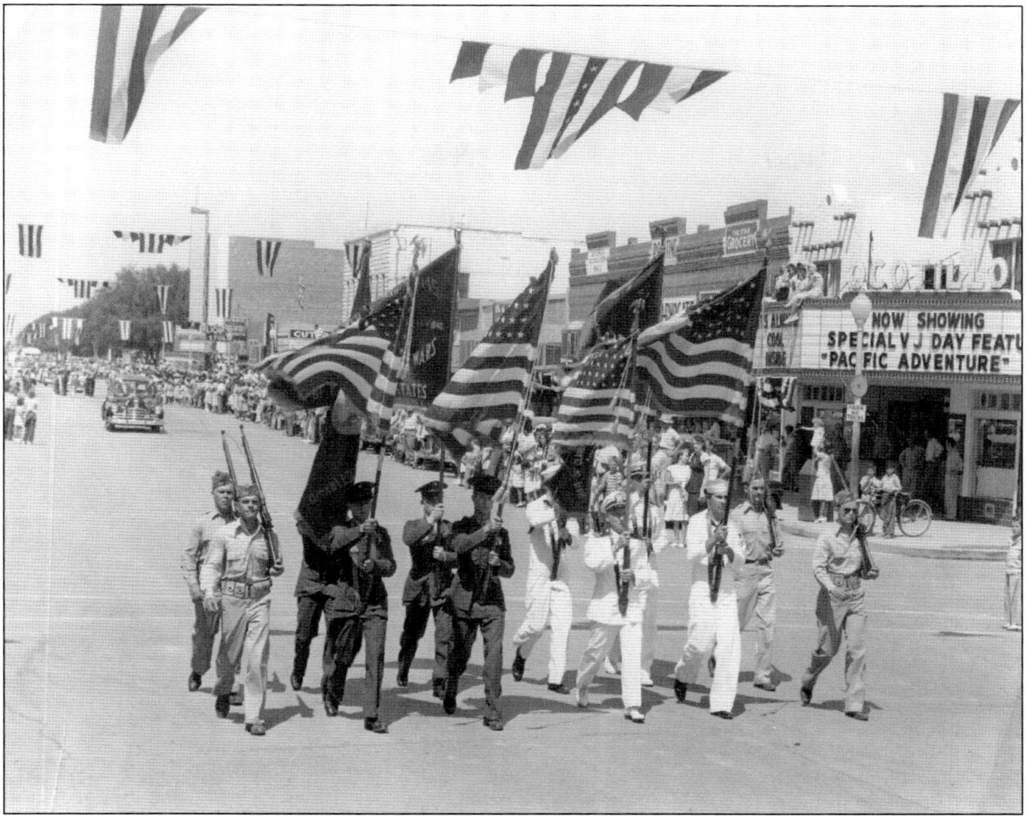

Artesia's V-J Day parade is shown in August 1948. V-J Day was celebrated to commemorate the World War II victory over Japan in 1945. Here, two views of the north side of Main Street are shown. In 1945, celebrations had taken place all over town throughout the day to celebrate the end of World War II. As these photographs show, everyone seems to have turned out for the festivities.

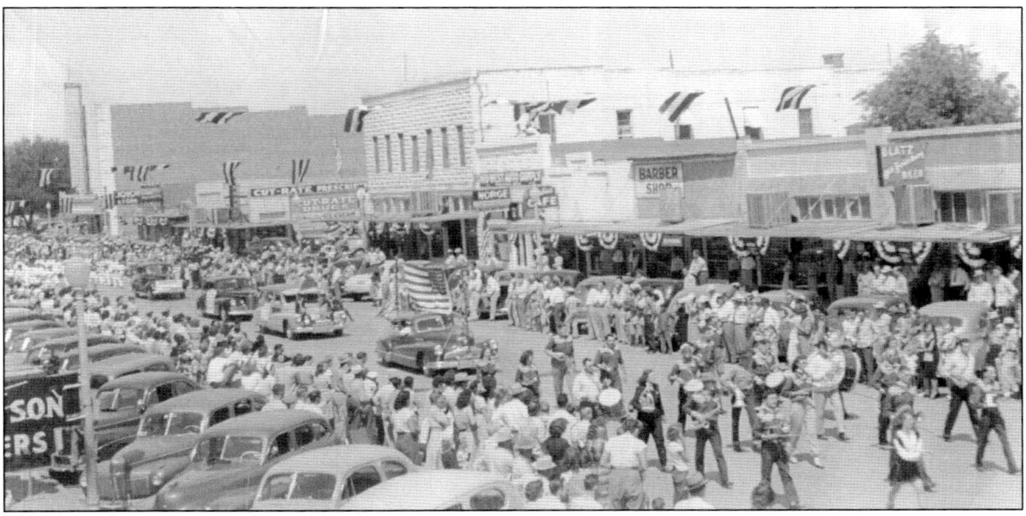

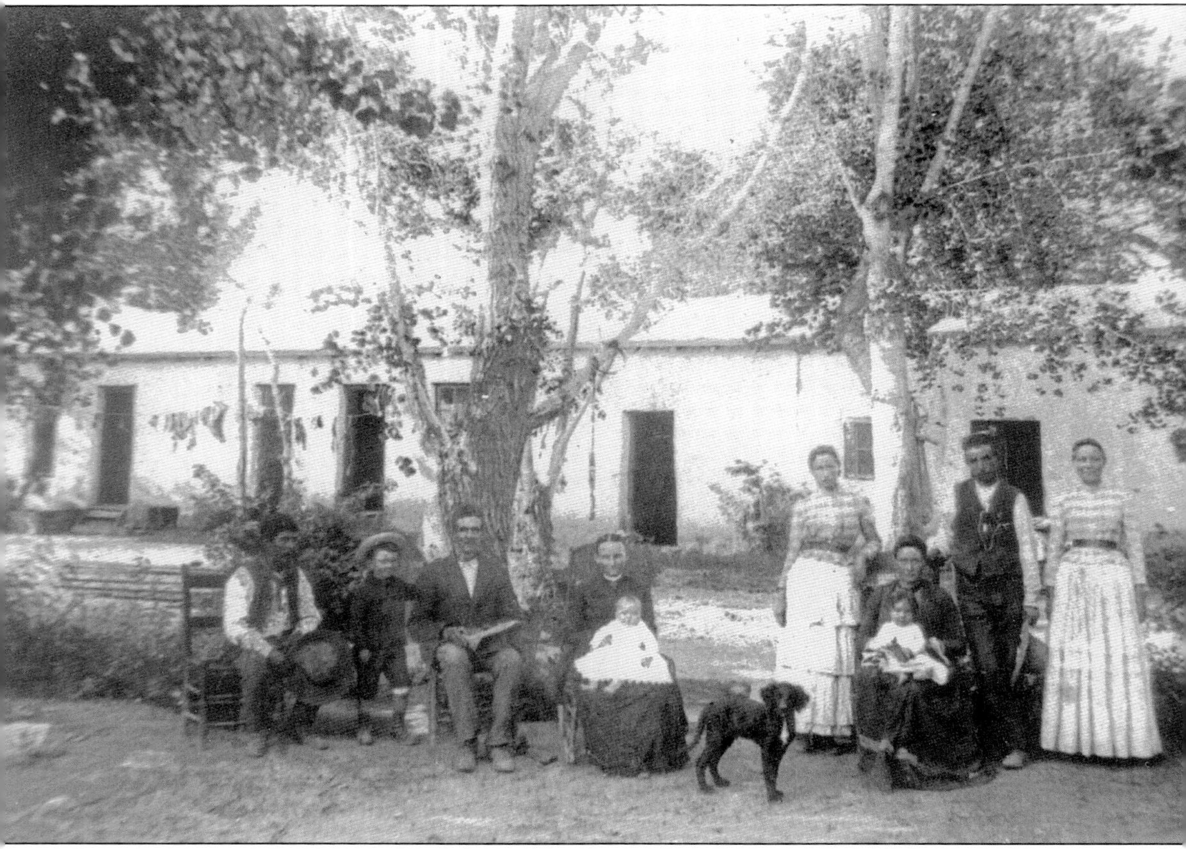

Before Artesia was founded, Robert and Lucy Gilbert operated a dinner station and overnight stop for the local stagecoach line at their home on the Penasco River about five miles south of present-day Artesia. The station was in business from 1874 until 1894, when the railroad came through the Pecos Valley and ended the need for stagecoaches. Billy the Kid shot the station's storeroom door in 1878, either over a Lincoln County War dispute or over Gilbert's refusal to sell him whiskey on a Sunday. The family hid in a cellar during Billy's visit, so no one was hurt. The Gilbert stagecoach station was known for its bountiful fruit orchards, pecan trees, and Mrs. Gilbert's roses. Here, the Gilbert family poses in front of their station in 1889. Seated, from left to right, are cook Alfonso "Fancy" Nuevo, Robert Jr., Robert Sr., Lucy, and baby Mary. The family group on the right is the Dalton family. They were staying at the station as they passed through the territory. It is believed that Mr. Dalton was a traveling sewing-machine salesman.

Seven

Going the Distance

As anyone who has ever visited southeastern New Mexico can affirm, transportation in the area can be a challenge even today. Dust storms, flash floods, occasional snowstorms, hail, and thunderstorms can still shut down roads pretty quickly. It must have been much worse for the earliest settlers in the Artesia area in the 1870s and 1880s. They had to face all of the weather conditions plus travel by horseback, wagon, foot, or stagecoach over dirt tracks. By the early 1890s, a railroad connected the Lower Pecos Valley towns; this made traveling or transporting goods convenient for those who were heading this way. Artesia's first automobiles arrived in the around 1905, and the first airport (called "a cow pasture with a windsock") was established in the late 1920s.

Before a numbering system for roads and highways was adopted in 1925, most roads had no standard numbers or names. Each map company had its own system, which resulted in a bewildering collection of signs at every crossroads. Confused travelers had to try to match a sign with their particular map. The advent of named highways in the late 1910s presented one solution to this problem. Soon after that, the Lincoln Highway, Dixie Highway, and Midland Trail, among others, crisscrossed the region.

The Ozark Trail Highway passed through the Lower Pecos Valley on its way from St. Louis to El Paso. This highway was designated by concrete markers placed along the route in the towns it passed through; in 1922, Artesia's marker was proudly placed smack in the middle of the intersection at Second and Main Streets. It was taken down in 1930 after a new highway was built. By then, the lights on the marker had failed, and enough motorists had crashed into it at night that it had been nicknamed "Artesia's tombstone." Today, the only remaining Ozark Trail Highway marker left standing in New Mexico is located in Lake Arthur—also right in the middle of the street.

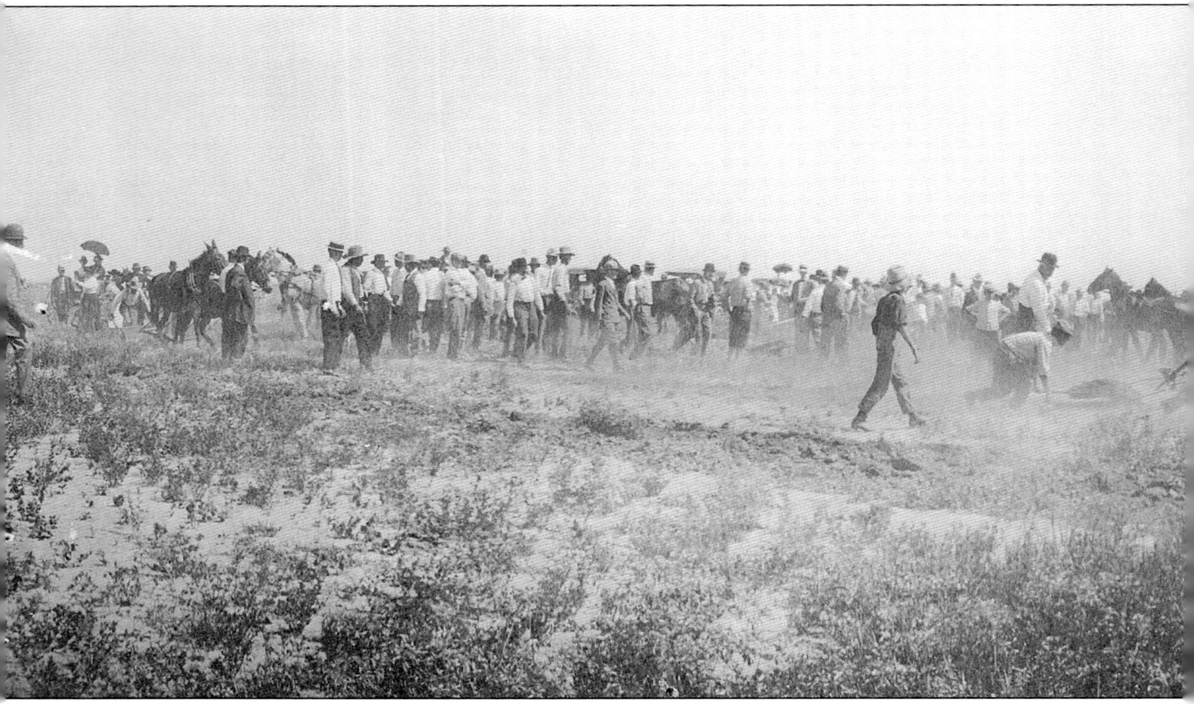

The town of Artesia quickly grew after the railroad came through the Lower Pecos Valley. The need for a railroad spur from Artesia to the town of Hope, 20 miles to the west, became apparent soon after, and by 1908, regional and foreign investors were trying to raise the funds to make this happen. When Artesia and Hope reached an agreement with the San Diego, El Paso & St. Louis Railway Company, things looked promising, and soon afterwards, the railroad's construction began. In this photograph, local residents are grading the route while being cheered on by the community and the local municipal band. But the railroad was never built. The San Diego, El Paso & St. Louis Railway Company went bankrupt soon after, and with the pre–World War I turmoil

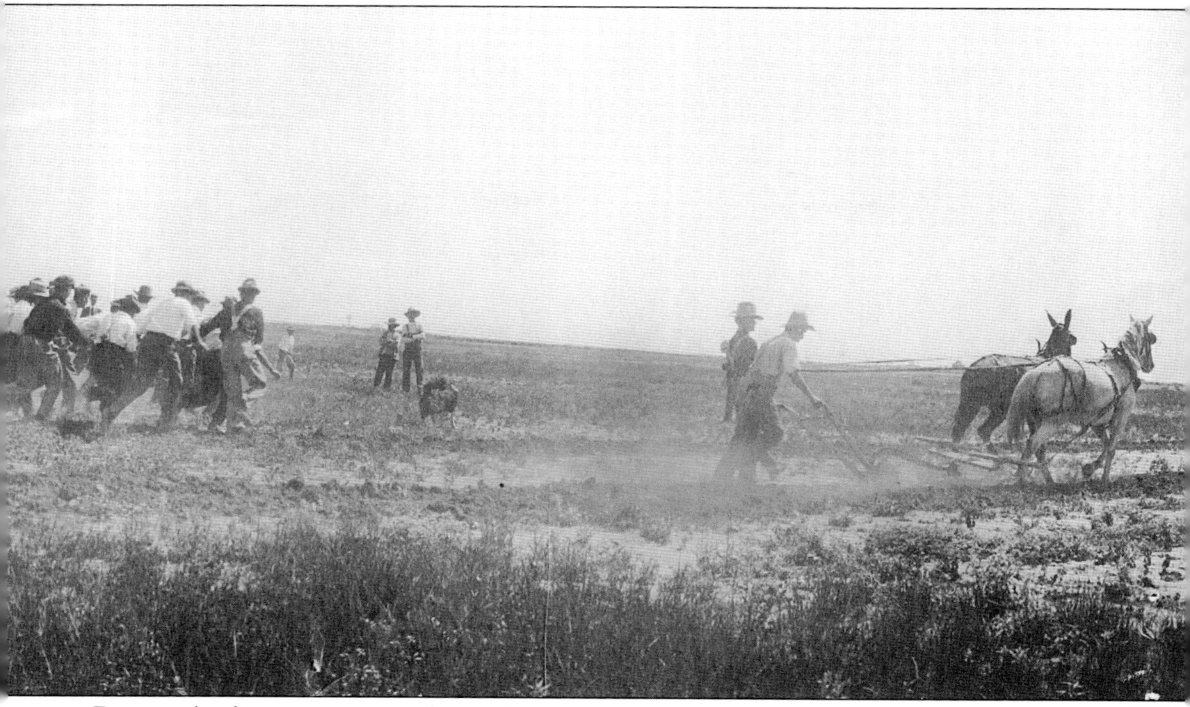

in Europe, the foreign investors changed their minds and withdrew their funds. A persistent myth lingers that the reason this railroad was never built was because the funds went down on the *Titanic* in 1912. This did not happen; the railroad project had already failed from a lack of funding by then. Lord Pearson, one of the European investors, later went down on the *Lusitania* in 1915, and this may be how the confusion started. Locals were left with the remnants of the graded land and the lost funds. A mock funeral was held for the spade that turned the first dirt for the "railroad that was not," and its headstone read, "Sacred to the Memory of the S.D. E.P. St.L. Railway, it died a'borning."

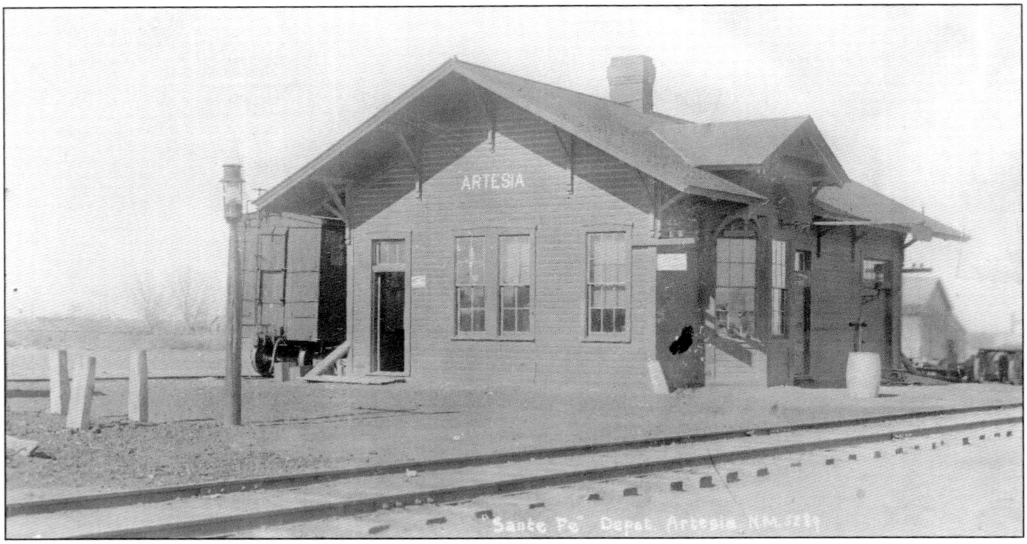

The original railroad depot in Artesia was a small, wooden building constructed in 1897 and remodeled in 1907. It was quickly outgrown because of Artesia's expansion, and in 1912, a new, improved passenger depot was built one block south of the original. After the new depot was constructed, the old one was used for freight only until 1940, when it was retired. It burned down in 1947. Passenger service to Artesia was discontinued in 1967 and the remaining depot shut down in 1988. The structure was fully restored in 2000 and today houses the Artesia Chamber of Commerce and Visitors Center.

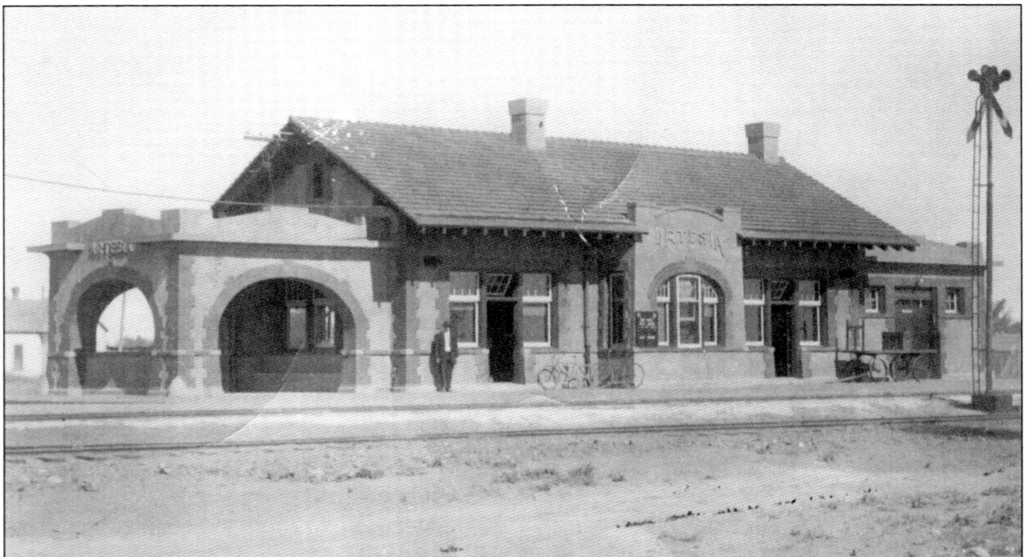

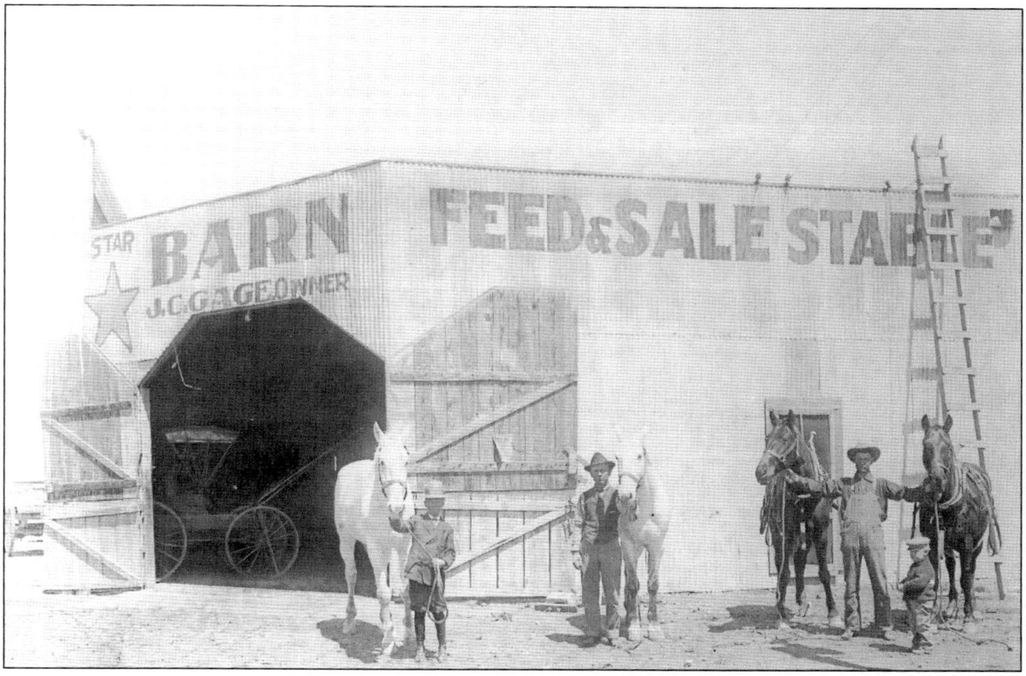

In the early years, Artesia had several livery stables like these two. The stables boarded horses for people who did not have a place for theirs at home and rented buggies, wagons, and teams as they were needed. The Star Barn seen above also sold feed. Owner J.C. Gage's family members are shown from left to right as follows: Floyd Snyder, J.C. Gage Jr. (he later married Floyd's sister Ola), Luke Gage, and Marion Gage. The Hart-Crouch Livery Stable pictured below was located on Second Street in Artesia.

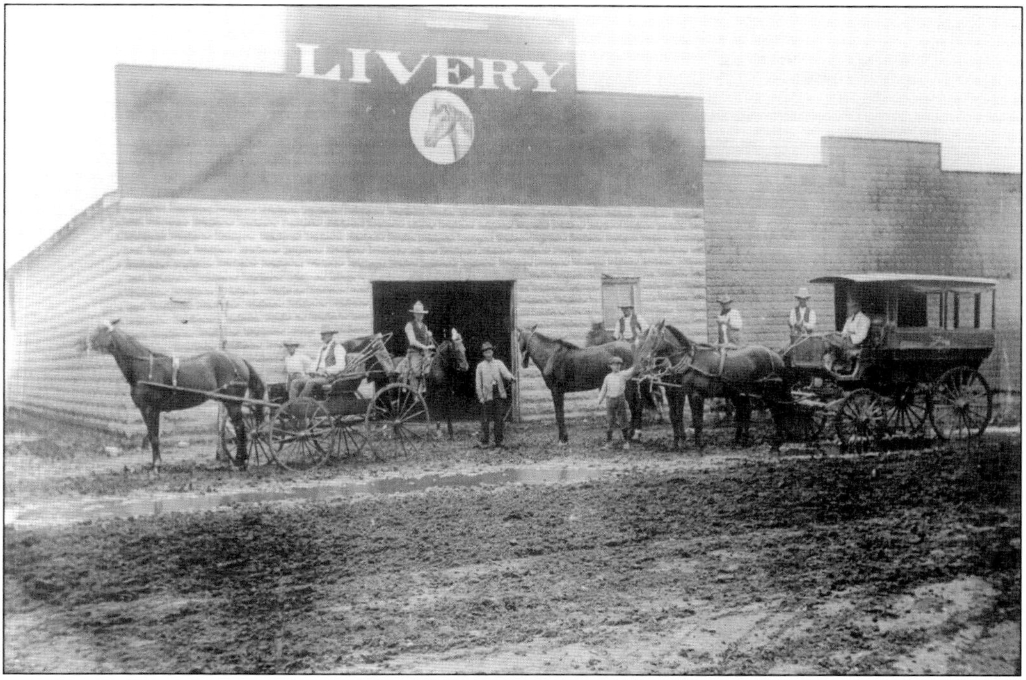

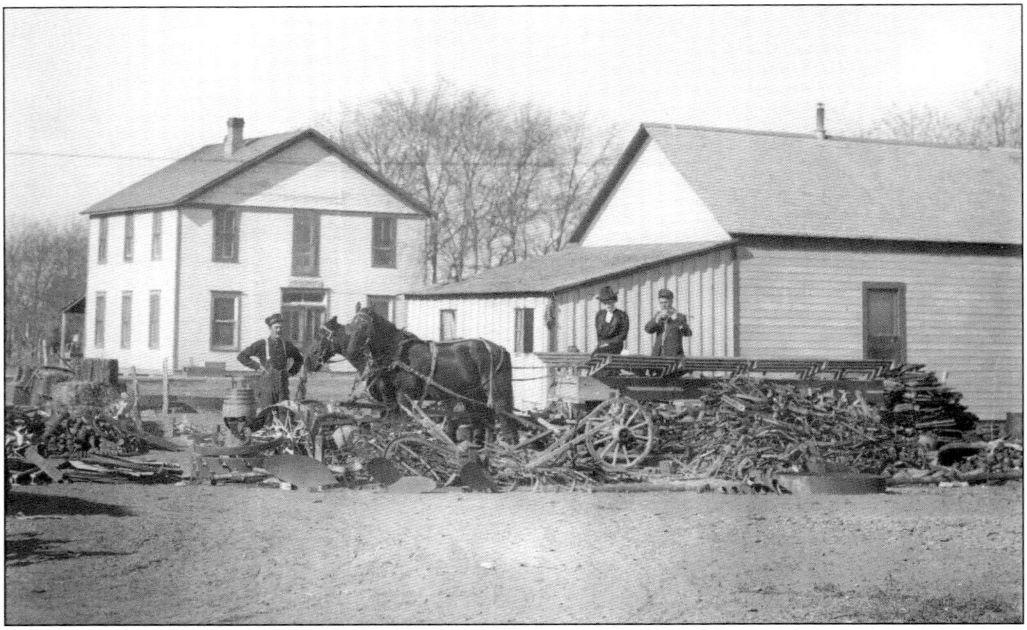

According to the 1917 *Artesia Advocate*, "You can't keep an honest junk man down, he will spread out." L.P. Evans was a pioneer in Artesia. Before settling here, he traveled with carnivals showing off an 18-foot-long snake. He began a scrap-metal business that quickly grew into a secondhand store, repair shop, and garage. By 1916, it was one of the most prosperous enterprises in the entire Pecos Valley.

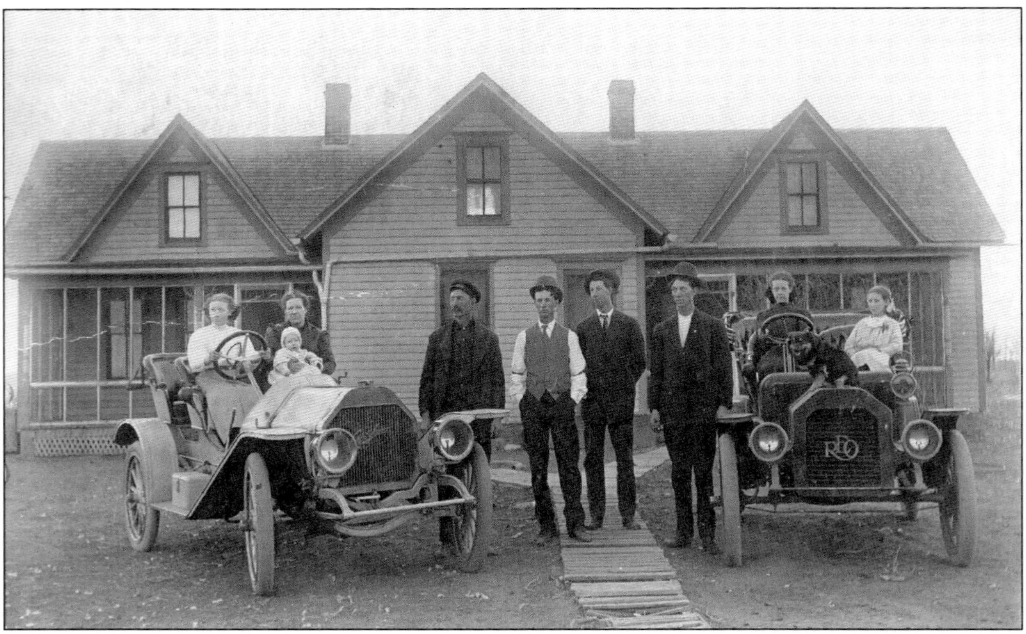

Pioneers show off their cars around 1905. The vehicle on the left is an early-model Overland. The Overland Auotmotive Division of Standard Wheel was bought by John Willys, whose Willys-Overland Company eventually became part of Chrysler. The car on the right is a REO Runabout. The REO Motor Car Company produced vehicles from 1905 to 1975; founder Ransom E. Olds's previous company eventually became Oldsmobile.

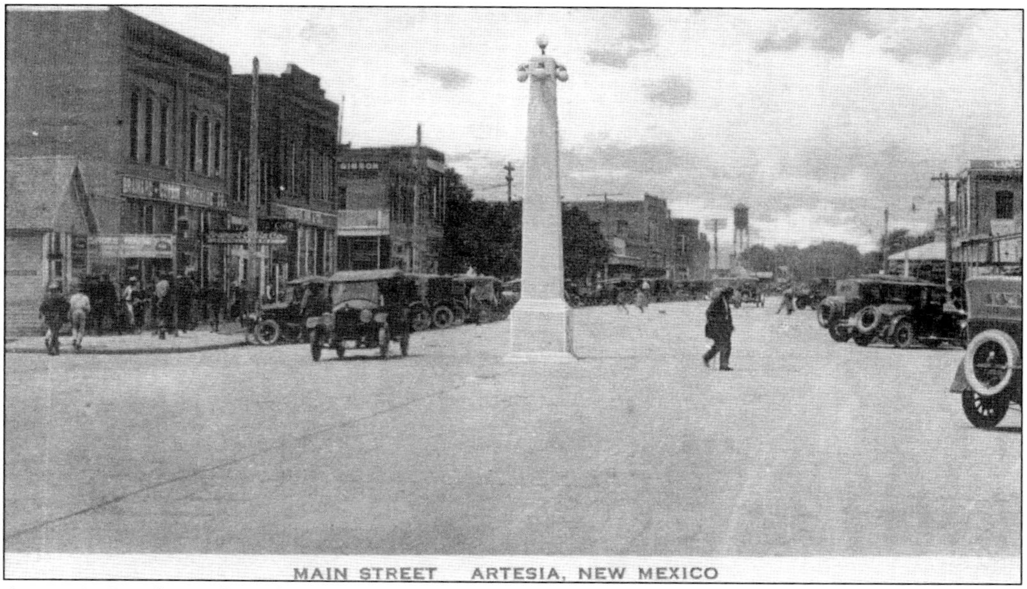

Artesia's Ozark Trail Highway marker stands in the middle of Main Street around 1923. The Artesia company of Matheson, Henrickson, and Brown made the local Ozark Trail Highway markers for $250 apiece. Each was made of reinforced concrete, measuring four feet square at the base and 21 feet high. As this photograph shows, it took up a lot of space in the street.

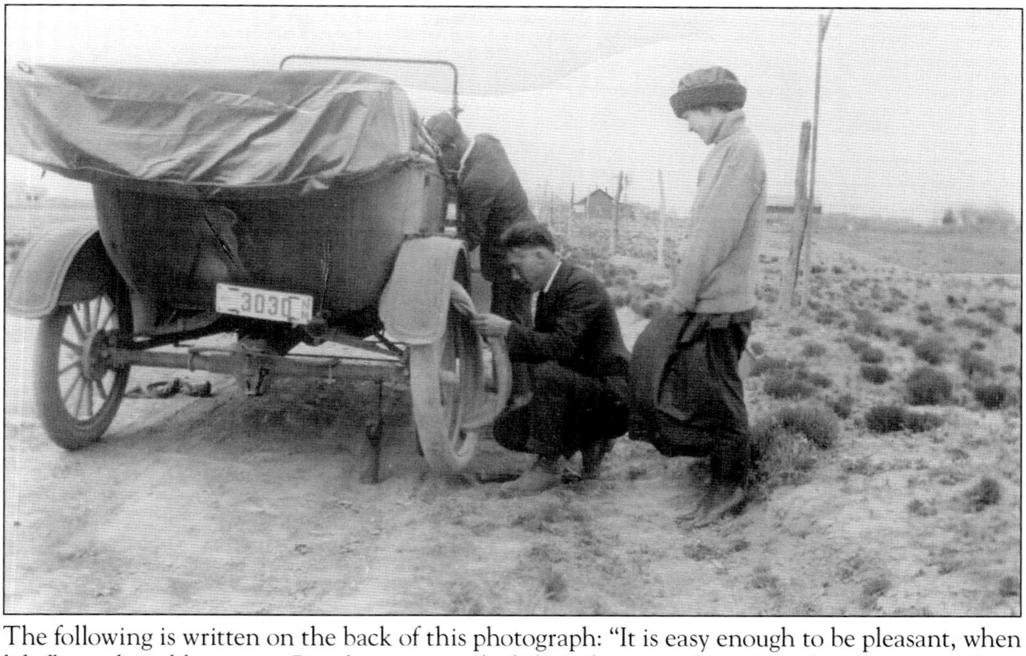

The following is written on the back of this photograph: "It is easy enough to be pleasant, when life flows along like a song. But the man worthwhile is the man who can smile, when everything goes dead wrong." ? Stirling (left), ? House (center), and Bernice Lee make an unscheduled stop while on a drive in the Artesia countryside in May 1920. Bernice must have been impressed by House's good humor—she later married him.

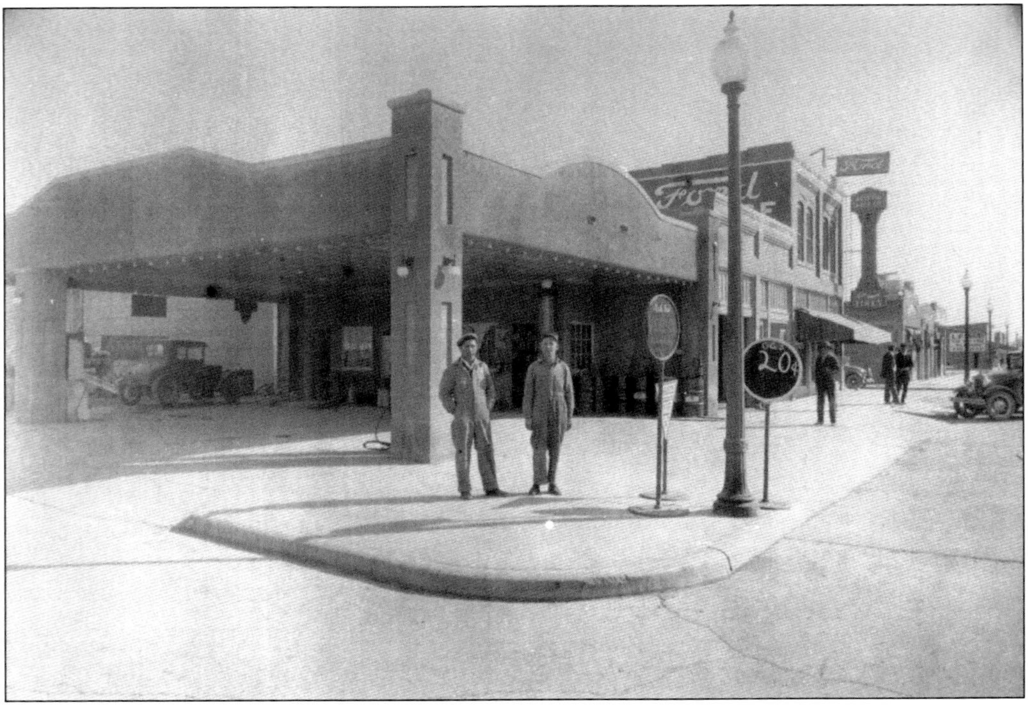

As automobiles became more and more popular, Artesia's livery stables were gradually replaced by gas stations. The station pictured above was located on the corner of Main Street and Roselawn Avenue, with the price of gas in the early 1920s shown on the sign. The Cave Brothers Grocery shown below is located at Second and Chisum Streets. Owners Jesse (left) and Olean Cave opened the grocery in 1925 and are pictured in this 1931 photograph with assistant Dick Graves (right). In addition to selling gas, the grocery also fixed flat tires, radiators, starters, and generators. It sold a variety of snacks and drinks at "a very economical prices," says an early advertisement, and emergency lodging was also available for 25¢ up to $1 per night depending on the accommodations required. The Caves retired in 1960.

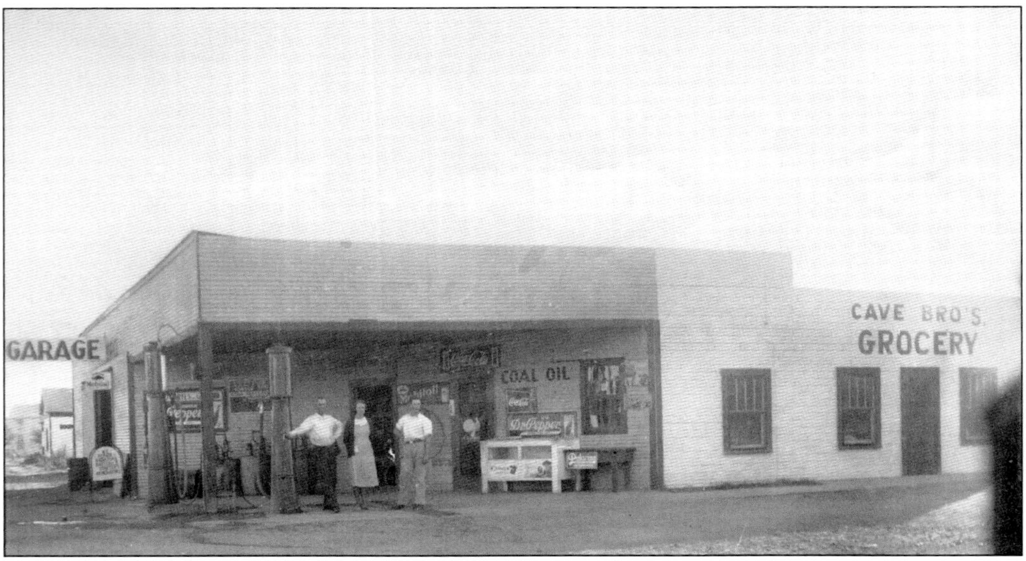

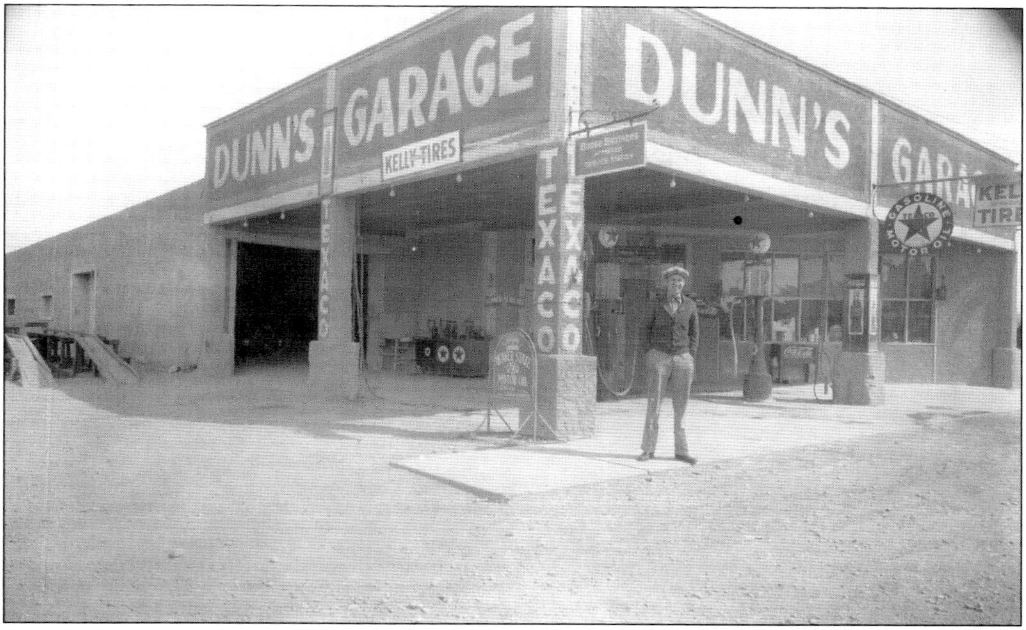

Dunn's Garage, in the photograph above, opened in the 1920s. Owner J.D. "Dude" Dunn is shown standing proudly in front around 1924. Like the Cave Brothers Grocery, Dunn's Garage offered a wide variety of products and services. In the photograph below, Reid Dowell's Magnolia Service Station crew is shown around the late 1940s. The station was built on the east side of First Street by Quay Avenue in 1930 and operated until 1974. The benefits of a full-service gas station such as this one included having an attendant pump the gas, clean windshields, and check the oil level and tire pressure. From left to right are Fred Sorrell, S.G. Davidson, Reid Dowell, and Elmer Thompson.

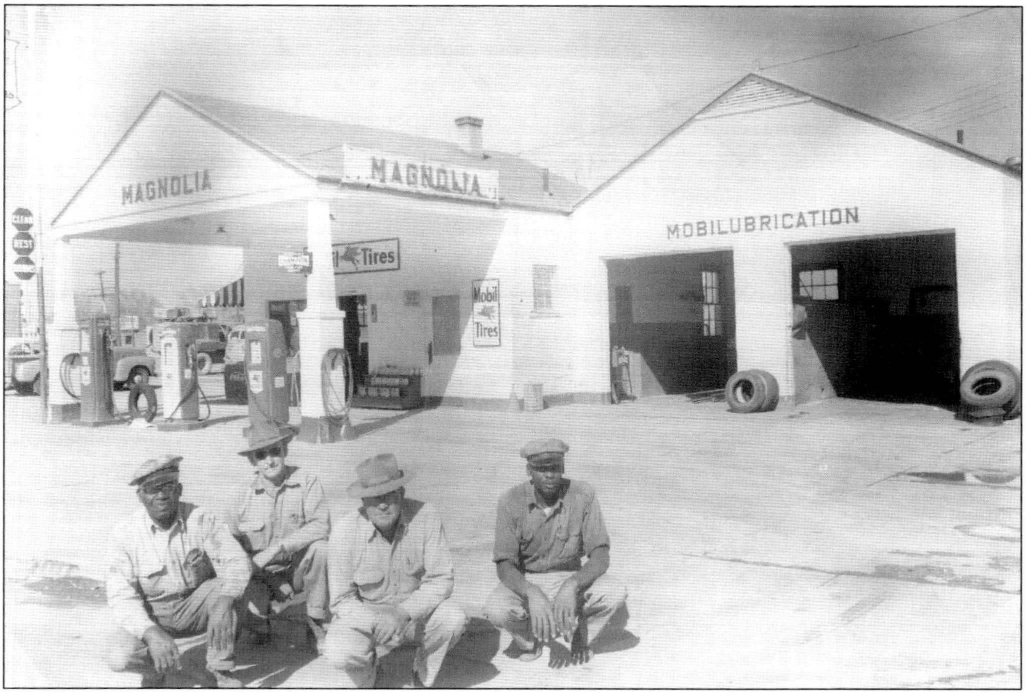

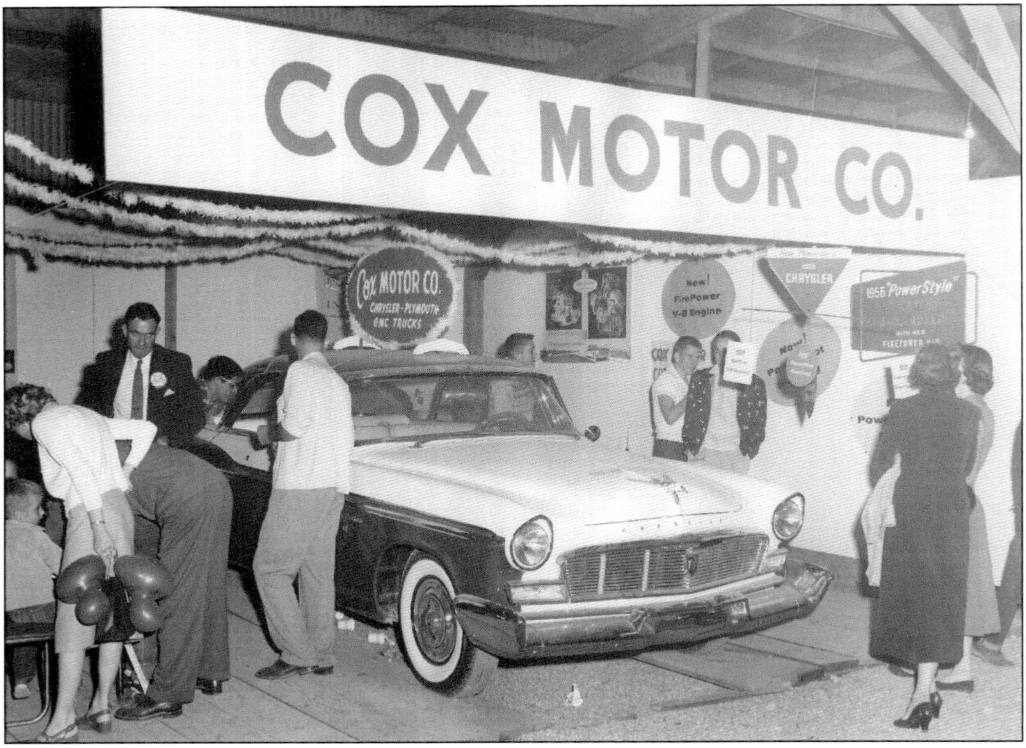

By the 1950s, automobile dealerships, such as the Cox Motor Company, were becoming more and more common because of the rise in automobile affordability. Cars were increasingly bigger with more luxury features. At the 1955 Home and Ranch Show, Cox Motor Company showed off the new 1956 Chrysler New Yorker.

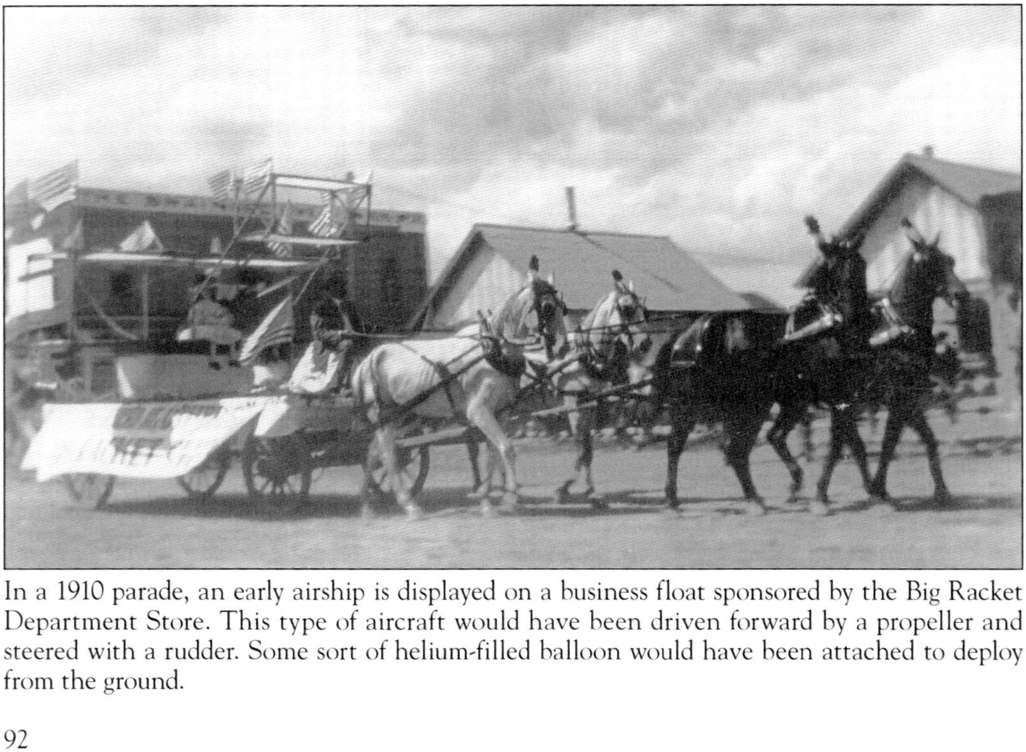

In a 1910 parade, an early airship is displayed on a business float sponsored by the Big Racket Department Store. This type of aircraft would have been driven forward by a propeller and steered with a rudder. Some sort of helium-filled balloon would have been attached to deploy from the ground.

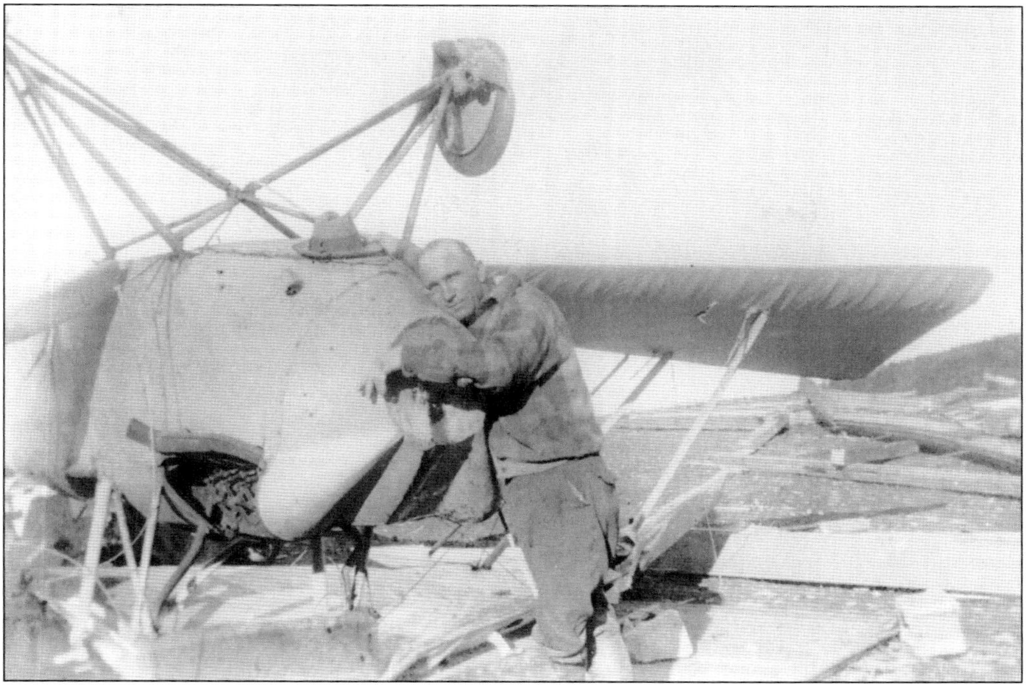

Jim and Olga Christman came to Artesia in 1928 where Jim had hopes of establishing an airport in a field north of town. However, Artesia was short of funds, so Jim performed in air shows and gave private flying lessons to support his family. The Christmans moved by air to Pennsylvania in 1932. Although Jim's dream of establishing a proper airport in Artesia was never realized, plans for Artesia's first airport were initiated after his death in an air crash in 1937. The new airport was established in the early 1940s and even housed a military glider school for a few months during World War II. Above, Jim Christman hugs the wreckage of his Hartman plane, destroyed by high winds in 1929. The photograph below shows his Standard airplane on the plains of New Mexico.

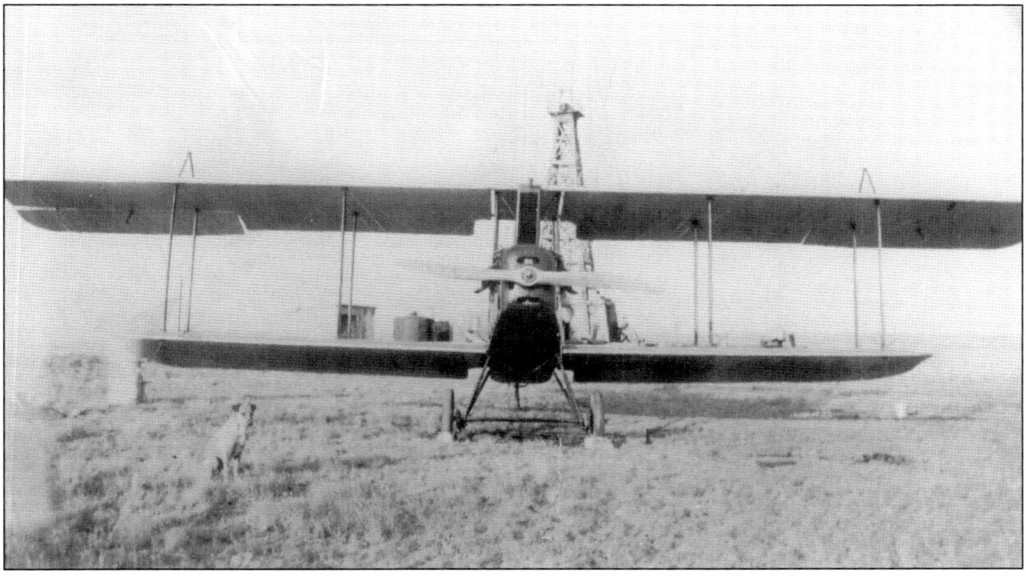

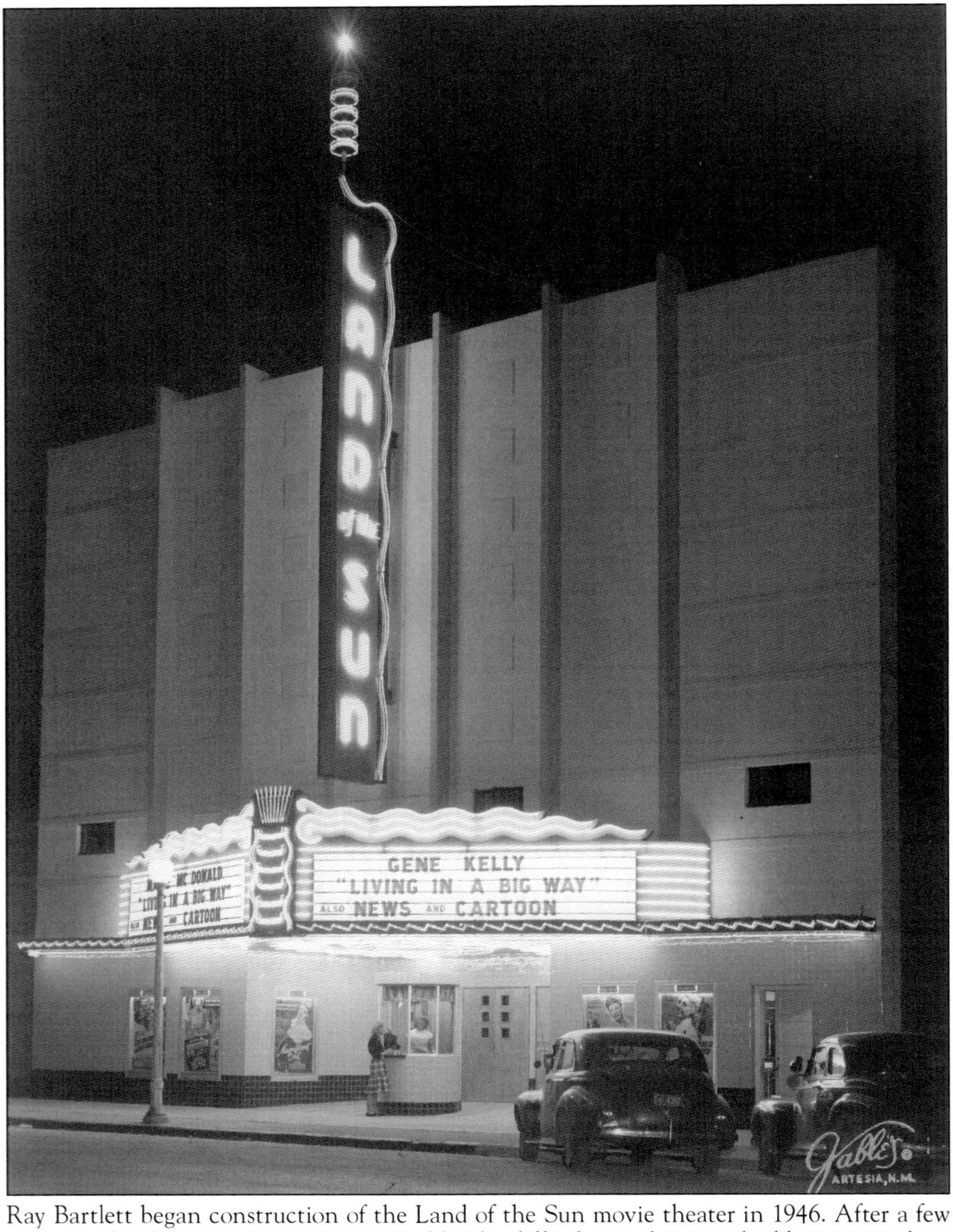

Ray Bartlett began construction of the Land of the Sun movie theater in 1946. After a few delays in the theater's construction caused by the difficulty in obtaining building materials in the post–World War II boom years, the new theater opened for business in August 1947. Locals immediately shortened the name to the "LandSun." The final cost for the structure was estimated at $150,000, and its furnishings were luxurious by the standards of the day. In this photograph, the LandSun Theater is shown three weeks after its grand opening. *Living in a Big Way* was star Gene Kelly's first film upon returning to Hollywood after serving in the military during the war, and it featured his all-time favorite musical number.

Eight

Enjoying Life

Since the first settlement of the area, finding ways to keep everyone entertained opened up the possibilities for many social activities and attractions. Just like today, going to the movies, enjoying a get-together with friends, visiting the parks, and having fun at dances were popular choices that the newly formed town had to offer in the early 20th century.

Social gatherings with friends always make the time fly by. All around Artesia, residents young and old could be found socializing with others at different hotspots. Gatherings at the local swimming pools were an all-time favorite. Over the years, Spring Lake, the Lanning and Oasis Swimming Pools, and the Municipal Swimming Pool gave everyone a chance to cool off in the heat of the summer. Picnicking in the parks and taking in the fresh air was a way to relax that everyone could enjoy.

Going to the movies was and still is a favorite to all, and Artesia has had its fair share of theaters. Throughout the years, C.W. Bartlett and his son Ray made a name for their family by bringing in the latest movies and catering to movies fans. C.W.'s Majestic Theater was the first one built in Artesia. It was replaced by the Bartletts' Ocotillo Theater, which offered a wide variety of entertainment besides films. Another Bartlett family venture was the Valley Theater located on Main Street. The Valley was opened in 1937 at a cost of $20,000. A unique feature of this venue was that it was open-air; it had no roof. The Valley Theater closed nearly two decades later. The Bartletts constructed the Land of the Sun Theater in 1947, which is still operating today—with some modifications. Another popular (and missed) theater that the Bartletts brought to town was the Circle-B Drive-In Theater, built in 1949.

As Artesia started to grow and change over the years, more attractions started to pop up. Even though some of the earliest eventually faded away, more opportunities for fun and entertainment are always coming up.

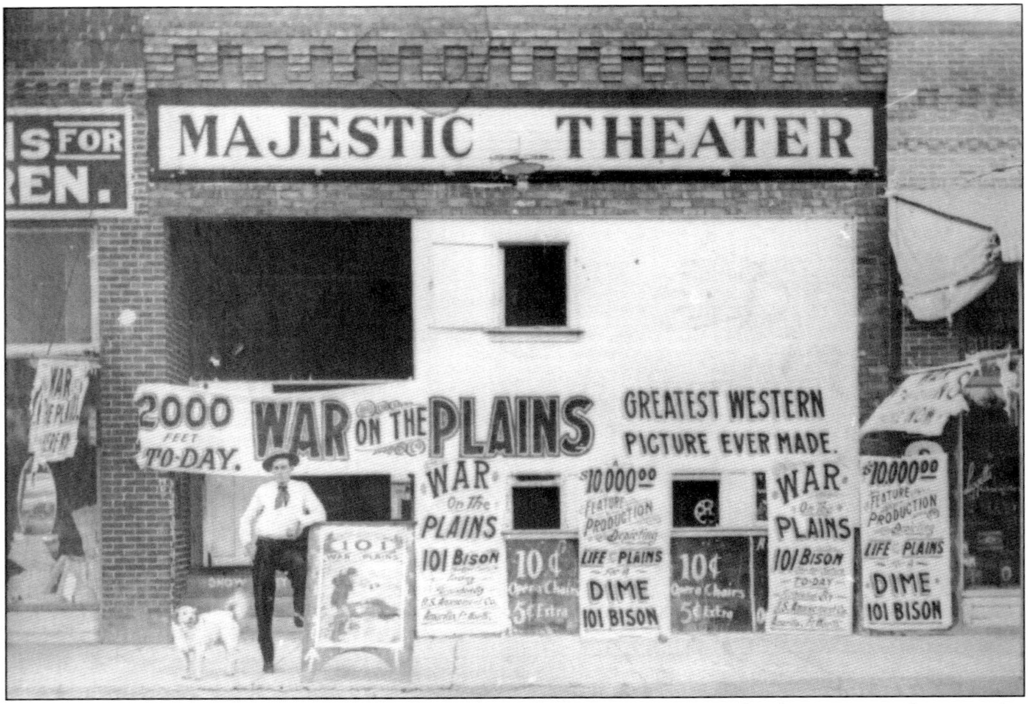

The first motion pictures were shown in Artesia in 1909. In 1911, the first movie theater, the Majestic, was built. The venue went through several name changes over the years, and C.W. Bartlett and his son Ray purchased it in 1923. In this photograph, early manager R.V. Hyatt is shown standing outside the theater to promote a Western in 1912.

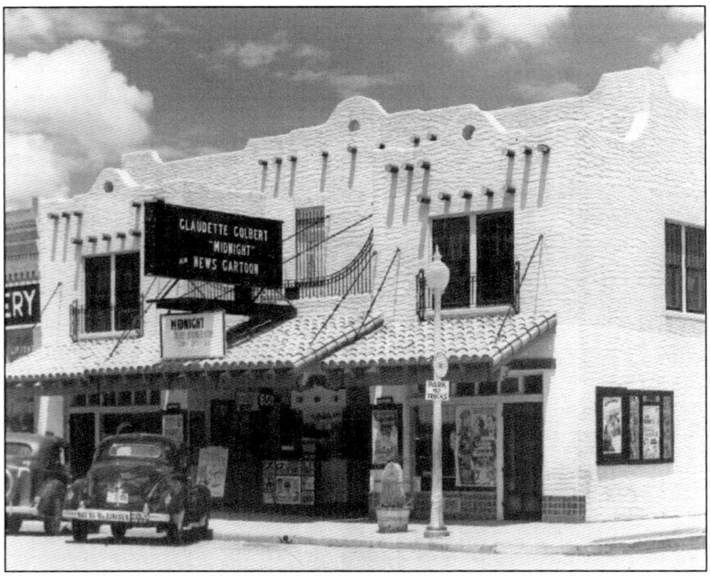

The Majestic Theater was torn down in 1935 to make way for a larger and more modern movie house. The Ocotillo Theater opened in May 1935, and owners C.W. and Ray Bartlett took pride in their new, $50,000 showplace. The Ocotillo seated 588 patrons, and the walls were decorated with eight murals of Native Americans and mountain scenes. C.W. was also the leader of Artesia's Municipal Band, which played many concerts at the Ocotillo.

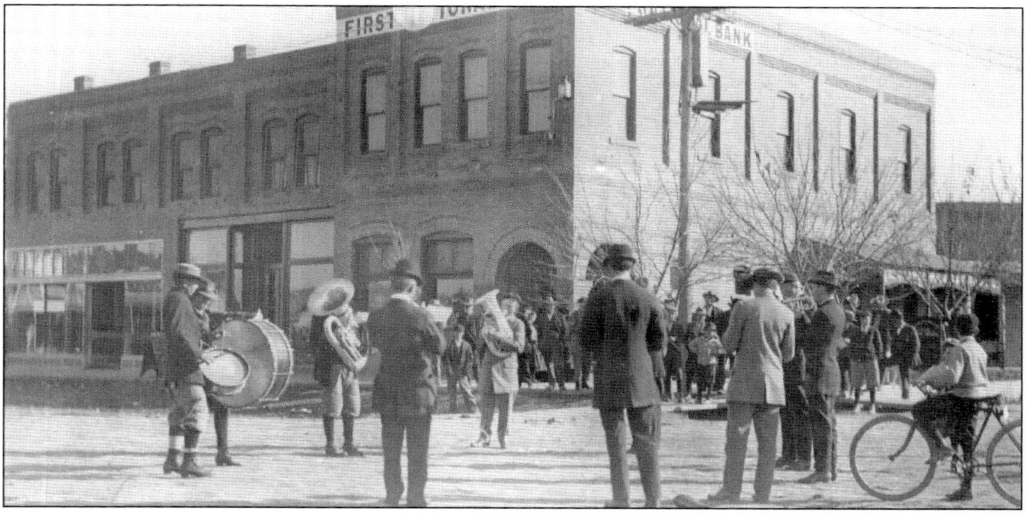

Artesia has a long history of loving music, and the Municipal Band was active throughout the community from the earliest days. The band performed at any and all events throughout southeastern New Mexico, including the ground-breaking for the Artesia-to-Hope railroad and ice-cream socials. Above, the band plays a concert at the intersection of Main Street and Roselawn Avenue in 1910. Below, Municipal Band members pose in 1910. Artesia High School also had an active band, whose concerts and performances were crowd-pleasers as well.

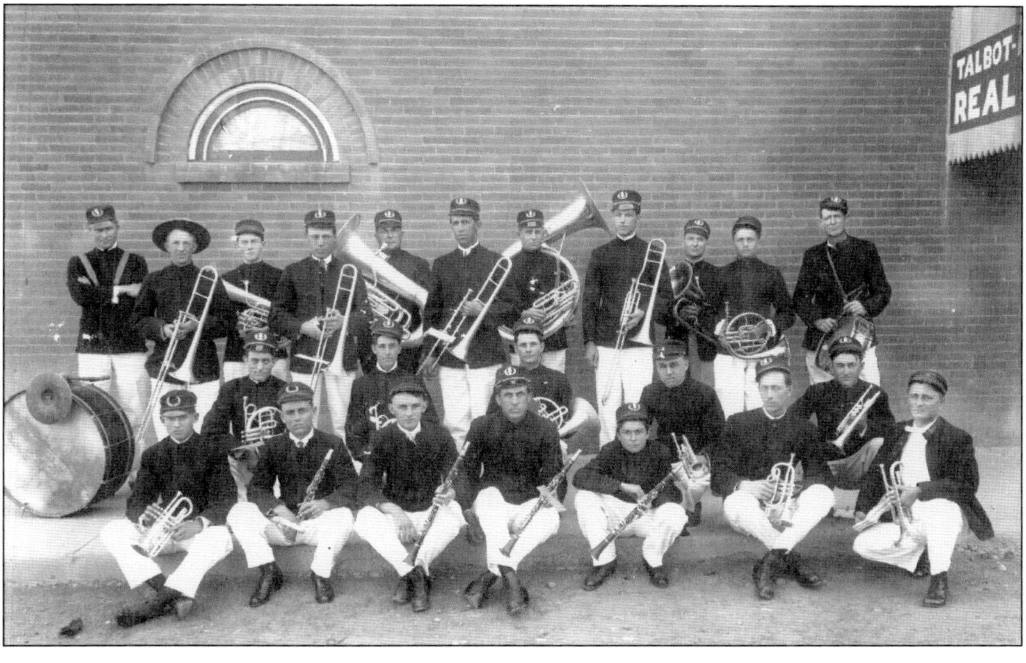

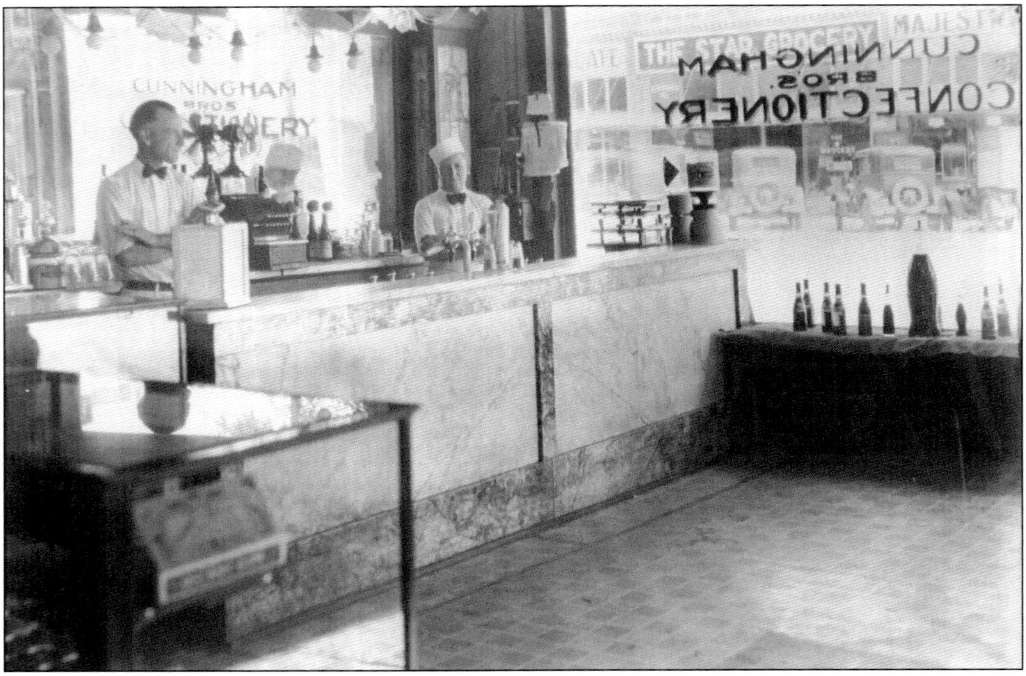

Local residents have always had their favorite places to hang out. Young people had soda fountains, older men had the local pool hall, and many women enjoyed their visits to the beauty shop. The Cunningham Brothers Confectionary was located at 309 West Main Street. Owner ? Cunningham (left) and soda jerk Jack Conner are pictured above in 1930. Besides ice cream and sundaes, the confectionary sold soft drinks and snacks. Below, a group of men plays cards in the Artesia Recreation Hall, also known as "the old pool hall," in the early 1970s.

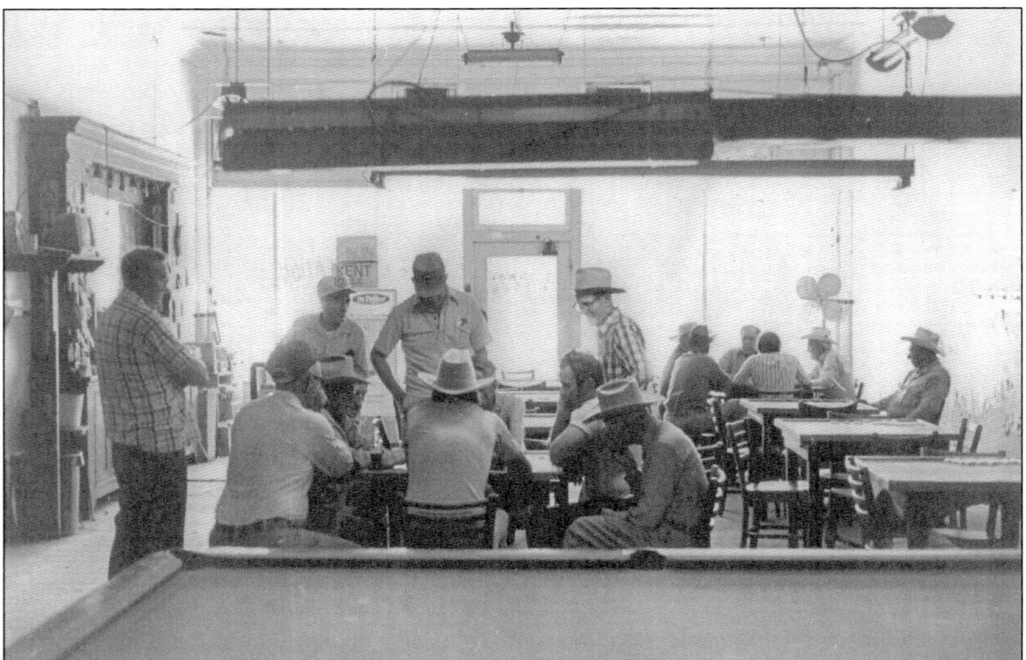

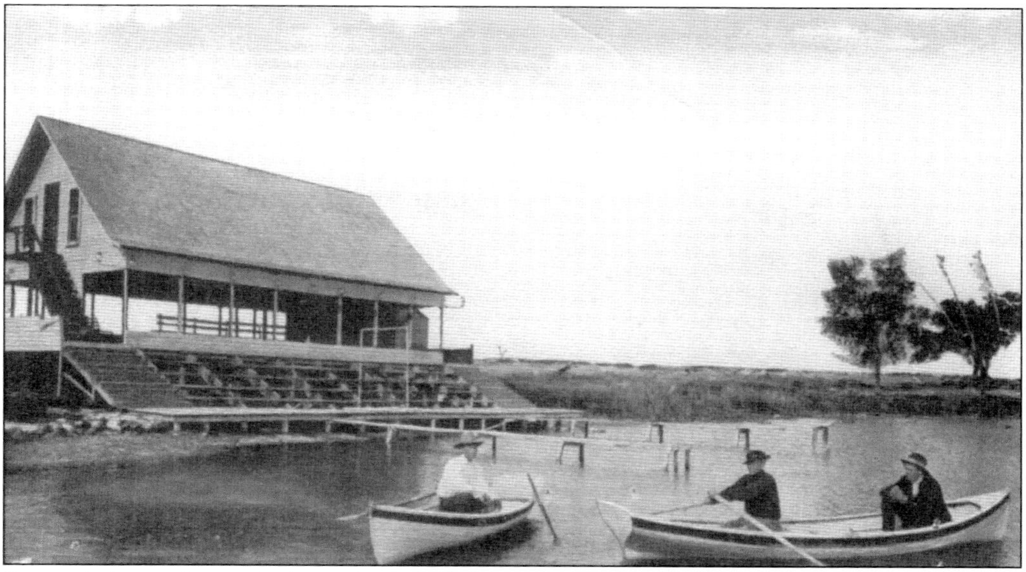

Spring Lake was located a few miles outside of Artesia and in the early days was a place to swim, boat, fish, attend a dance, watch fireworks, enjoy baseball games, or hold picnics, parties, and other gatherings. In this photograph, the pavilion and grandstand at Spring Lake are shown around 1910. With the overuse of area artesian wells, the springs that fed Spring Lake dried up, and the lake disappeared.

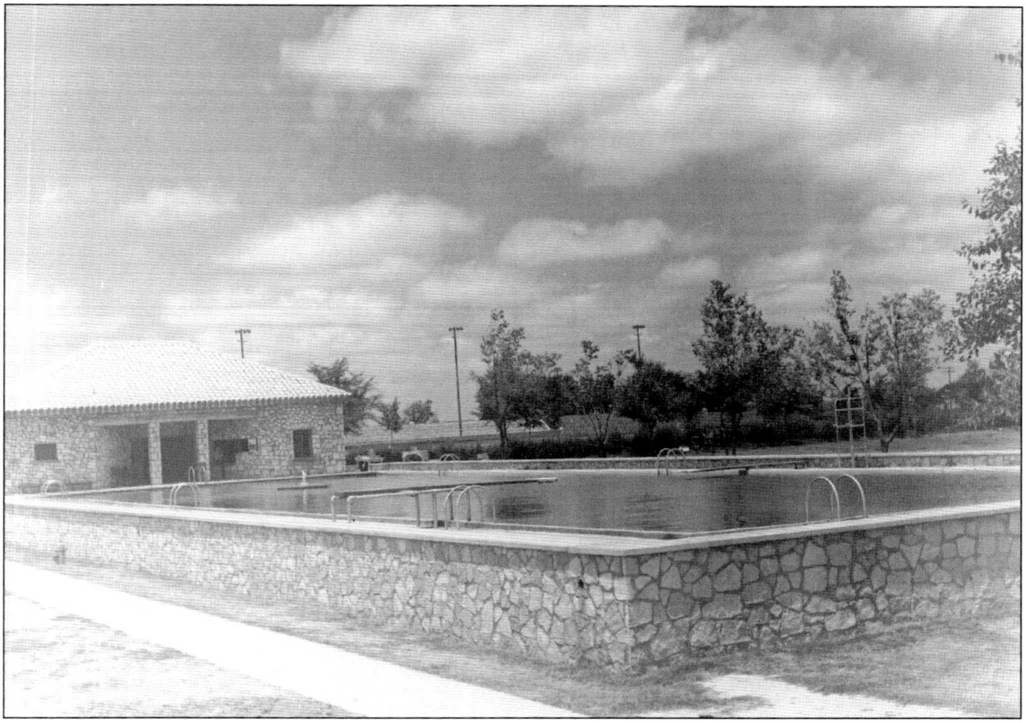

The Municipal Swimming Pool, located at Artesia High School, opened in June 1939. The pool was a special project of city manager P.V. Morris and mayor Hollis Watson and was built with Works Progress Administration (WPA) labor. The pool was the coolest place in town to hang out in the summer until it closed in 1977.

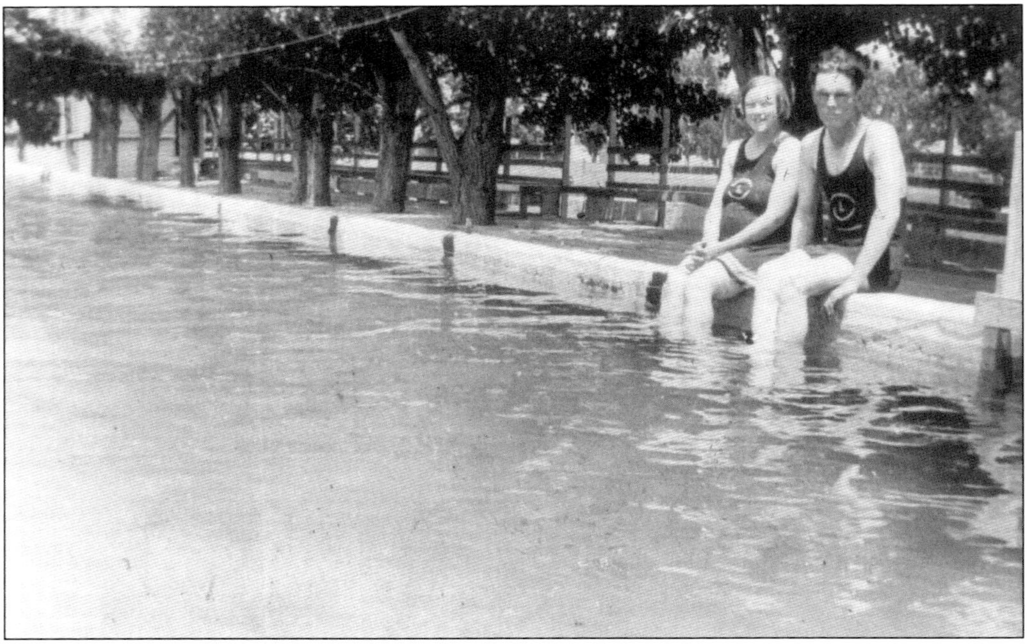

The Lanning and Oasis swimming pools both opened to the public in the summer of 1925. The Lanning Pool (above) featured two separate sections—the shallow side was for children. Its slogan: It's Always Cool at the Lanning Pool. Freshwater circulated throughout both pools constantly. The Lanning Pool was a popular attraction until 1930, when the farm was sold and the pool closed. The Oasis Pool (below) featured a concrete pool that was arranged so that freshwater ran through daily. The Oasis also had an open-air dance pavilion and concession stand. A dwindling water supply and stricter health laws led to the pool closing in the 1940s.

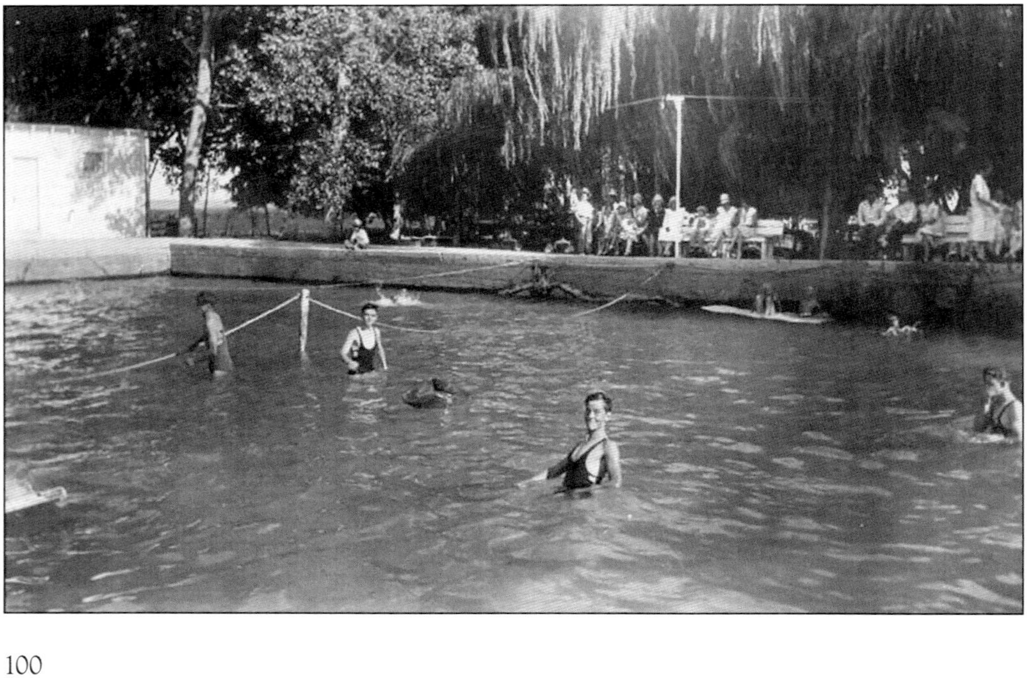

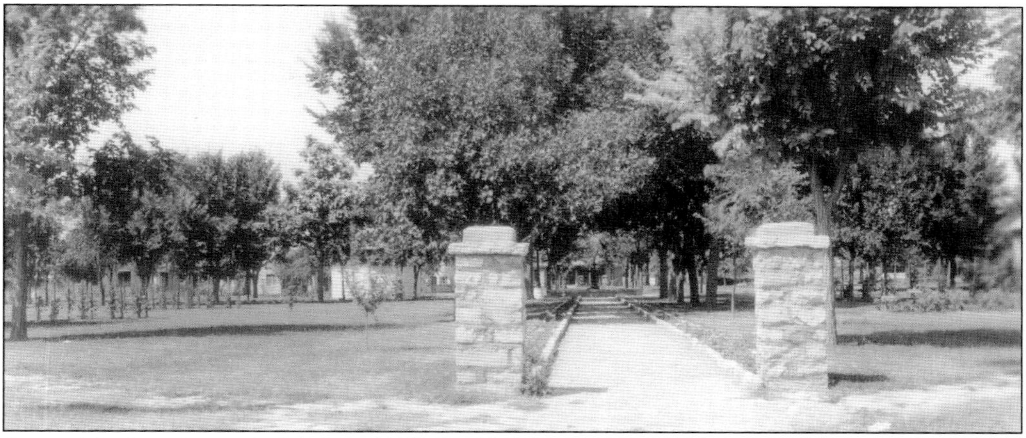

Central Park is Artesia's oldest park, dating back to the early 1900s. An early artesian well was located here. Local volunteers, women's groups, and children volunteered to keep the park clean in the early years. Over the decades, the park has seen many additions and subtractions. This late-1930s photograph shows WPA improvements.

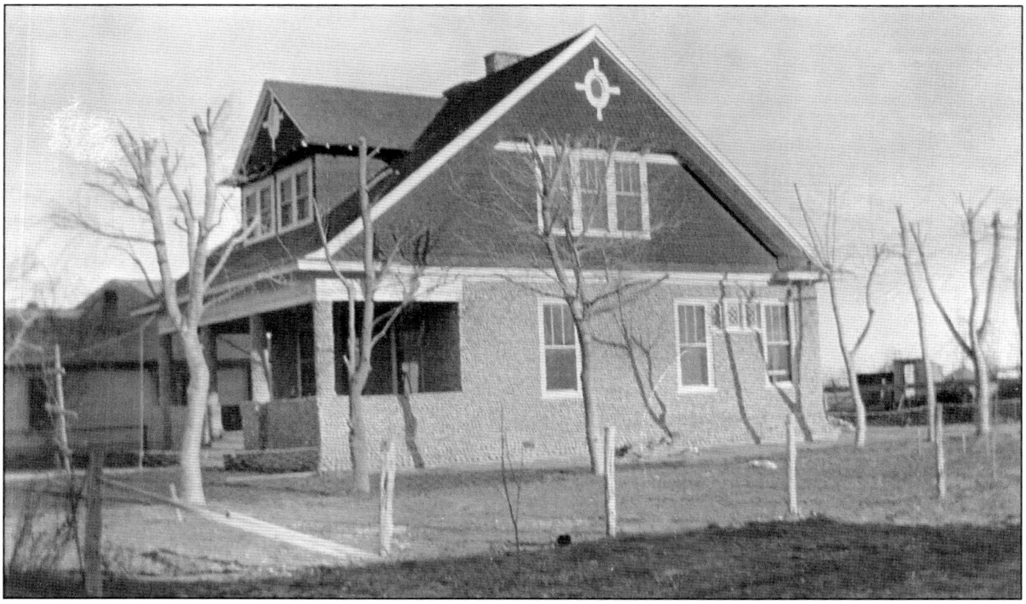

The Moore-Ward house is shown in 1911. Today, the Artesia Historical Museum and Art Center is located in this house. The young pecan trees shown in this photograph are still alive and doing well, and their pecans are prized by locals. Many locals and tourists enjoy visiting the museum each year to learn about Artesia's history.

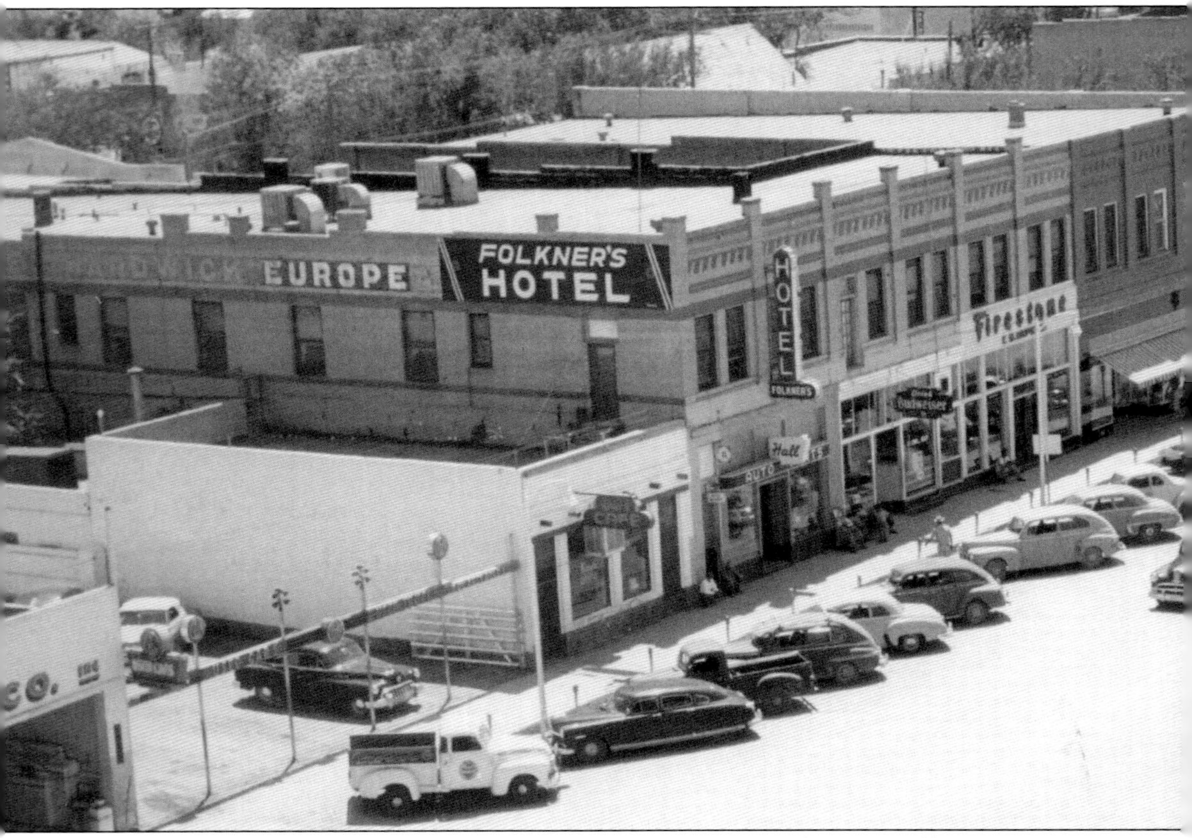

Built between 1906 and 1910, the Hardwick Hotel was purchased by L.E. Folkner in June 1928. It was located on the south side of Main Street between First and Second Streets. L.E. finally got around to changing the name to the Folkner Hotel in June 1948, some 20 years later. Besides rooms to rent, the hotel offered the King's Café and, by 1949, the Owl Bar downstairs. The hotel was a popular place for oil-field roughnecks to stay on weekends during Artesia's oil-boom days. During Prohibition, it was not uncommon to find men passed out in the halls on Sunday mornings after drinking bootleg liquor all nightlong on Saturday. L.E. was tolerant of this behavior, as he was an oil-field investor and had his own oil-tank company until 1940. Thus, he was personally acquainted with many of the men who overindulged. L.E.'s Folkner Bar was the first to reopen in Artesia after Prohibition was repealed in 1933.

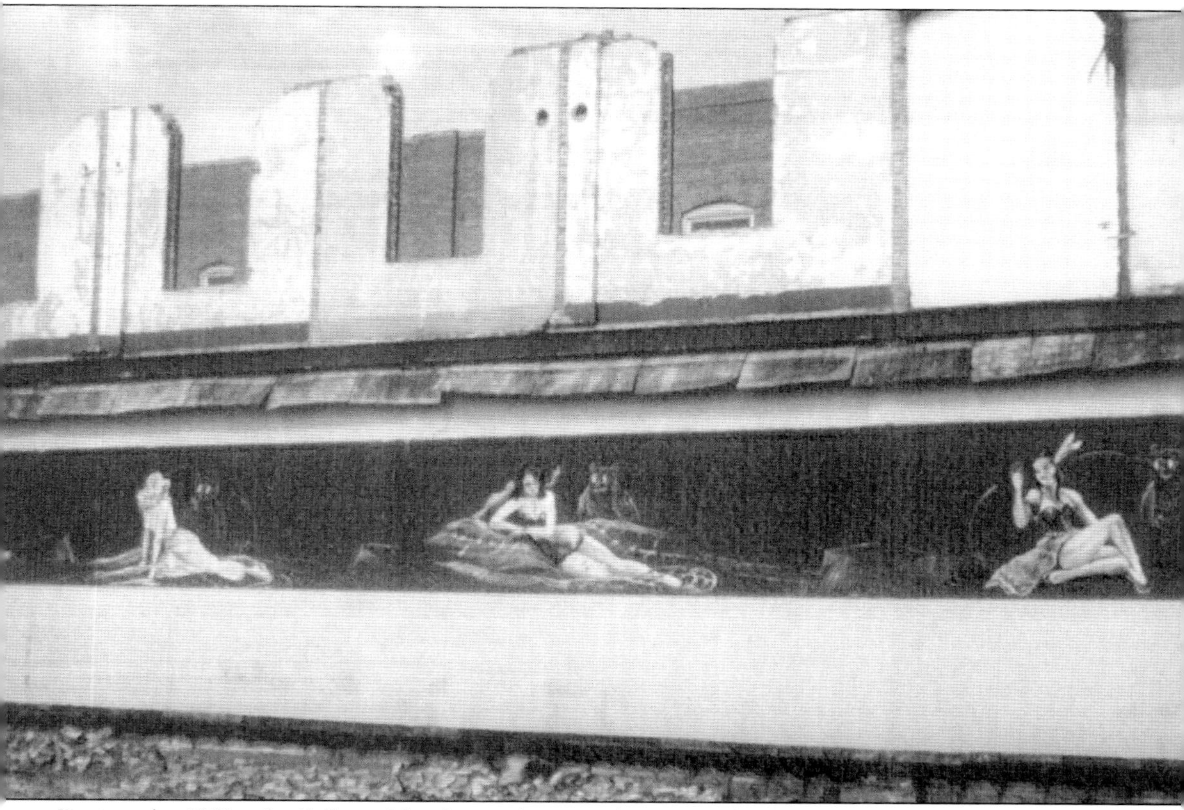

During the 1950s, the Folkner Hotel rented many of its rooms by the week or by the month. A resident who was fond of frequenting the hotel's Owl Bar found himself unable to pay his hotel room bill one day. The indigent resident was an unemployed artist, so he bartered his services to L.E. and Lou Ola Folkner instead of coming up with the cash for his hotel bill. The resulting painting, *The Cowboy and the Dude*, is now owned by L.E. and Lou Ola's granddaughter, and a print of it hangs upstairs in the Artesia Historical Museum and Art Center. This same impoverished artist had also managed to run up quite a large tab in the Owl Bar, so to pay for that, he painted a large mural on the inside wall featuring pinup girls. The Folkner Hotel's east end was torn down in the early 1970s, and the Owl Bar's murals were visible for a day (pictured) before being completely destroyed.

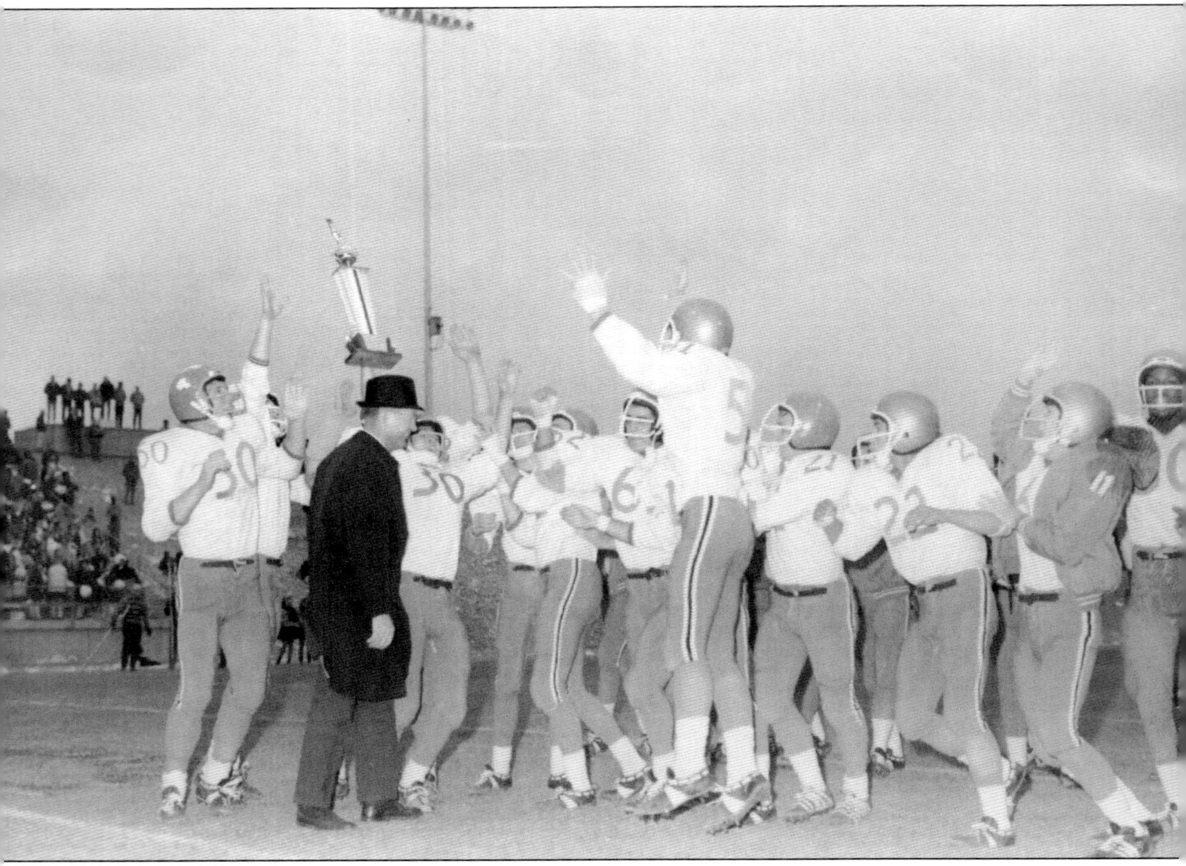

Pictured here, the Artesia High School Bulldogs football team celebrates a sixth championship victory in 1969. The Bulldogs have won many state titles since their first championship in 1957. Artesia's first football field was finished in 1939 and named Morris Field after city manager P.V. "Pearly" Morris. It was built at a cost $48,026.18, and Pearly personally visited quarries all over New Mexico to select the native stone used in the construction. In 1939, Artesia hosted the state's first high school championship game, the Gateway Bowl. The Bulldogs did not qualify to play that year, but Artesia went on to host the Gateway Bowl in 1940 and 1941. Following World War II, championship high school football was finally revived in New Mexico in 1953, and the Bulldogs played their last game in Morris Field in November 1966, beating the Highland Hornets 40-14 for the state championship.

Nine

Sports—The Tradition Continues

Artesia is known as the "City of Champions" and is famous across the state for its high school football program, but Artesia also has had champions in other sports. The easiest way to spot a Bulldog team member is by uniform color. From 1909, the school colors were orange and black, chosen to match those of Princeton University. Sometime in the 1950s, the colors switched to orange and white (with black as an accent). White or black, it doesn't really matter—what matters is the orange.

Since 1957, the Artesia Bulldog football team has won many state championships: 1957, 1964, 1966, 1967, 1968, 1969, 1974, 1975, 1976, 1978, 1980, 1982, 1983, 1984, 1987, 1992, 1993, 1994, 1996, 1997, 1998, 2001, 2003, 2004, 2006, 2007, 2010, 2014, 2015, and 2017—with the hope of many more to come. Several former Bulldogs have gone on to play in college and professional football.

Artesians Fred Brainard and Carl Manda both succeeded in professional baseball careers. Fred played baseball after graduating from Artesia High School in 1910 and then again after serving in World War I. Carl started his professional minor-league career in 1909 with the Kansas Lyons, playing second and third base. In 1914, Carl made his major-league debut with the Chicago White Sox. He retired in 1925–1926 and returned to Artesia.

Although Artesia was never able to support its own professional major-league baseball team, the town did get a glimpse of it with the Artesia Giants and Artesia Dodgers; both teams were part of the class D Sophomore League. The Giants were here in 1958–1960 and were affiliated with the San Francisco Giants. The Dodgers played in Artesia during 1960–1961 and were affiliated with the Los Angeles Dodgers.

In the 1950s, Artesia also had its own basketball team, the Artesia Travelers. The team was part of the Amateur Athletic Union.

Soccer, golf, and tennis are all popular sports in Artesia today, as are hunting and sport shooting. As always, Artesia has something for everyone.

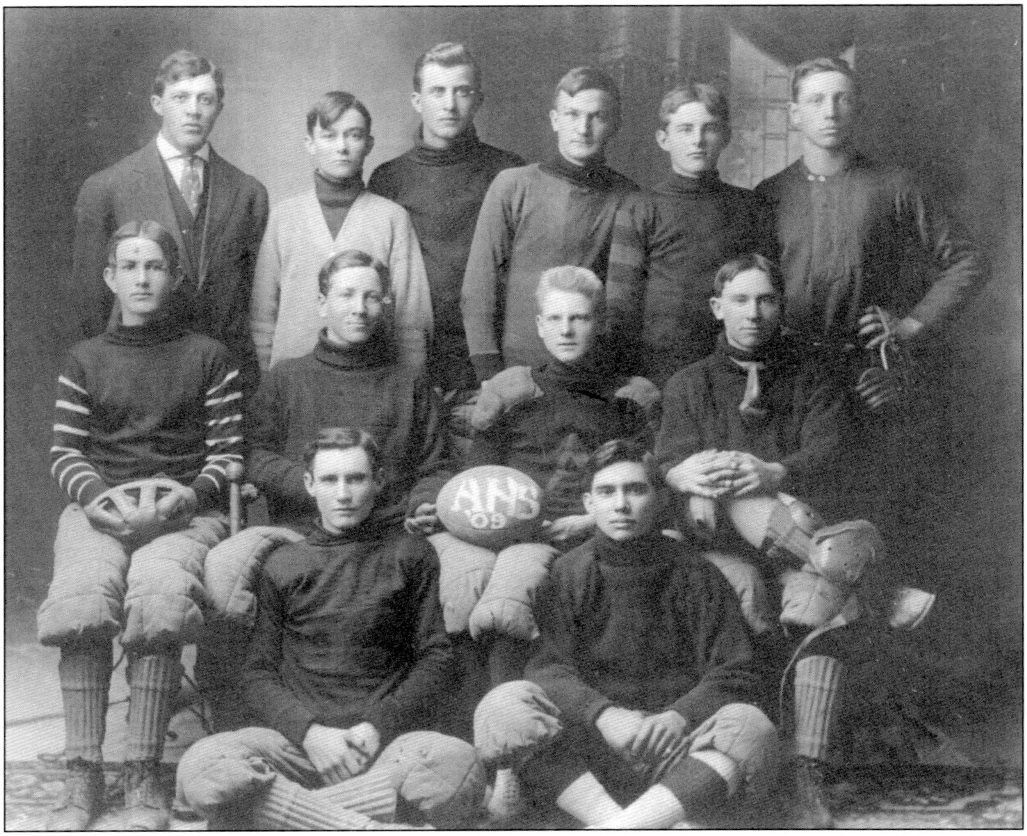

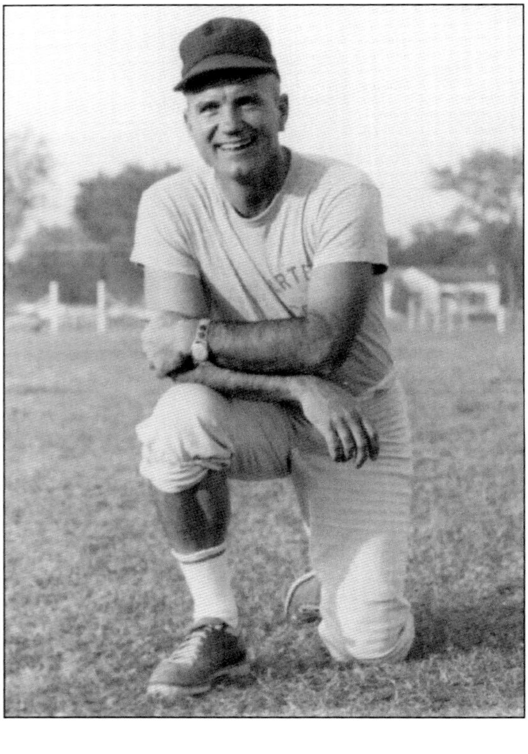

The first Bulldog team and coach are pictured in 1909. From left to right are (first row) right halfback Lafayette Greicher and left tackle Molar Temple; (second row) left end Oscar Harper, right tackle George Threlkeld, quarterback Noble Brainard, and left halfback Robert White; (third row) coach ? Rose, center Collin Gerrells, right guard Adlai Feather, left guard and team captain Clarence Kepple, right end Frank Daniels, and fullback Fred Brainard.

The Bulldogs have had many excellent coaches throughout the years. Coach L.G. Henderson, pictured here in 1963, led the Bulldogs to five state championships during his career in Artesia from 1960 to 1973. Mike Phipps, a former Bulldog player, succeeded L.G. as coach and won seven more championships. L.G.'s son Cooper Henderson followed the lead of L.G., Mike, T.W. Harvey, and Barry Coffman as coach in 1989.

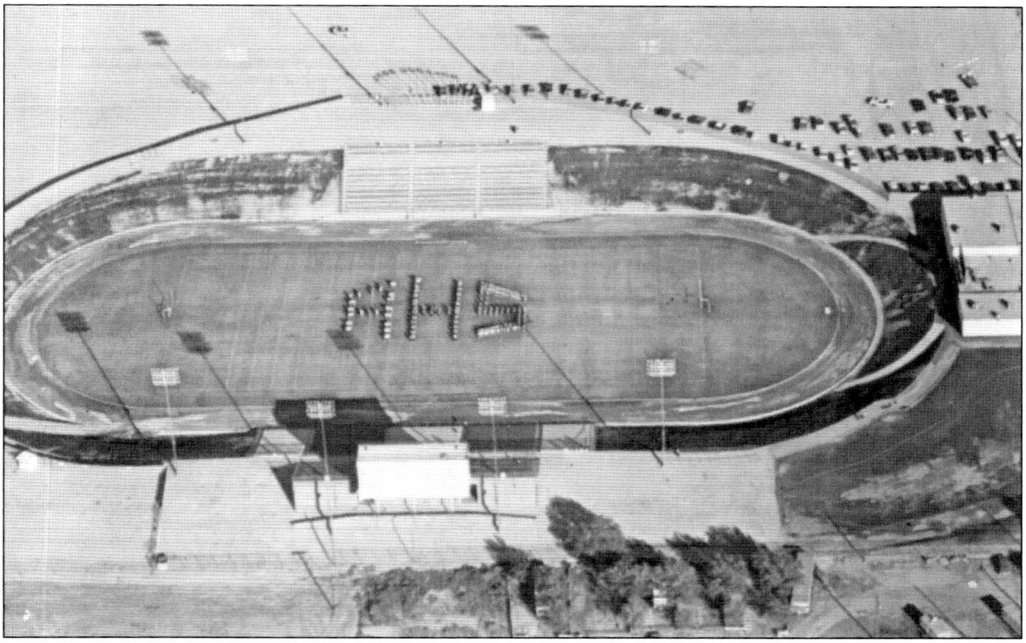

In the photograph above, Artesia's Bulldog Bowl is shown soon after construction in 1967. The stadium provided a newer and larger location for Artesia Bulldog football games. Below, Artesia High School's 1924 football team poses with its coach, H.J. Kaiser. As evident in the photograph, players' helmets at that time were made of leather.

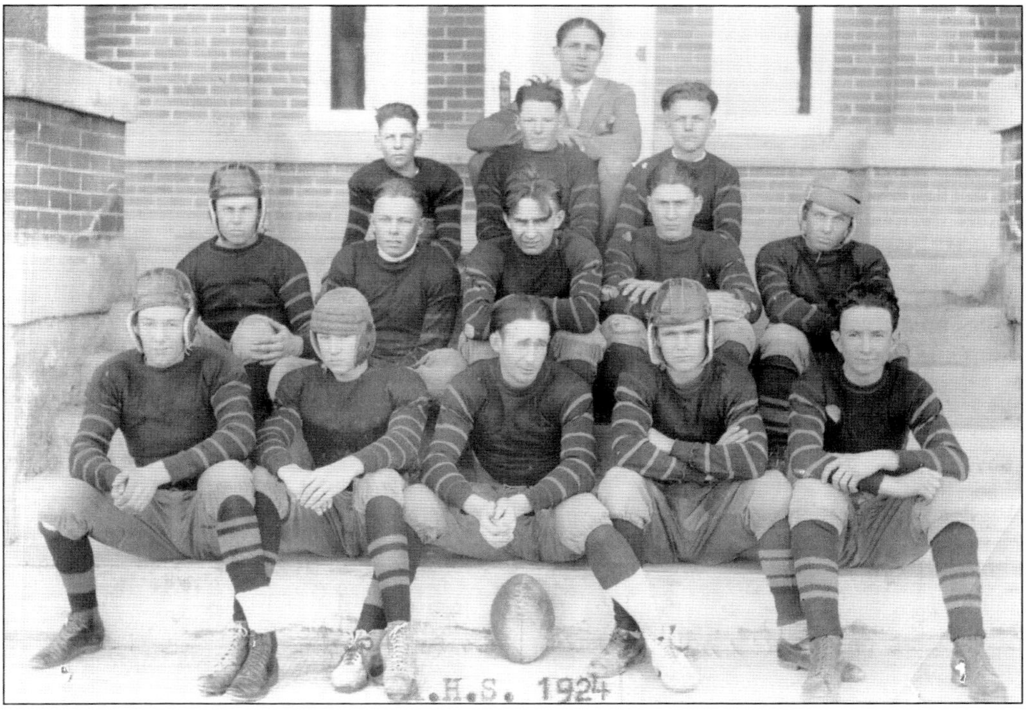

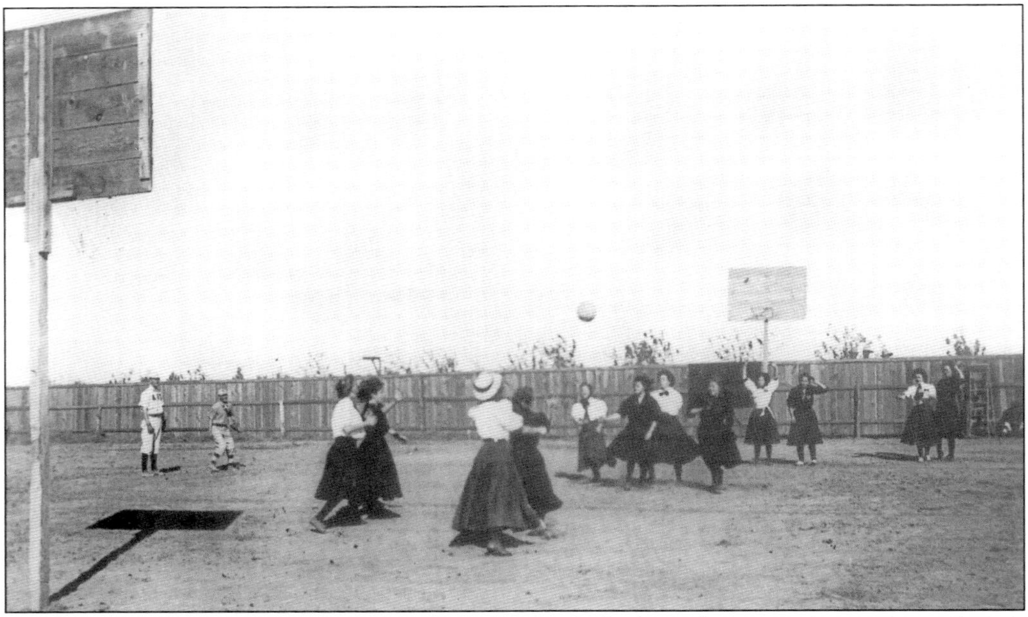

In the photograph above, the Artesia High School girls' basketball team is playing Roswell High School's team in October 1908. Artesia is in the dark tops, and the girls' uniforms include skirts. The 1910 Artesia High School girls' basketball team is shown below. From left to right are Bertha Speck (goal), Beulah Stagner (center), Valeria White (jumping center), Margaret Owen (guard), Gertrude Shockley (substitute), Helen Springer (guard and team captain), and Ola Acord (goal). A note written on the back of this photograph indicates that Valeria is the best player on the team, although Helen is also cited as a fine player.

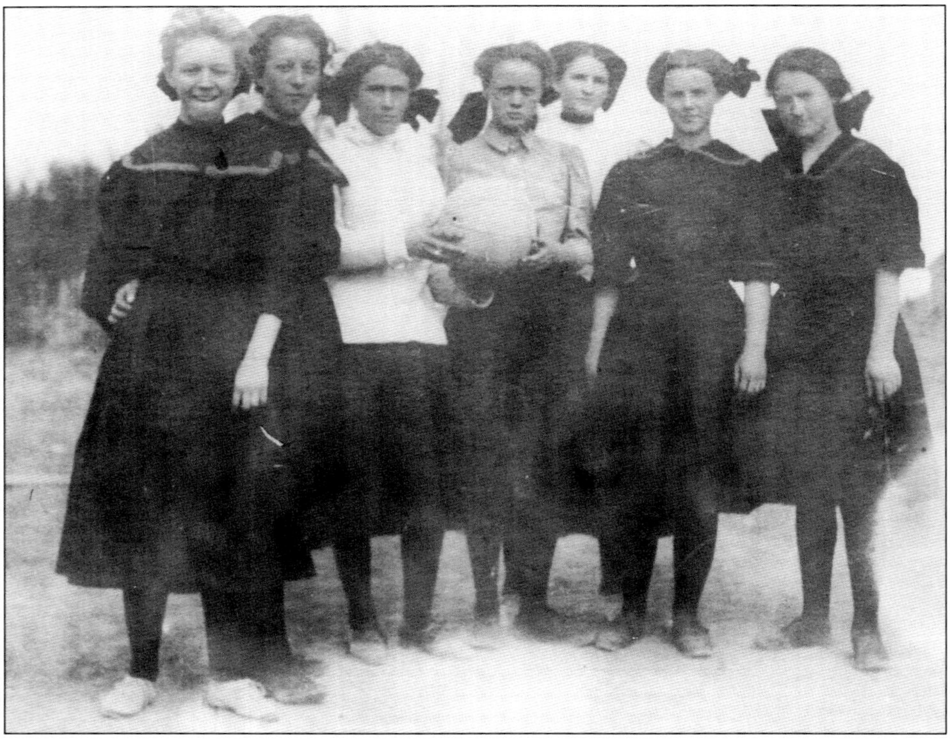

Over the years, uniform requirements for girls have changed. In this photograph of the Artesia High School girls' basketball team of 1919, the uniforms have changed from skirts to bloomers and from fitted shirts to looser blouses. From left to right are (first row) Gladys Cowan and Alva Lee Morthland; (second row) Bertha Shattuck, Mary McCaw, and Velma Smith; (third row) Etta Burns, Ethel Bullock, and Mary Awalt.

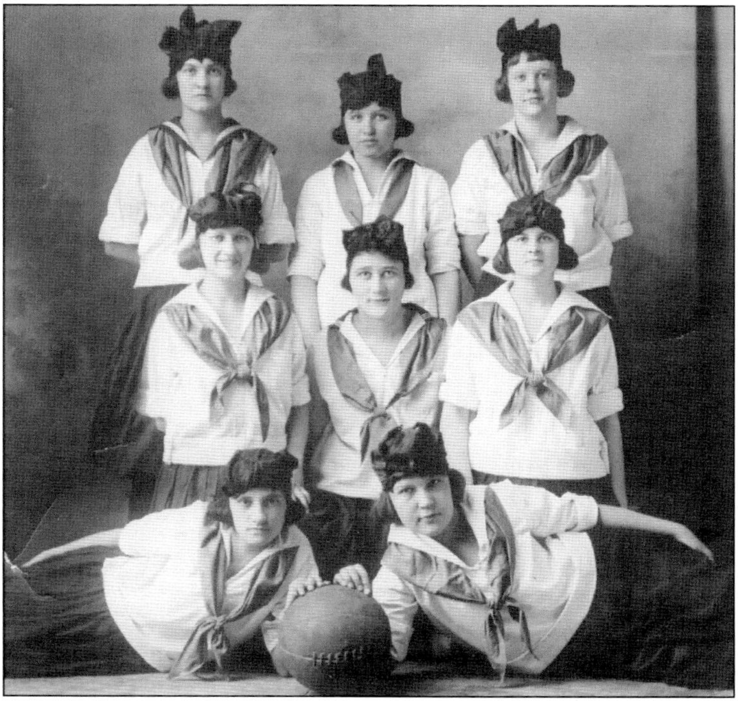

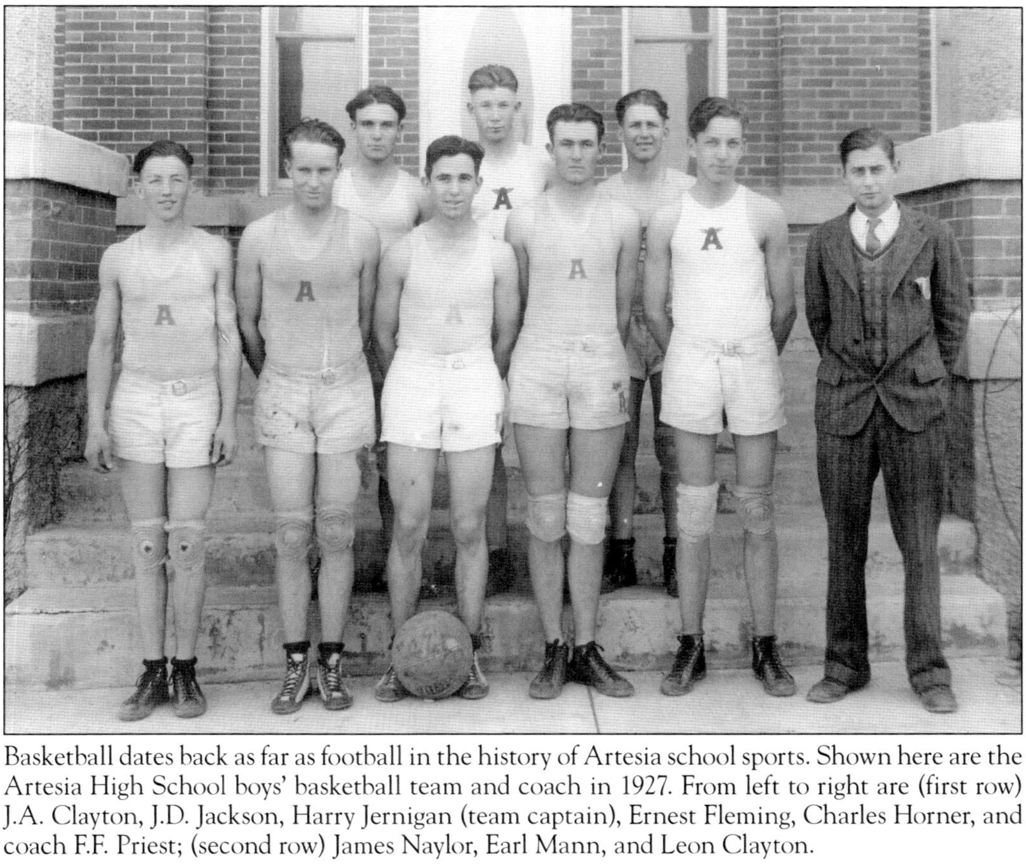

Basketball dates back as far as football in the history of Artesia school sports. Shown here are the Artesia High School boys' basketball team and coach in 1927. From left to right are (first row) J.A. Clayton, J.D. Jackson, Harry Jernigan (team captain), Ernest Fleming, Charles Horner, and coach F.F. Priest; (second row) James Naylor, Earl Mann, and Leon Clayton.

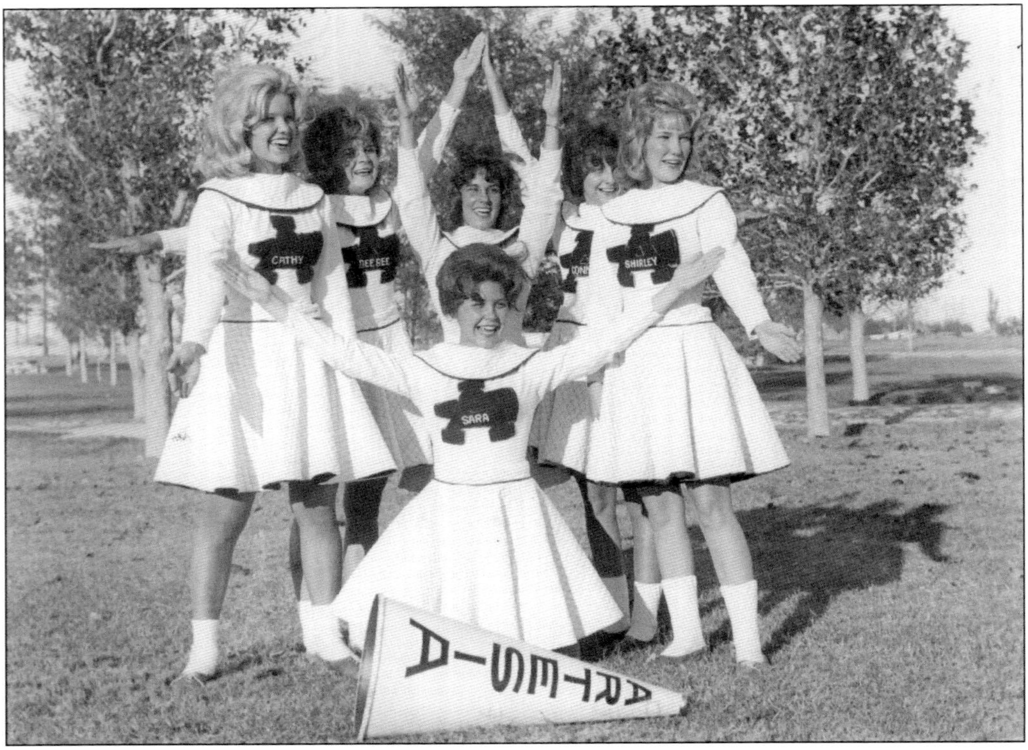

Along with the fans cheering on the team, there is always a cheerleading squad guiding spectators and entertaining them with their routines. Above, Artesia High School's 1963 cheerleaders strike a pose in their new uniforms. They are (first row) Sara Stromberg; (second row), from left to right, Cathy Parry, Dee Bee Worthington, Barbara Landrum, Connie Taylor, and Shirley Compton. Besides cheering at all the games, cheerleaders are also responsible for leading pregame pep rallies. In the photograph below, Artesia High School cheerleaders lead a pep rally in 1987. The differences in the uniforms from 1963 to 1987 are apparent.

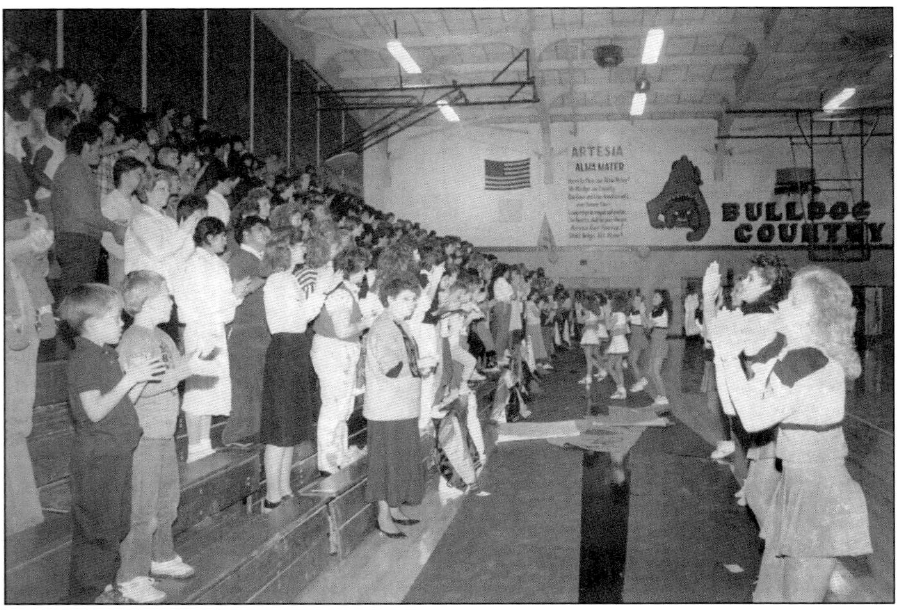

Fred Brainard played on Artesia High School's original Bulldogs football team, and after graduating became a professional minor-league baseball player. In the photograph at right, Fred is shown during his time playing for the New York Giants around 1915. Below, Fred is pictured with fellow New York Giants players in 1915–1916. From left to right are George Kelly, Jim Thorpe, Fred, and an unidentified teammate. After serving in the Army during World War I, Fred returned to playing baseball and later managed the Newark (New Jersey) Bears and the Dallas (Texas) Steers. Artesia's Brainard Park baseball field was named after Fred and dedicated in 1951.

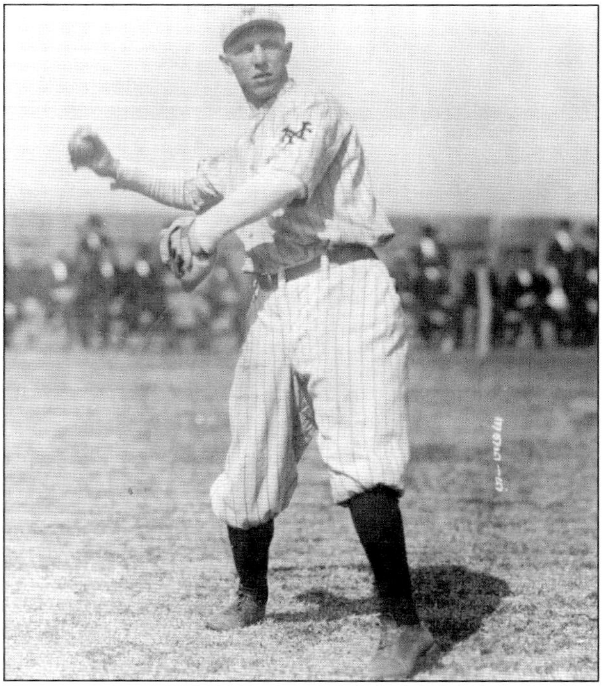

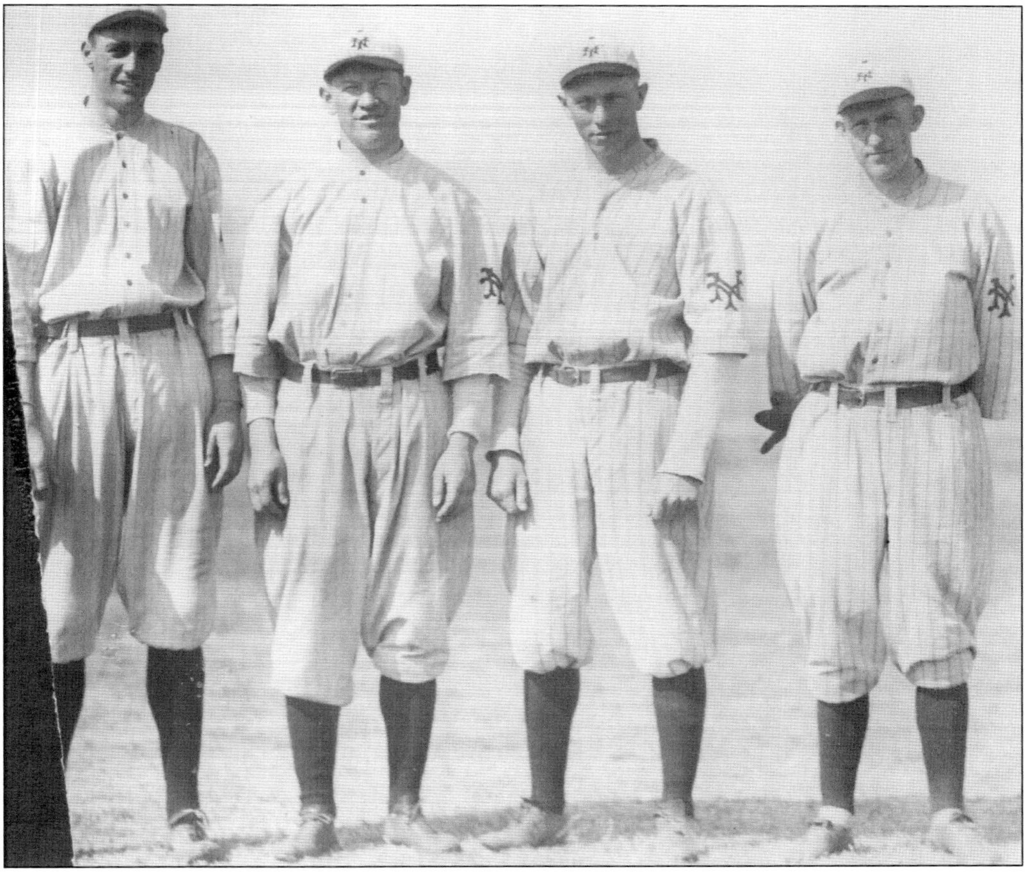

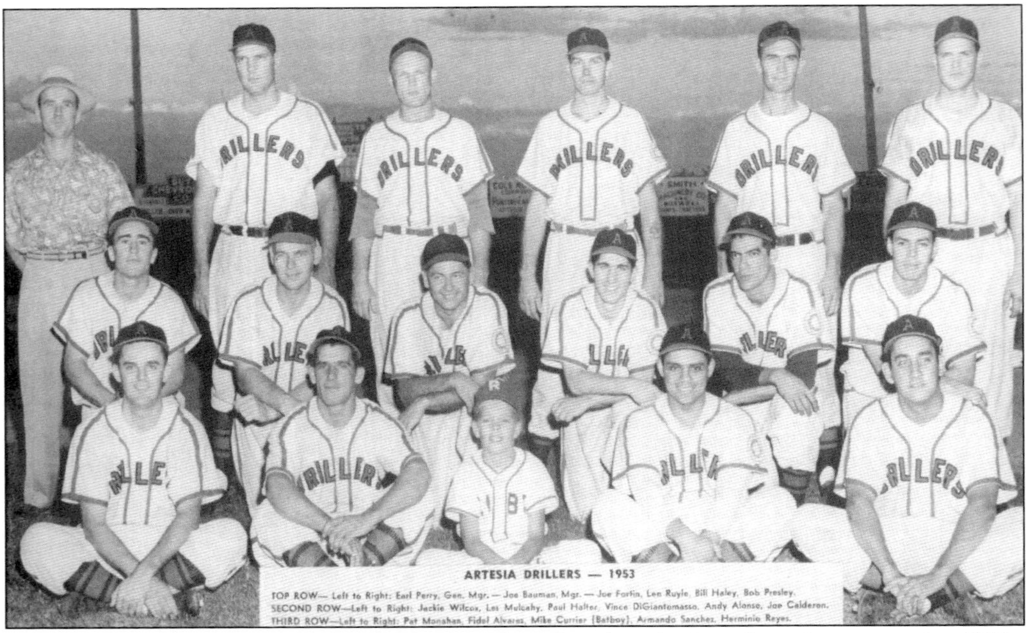

Artesia had two minor-league baseball teams that played in the Longhorn League in the 1950s. The Artesia Drillers were active in 1951–1953. The 1953 team is pictured above, including record-setter Joe Bauman, second from the left in the third row. Bauman's achievement of the greatest number of home runs in a single season was set a year after leaving the Drillers, although he made the record-setting hit during a game at Artesia's Brainard Park when playing for the Roswell Rockets. Bauman's mark of 72 was not toppled until 2001 (by Barry Bonds). The Artesia Drillers became the Artesia Numexers in 1954, and the team was active for another year before it disbanded. Below, the Numexers are shown in 1954. Both teams had a loyal batboy in Mike Currier, who is seated in the center of the first row in both photographs.

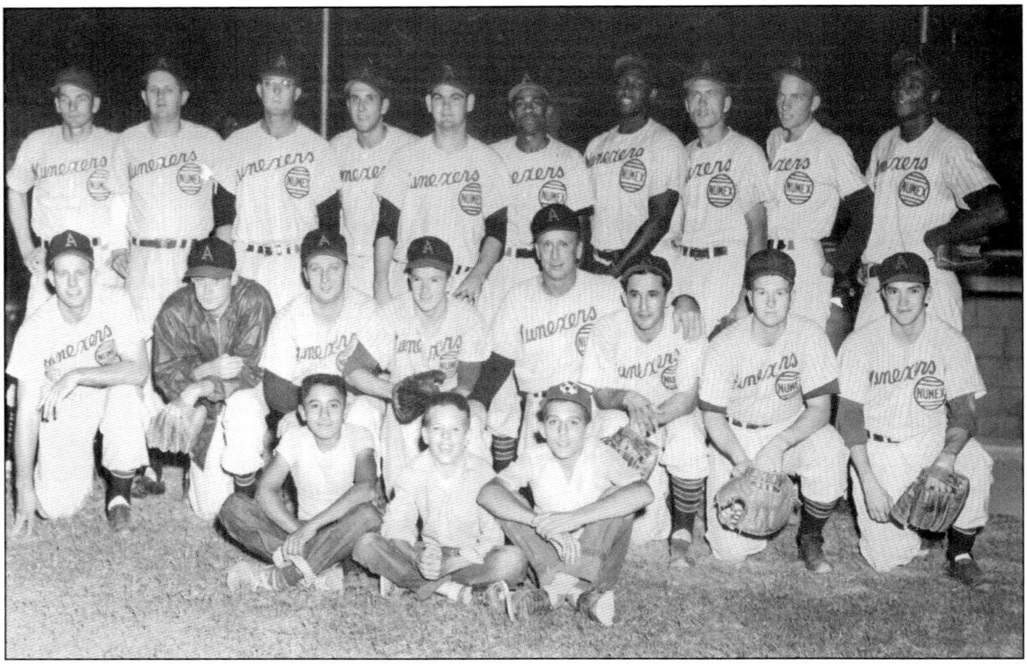

Not only are organized sports popular in Artesia, but fishing has always been a favorite of families and friends. At right, Joe Clayton (far left) is shown in the early 1900s with a group of friends after a day of fishing at Lake McMillan, about 20 miles south of Artesia. The Pecos River fed into Lake McMillan, which supplied irrigation water to farmers in Carlsbad after the artesian well aquifer dried up south of Artesia. Seen below, Lake McMillan was a very popular fishing spot. And by late summer, when the water level dropped because of irrigation, people joked that they could wade out and grab the fish by hand.

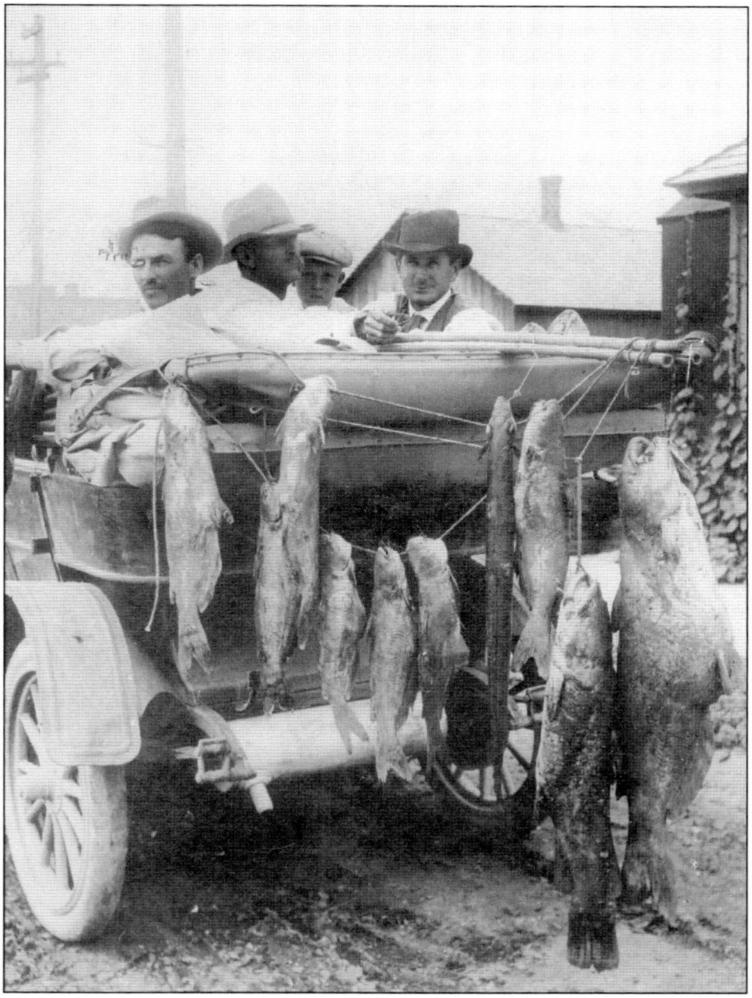

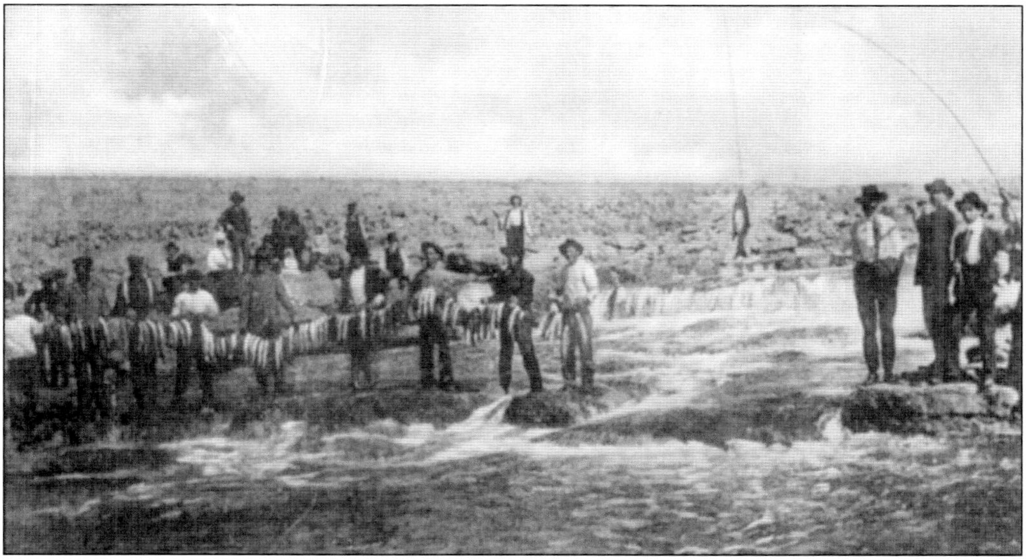

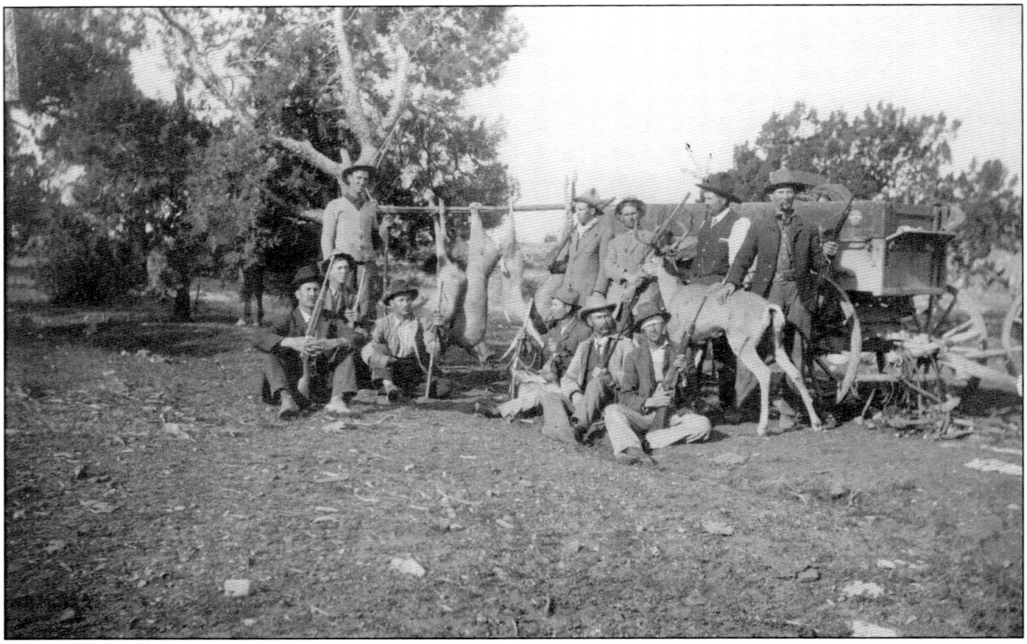

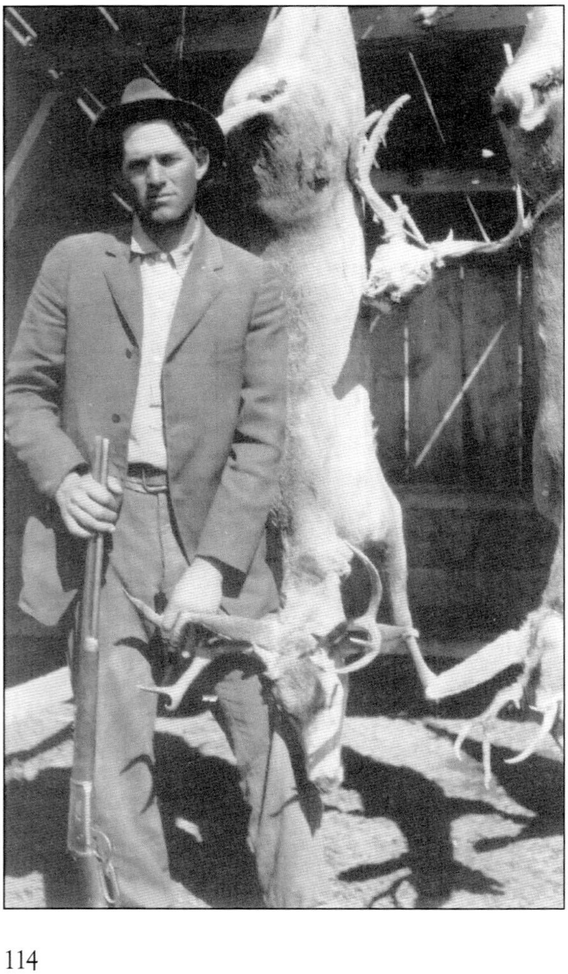

Along with fishing, hunting for wild game in the area around Artesia has always been popular. Hunters could find a wide variety of quarry in the plains of southeast New Mexico and in the neighboring mountains. Many sportsmen took great pride in their trophies. Organized hunting parties were a chance for groups of friends to get together and enjoy a camping trip. In the photograph above, a hunting party hosted by Harvey Muncy enjoys time in the mountains in 1910. In the photograph at left, Albert Richards shows off his trophy around 1911.

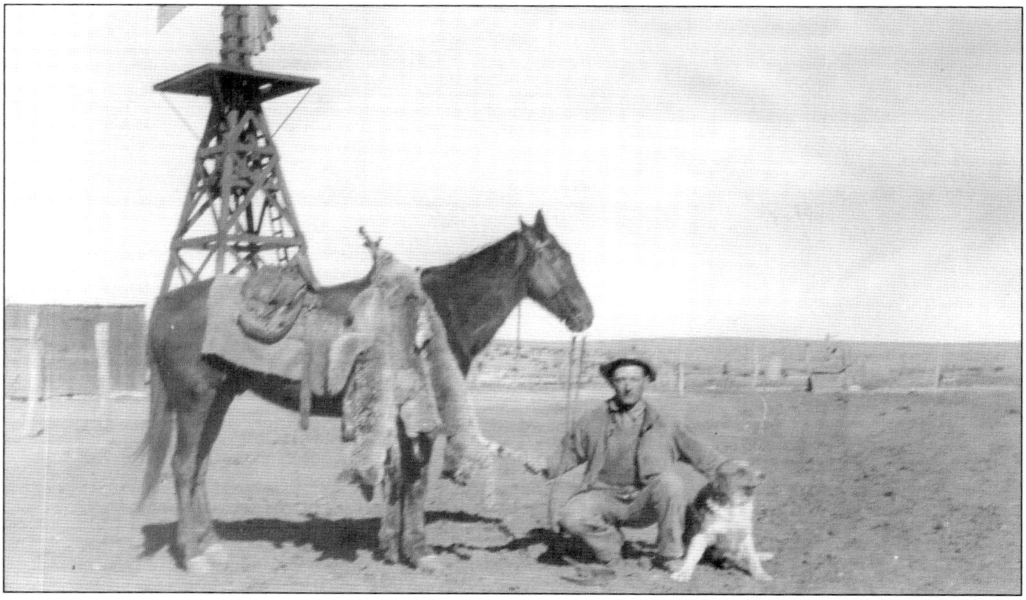

Above, E.P. Tatman displays his hunting trophies in 1923. Instead of more traditional game, E.P. chose to hunt predators that were a danger to his farm animals. Besides the recreation of hunting, local sportsmen also enjoyed the variety of meat their game provided to their diets. In the early days, hunters skinned and prepared game themselves. Later, the Artesia Locker Plant provided this service for them. The locker plant also offered Deepfreeze storage of meats and would grind sausage to order. Shown below around 1950 are, from left to right, C.H. Winters, Allen Pears, and owner Sie Hogsett.

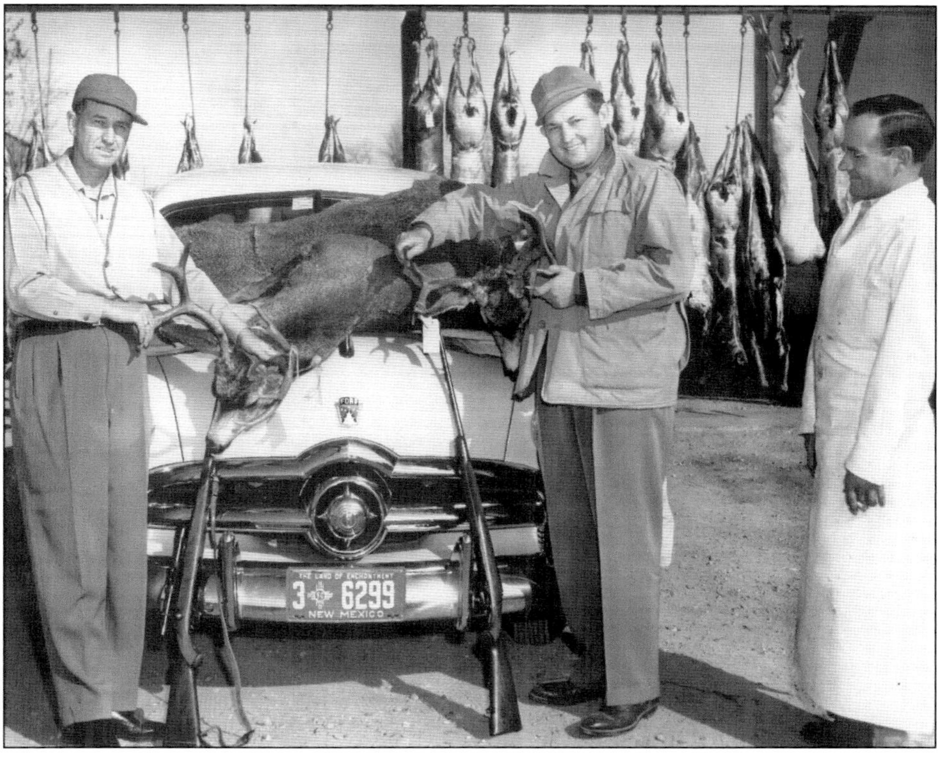

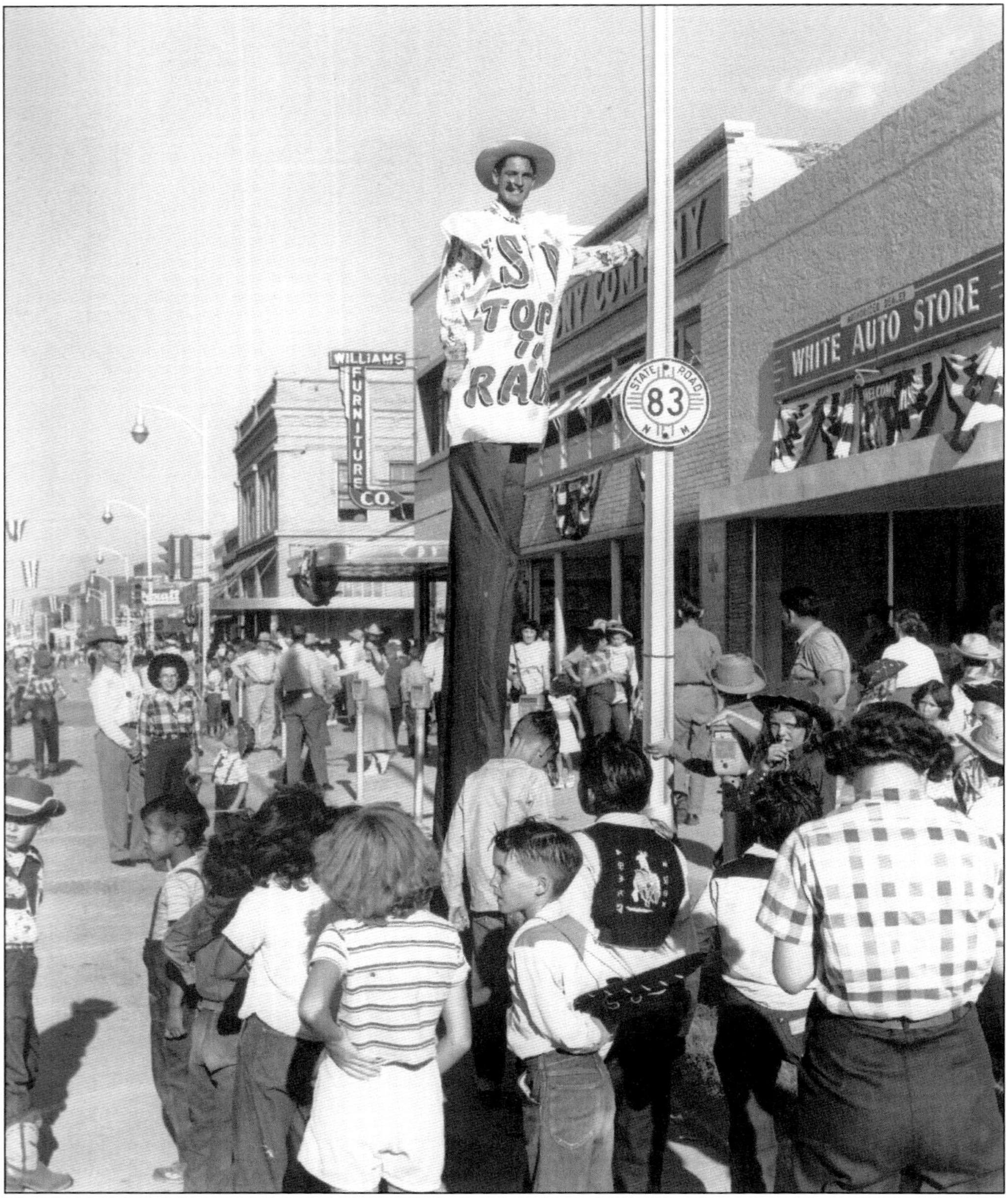

Community celebrations have always been popular in Artesia, and parades remain a local crowd-pleaser for adults and children alike, giving everyone a chance to socialize and catch up on each other's news. Here, many local residents have turned out to watch a rodeo/county fair parade in the early 1950s. This gave some people a chance to dress up in their best Western outfits. Local businesses, such as radio station KSVP, took advantage of events like this one to advertise their services and specials to the public, whether through signs displayed in business windows or worn by Jack Knorr on stilts—"KSVP Tops in Radio."

Ten

Celebrations of Yesterday and Today

Artesia has always celebrated local and national events in style. From the earliest agricultural festivals to civic achievements to commemorations of important milestones in local and national history, every festivity has included a wide variety of activities designed to please and entertain everyone in the community. Every theme has been different, and each occasion has included specifically designed events. Just about every important celebration has been kicked off with a parade on Main Street—but not all. Another important component has been food; barbecues and cook-offs have always been crowd-pleasers and have drawn in those who like to cook and as well as those who like to eat!

Monumental anniversaries are more than enough reason to have a good time. Artesia's Golden Jubilee celebration in 1955 included a 1905 fashion show—with many residents showing off their keepsake wardrobes—and many other activities. In August 1967, the city commemorated cattle king John Chisum's arrival in the Lower Pecos Valley with the Chisum Trail Centennial, featuring two full days of events at various locations. A horseshoe-pitching contest took place both days in Central Park, along with an Old-Timers Reunion. Central Park hosted fashion shows, put on by Chisum Centennial Queen candidates, of historic and modern clothes; and Miss New Mexico 1967, Rosemary Brown of Carlsbad, made a special appearance along with the Country Folks, who performed a selection of Western music. The Waterdogs swim team put on an exhibition at the municipal swimming pool, and the College of Artesia Drama Group performed two evenings of "old-time mellerdramas." A fiddling contest was held at Morris Field along with a big barbecue.

Artesia's celebration of the American bicentennial in 1976 featured a formal flag-raising ceremony and a memorial tree-planting dedication in Eagle Draw Park. Also, the Artesia Arts Council and the Artesia Bicentennial Committee presented a special performance titled *Behind the Front*.

New Mexico's statehood centennial in 2012 is the latest event to spark the need to celebrate, and Artesia's festivities will no doubt be memorable.

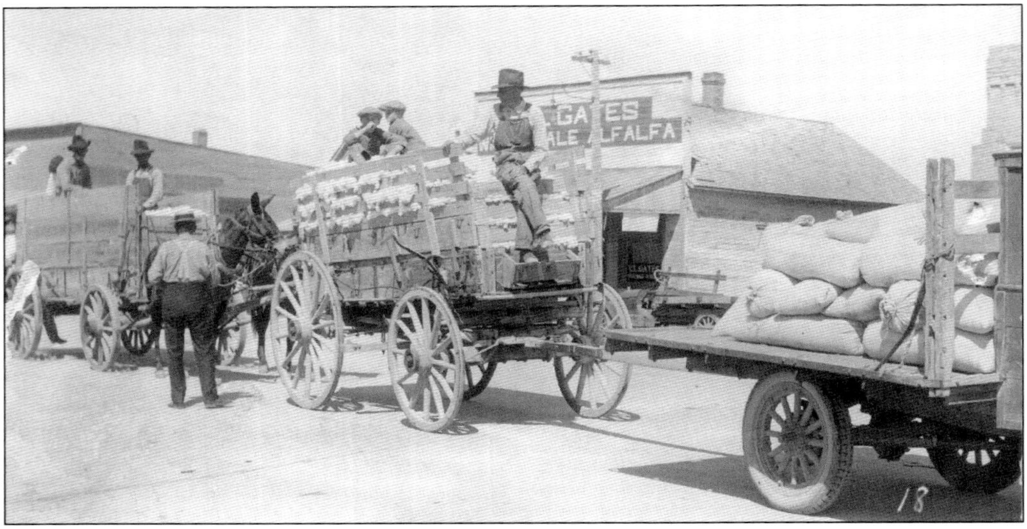

The Cotton Festival was one of Artesia's earliest community celebrations in the 1900s. Farmers proudly displayed their cotton crops in a procession down Main Street, as shown above. The Cotton Festival quickly evolved into the Alfalfa Festival after farmers realized that alfalfa was outgrowing cotton. The first Alfalfa Festival took place in 1907 with the parade down Main Street shown in the photograph below. After the parade, residents had the opportunity to view and participate in rodeo competitions, baseball games, horse races, footraces, and livestock shows. There was also a carnival with games, a flower show, and music provided by Artesia's Municipal Band.

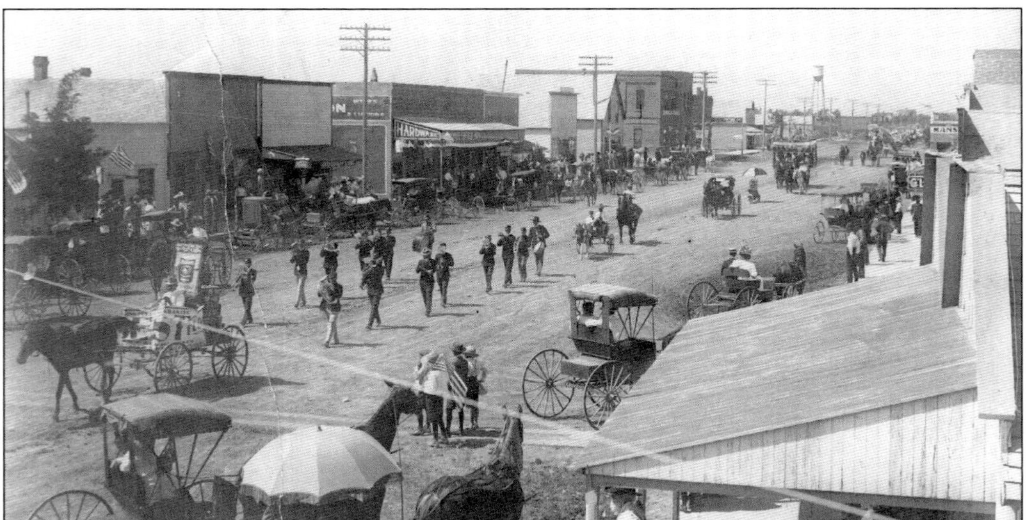

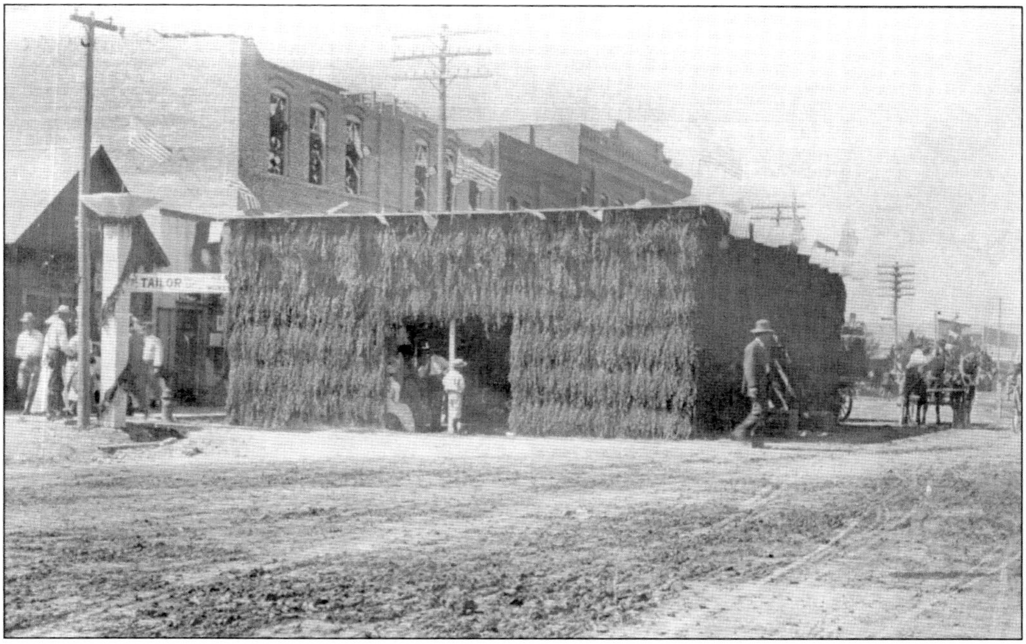

The Alfalfa Festival grew annually, bringing in more and more out-of-town visitors each year thanks to the special fares offered by the Santa Fe Railway. The Pecos Valley Press Association met in Artesia during the festival each year to ensure the event received maximum publicity. The Phantom movie theater offered free shows, and the Spring Lake Spa held special dances and fireworks displays. In 1915 and 1916, the event was renamed the Eddy County Fair and then patriotically postponed until the end of World War I. A featured exhibit in 1915 was the House of Hay on Main Street.

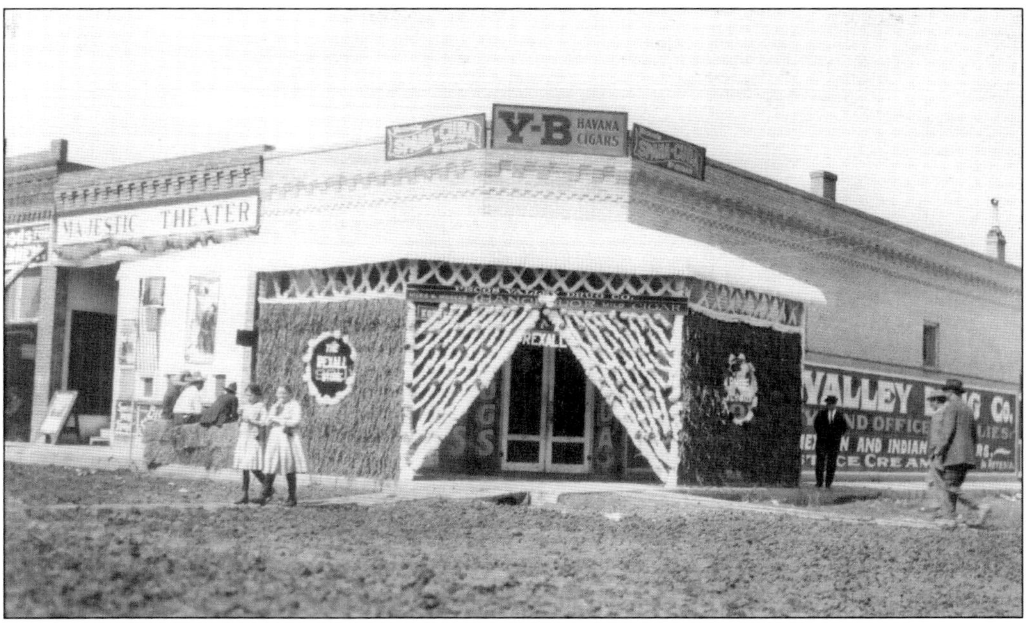

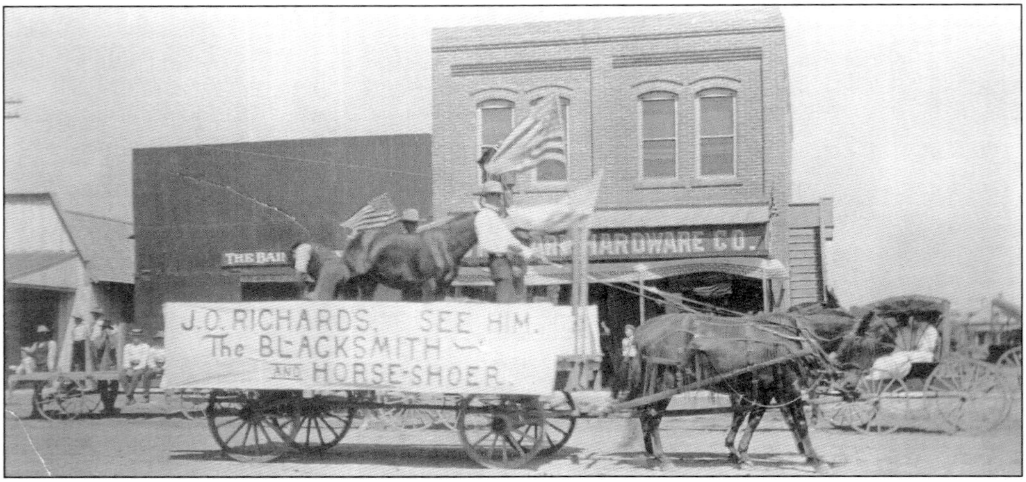

Artesia's Alfalfa Festival was revived in 1923, and things were bigger than ever. In 1923, an automobile was given away in a drawing and the always popular Women's Flower Show was expanded to include fine arts, curios, and cooking demonstrations in the exhibit hall. The Children's Division was also expanded, with an emphasis on agriculture. Prizes were given for the best parade floats and for the "best representation of a fruit, vegetable, or flower in costume" by a child, according to the *Artesia Advocate*. Yet, all this was not enough to save the revived Alfalfa Festival. Oil production had replaced agriculture as the no. 1 industry in the Lower Pecos Valley, and many area artesian wells were starting to dry up and cause a water shortage for large farms.

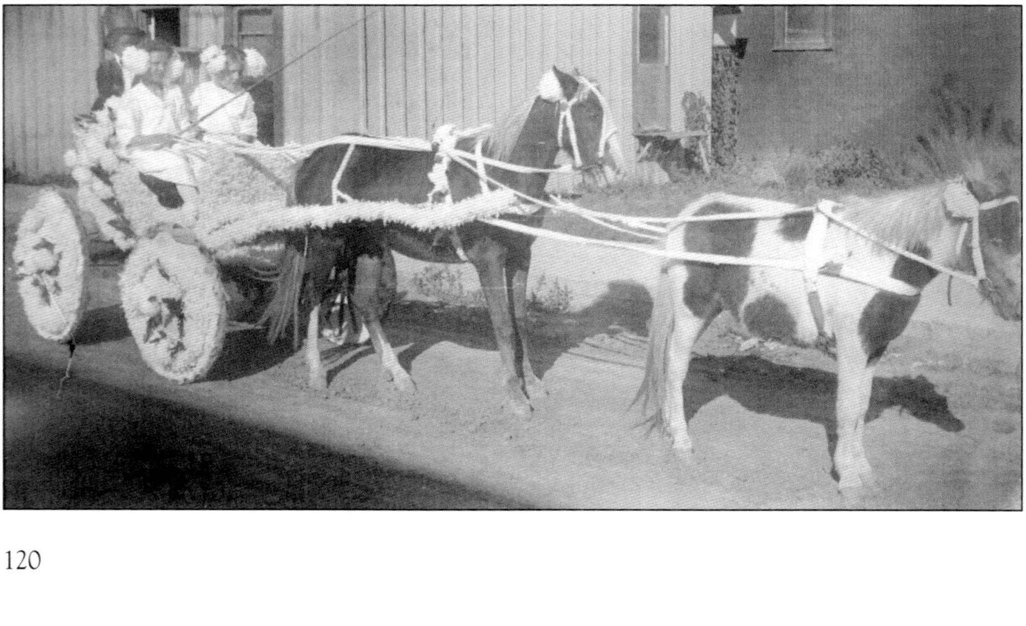

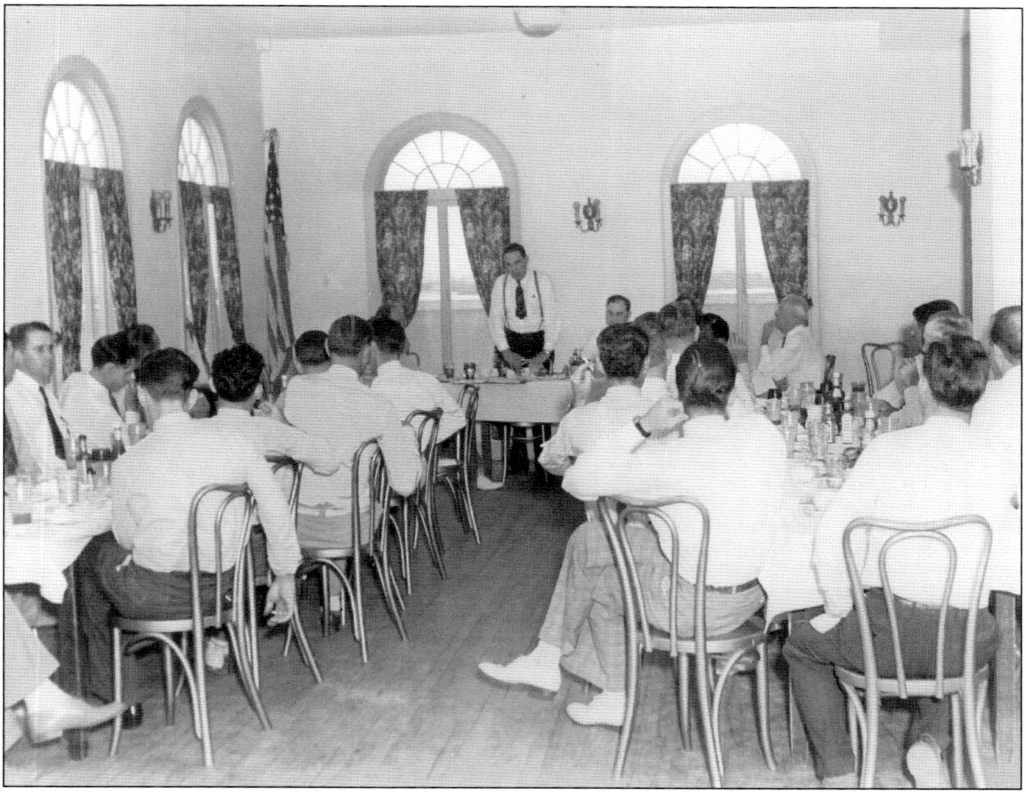

The Civilian Conservation Corps had a camp in Lake Arthur near Artesia, and Artesia received several Work Progress Administration public projects: a municipal swimming pool, new police and fire stations, a new hospital and city hall, a new high school, Morris Field, and a face-lift for Central Park. To celebrate the completion of these projects, Artesia threw a huge party in August 1939, and New Mexico governor John Miles was an honored guest. A luncheon was held in the Artesia Hotel's banquet room, and a community barbecue took place at Central Park for over 4,000 people. Today, several of these sites are still in use, but others have since been torn down.

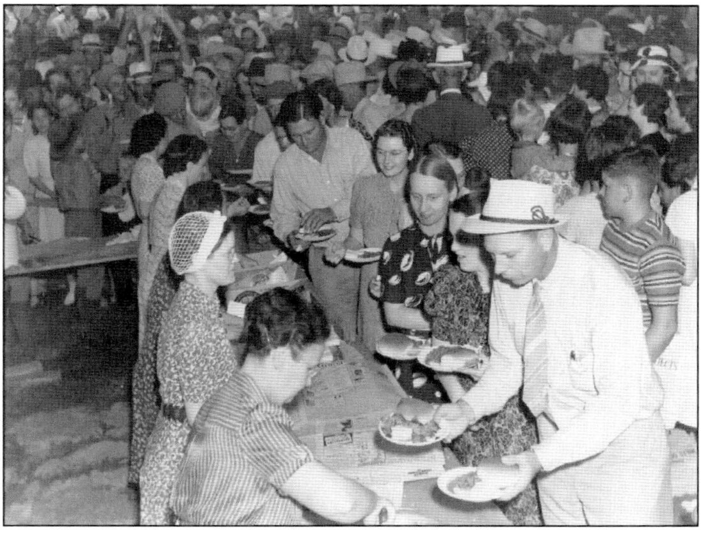

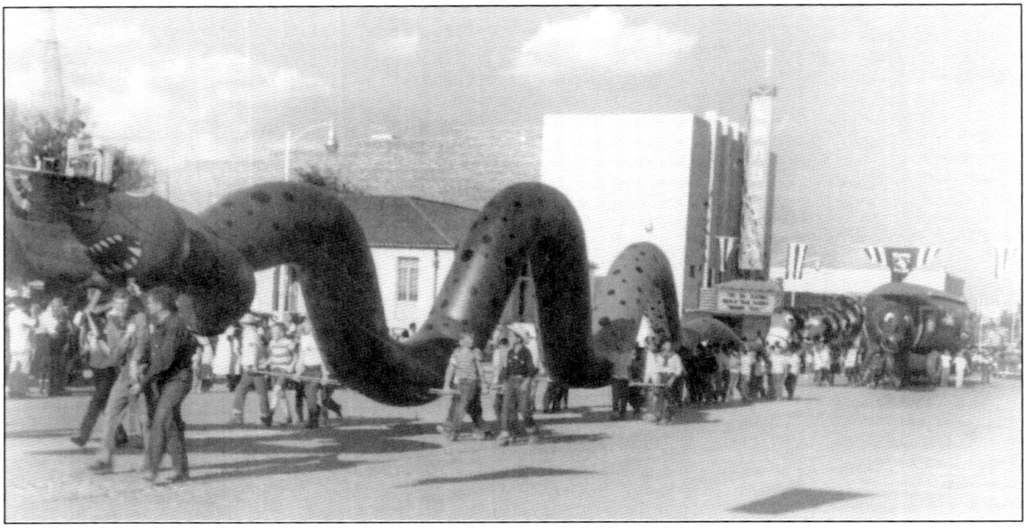

Not every parade in Artesia is the same. Rodeo parades feature livestock, floats, and farm equipment, while homecoming parades focus on sports and student organizations and achievements. Parades for more specialized events, such as a car show, target different audiences and are a great way to advertise at little to no cost. As shown in these photographs, Artesia's 1950 Fourth of July parade, which featured a series of large balloons, was unique. It was considered a great honor for the youngsters of Artesia to be one of the selected handlers of the balloons.

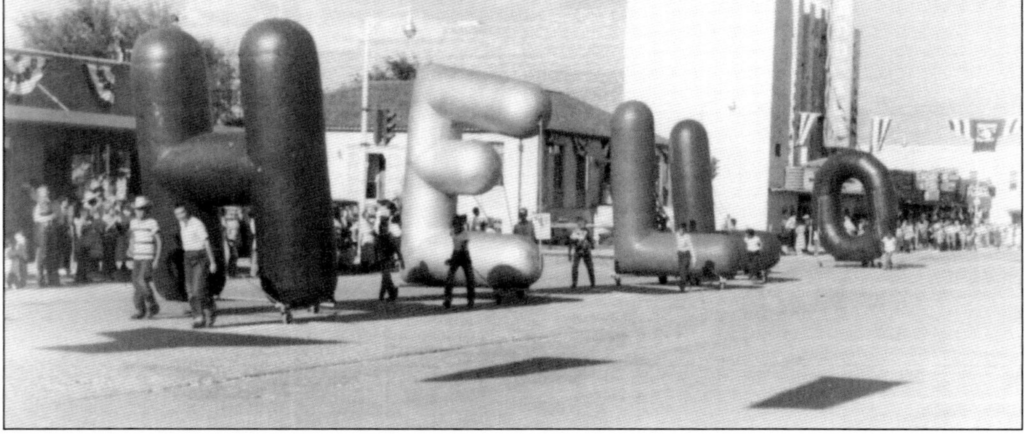

Artesia celebrated its Golden Jubilee in August 1955 with two days of activities. Several competitions were held throughout the celebration. Local men competed in a whisker-growing contest; there were several categories, including the longest, handsomest, and ugliest whiskers and the most impressive mustache. Here, Ernest Scoggin, M. Anderson, and Andy Corbin show off their efforts.

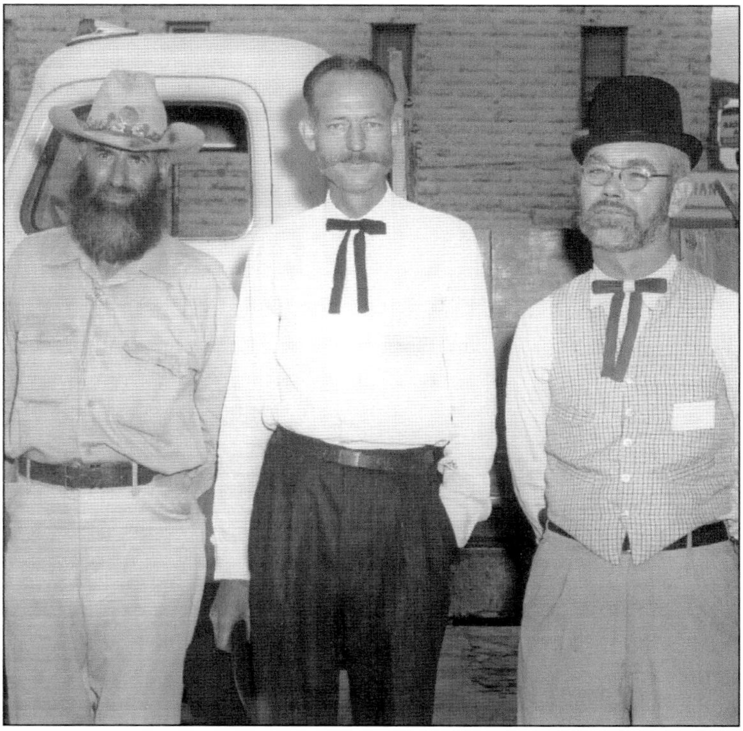

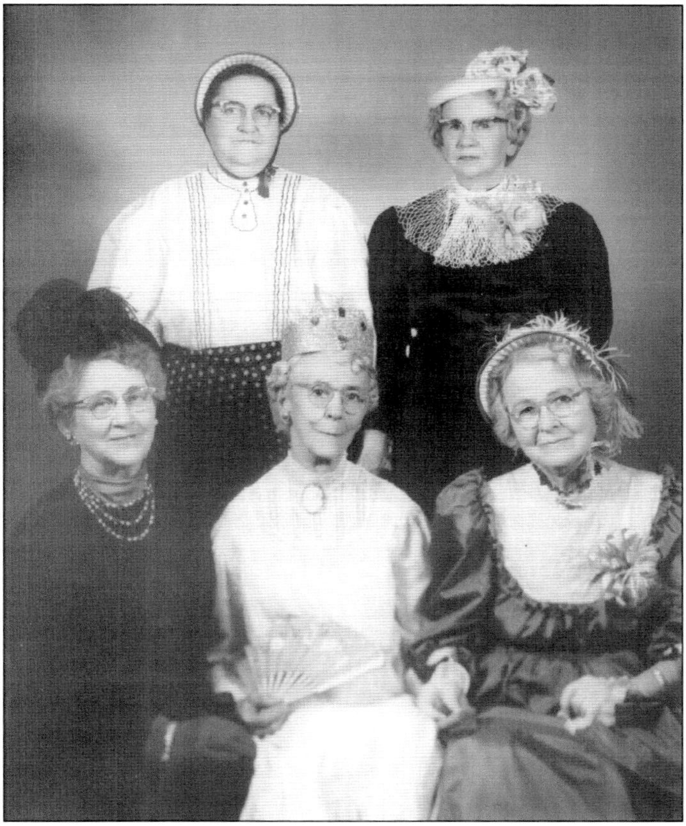

Artesia's Golden Jubilee celebration also included an Old Settler's Picnic, Old-Timer's Reunion, a band concert, several parades, cookouts, and rodeos, and dances each day. A children's swim meet took place at the municipal swimming pool, and a Golden Anniversary Queen was crowned. From left to right are (first row) Nora Clayton, queen Mary Gilbert, and Vena Newman; (second row) Ruby Turknett Amstutz and Dora Carder.

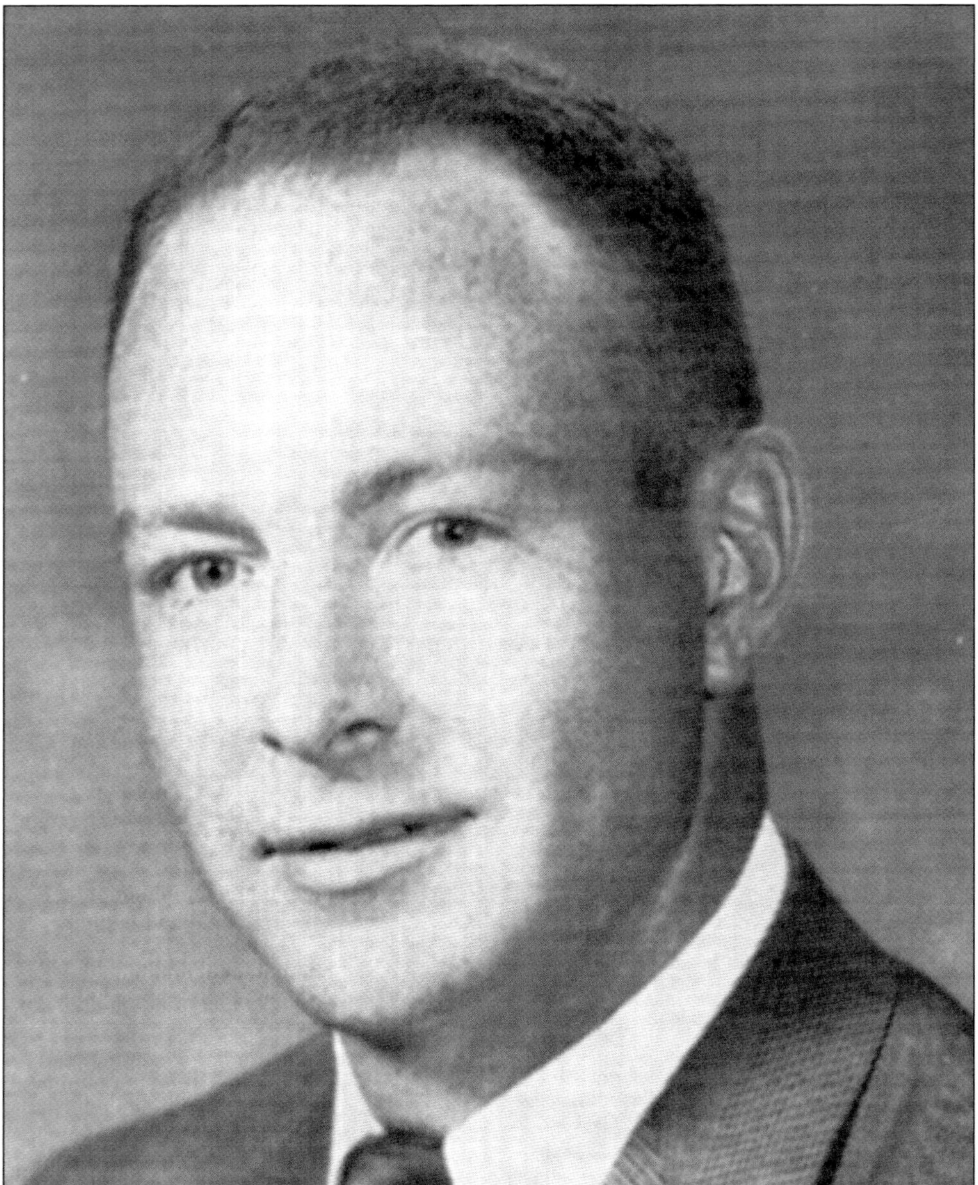

Apollo 14 astronaut Edgar Mitchell graduated from Artesia High School in 1948, and the yearbook listed his hobby as flying. As a student, Edgar had a rival for his girlfriend who tried to scare Ed off by taking him up in a small crop-dusting airplane and doing stunts. Instead of being scared, Edgar landed with a new love—being airborne. After graduation, he earned degrees in industrial management and aeronautical engineering, as well as a doctorate in aeronautics and astronautics. Edgar was one of the men in mission control who helped the troubled Apollo 13 mission make it home safely and was the sixth man to walk on the moon on the Apollo 14 mission in February 1971. Artesia celebrated Edgar Mitchell Day on March 15, 1971, and dedicated the stretch of Highway 285 from Carlsbad to Roswell as the Edgar D. Mitchell Highway. Ed spoke to students and the public that day and participated in a parade in his honor, and the *Artesia Daily Press* also published a special edition for his homecoming.

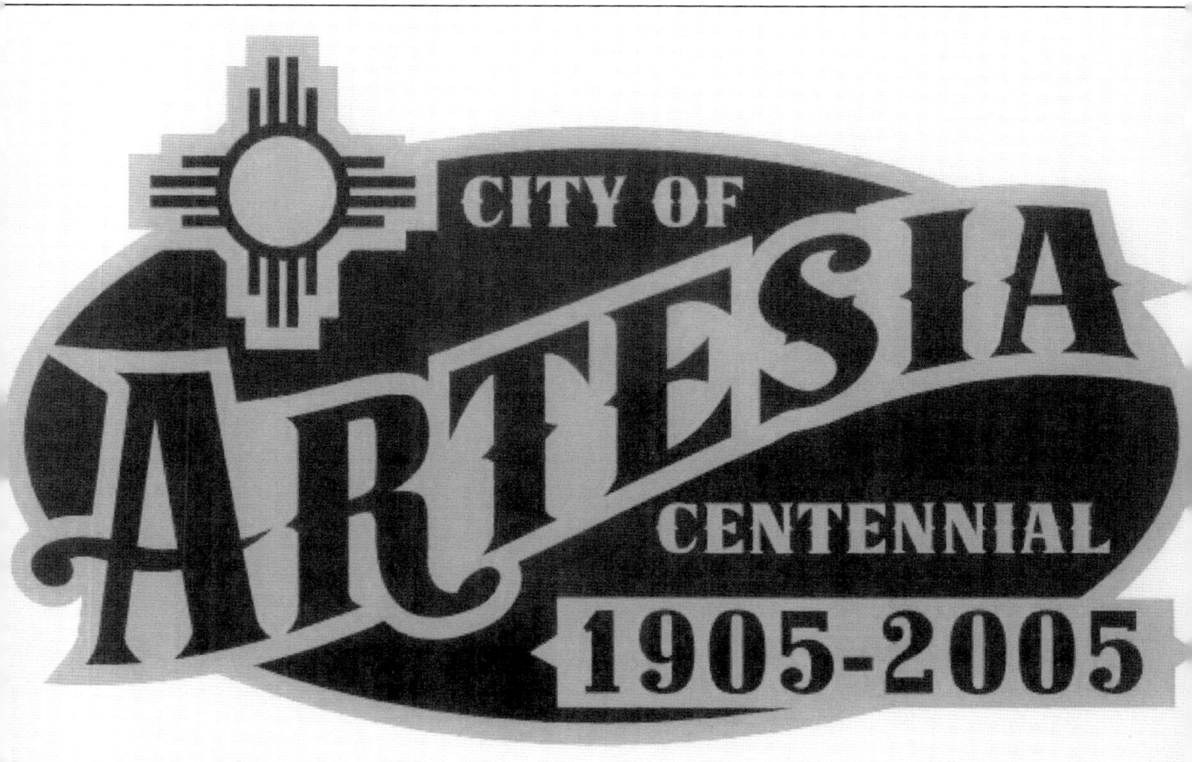

In 2005, the City of Artesia celebrated its long-awaited 100th anniversary with a year's worth of events and activities. The year kicked off with Artesia MainStreet's free New Year's Eve concert featuring the Charlie Daniels Band, and the city threw itself a community birthday party in February that featured a costume contest for the best outfits depicting 1905 fashion. Funding was available from the City of Artesia to help clubs and organizations turn their annual events into centennial-themed celebrations, and the Artesia Historical Museum and Art Center displayed Artesia A–Z, with student art panels illustrating aspects of life in Artesia for every letter of the alphabet. The extravaganza of the year was a four-day celebration over the Fourth of July weekend featuring a parade, crafts fair, sculpture dedication, sports competitions, free concerts, a Sunday-morning sunrise service, a fabulous fireworks display, and many other unforgettable events.

Bibliography

Bidal, Lillian H. *In Pursuit of a Railroad*. Cloudcroft, NM: Sacramento Mountains Historical Society, 1990.

Hopkins, Ellen M. *Yates: A Family, a Company, and Some Cornfield Geology*. Artesia, NM: Yates Drilling, 2000.

———. *A History in Bronze*. Artesia, NM: Artesia MainStreet, 2000.

Julyan, Robert. *The Place Names of New Mexico*. Albuquerque: University of New Mexico Press, 1996.

Katz, Susana R. and Paul. *Pecos Past*. Amarillo, TX: US Department of the Interior, Bureau of Reclamation, Southwest Regional Office, 1985.

———, eds. *Advances in Middle Pecos Archaeology (Proceedings of a Symposium Held at the Fourth Jornada Mogollon Conference, Tularosa, New Mexico, on October 12, 1985)*. Carlsbad, NM: US Department of the Interior, Bureau of Reclamation, 1987.

Waltrip, Lela and Rufus. *Artesia: Heart of the Pecos*. Canyon, TX: Staked Plains Press, 1979.

Weigle, Marta, ed., with Fran Levine and Louise Stiver. *Telling New Mexico: A New History*. Santa Fe: Museum of New Mexico Press, 2009.

About the Museum

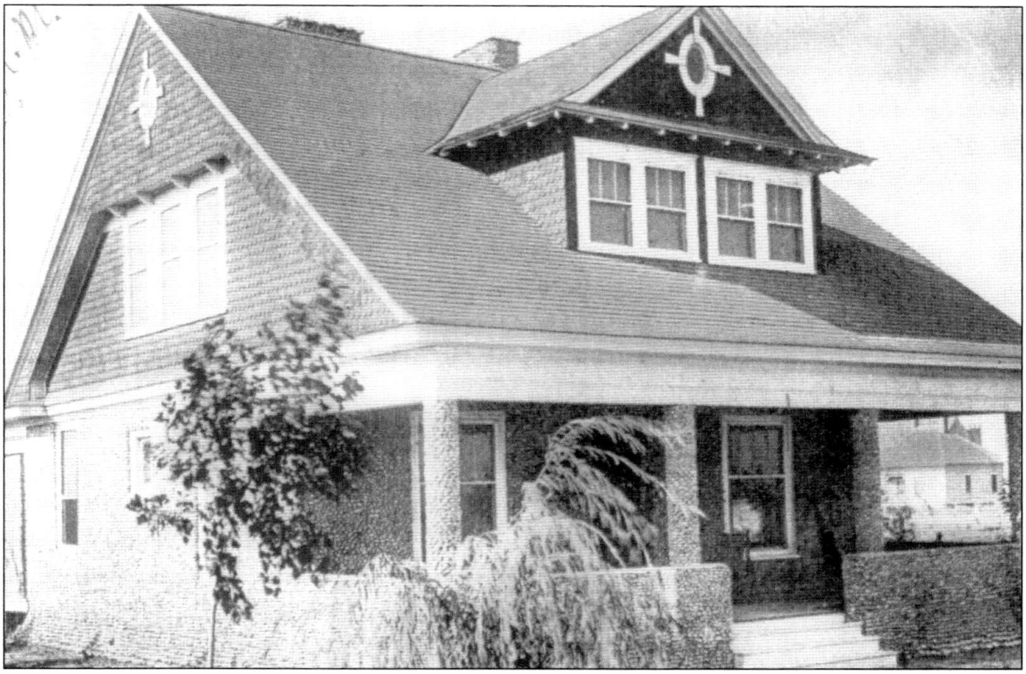

The Artesia Historical Museum and Art Center is located in the Moore-Ward cobblestone house. This unique residence was built for Charles and Anna Moore in 1904–1905. The house itself is constructed with a wooden frame and a cobblestone facade. The stones are river rocks hauled in by wagon from the Rio Penasco. It took nearly two years to cement them in place. The home cost $5,200 to build, and when it was completed, the local newspaper boasted that while it was not the biggest house in town, it certainly was the prettiest.

The Moores sold the house to the S.S. Ward family in 1906, and when Mrs. Ward passed away in 1967, her heirs gave the house to the City of Artesia to be used as a museum. The Artesia Historical Museum officially opened on March 1, 1970. The Moore-Ward House was entered into the New Mexico Register of Cultural Properties in 1976 and was placed in the National Register of Historic Places in 1984. The Artesia Historical Museum and Art Center is located at 505 West Richardson Avenue, Artesia New Mexico, 88210 and can be reached by telephone at (575) 748-2390.